W9-BLP-595

SELF-DIRECTED LEARNING: CONSENSUS & CONFLICT

WITHDRAWN

Huey B. Long and Associates

WITHDRAWN

Please remember that this is a library book,
and that it belongs only temporarily to each
person who uses it. Be considerate. Do
not write in this, or any, library book.

B74
5465
1991

Copyright @ 1991 by Oklahoma Research Center for Continuing Professional and Higher Education of the University of Oklahoma.

No part of the work covered by copyright hereon may be reproduced or used in any form by any means-graphic, electronic, or mechanical, including photocopying, reading, or information storage and retrieval systems-without the written permission of the publisher.

Manufactured in the United States of America.

International Standard Book Number ISBN 09622488-3-5
Library of Congress Catalog Card Number # 90-063989

TABLE OF CONTENTS

Part I - Theoretical Concerns

Part III - Practice

TABLES AND FIGURES

Tables

Figures

PREFACE

Self-Directed Learning: Consensus and Conflict is the fourth
book based primarily upon papers originally presented at the
International Symposium on Adult Self-Directed Learning.
This publication is based on papers presented at the Fourth
International Symposium on Adult Self-Directed Learning
convened, as were the second and third symposia, at the
University of Oklahoma. Manuscripts selected for inclusion
as chapters in this book went through two refereed processes:
first as a paper selected for presentation at the symposium,
and second as a chapter in this book.

The International Symposium on Adult Self-Directed
Learning is designed to accomplish several purposes, namely,
to encourage research into self-directed learning by providing
a forum for professional exchange of current procedures,
findings, theory and application. It is also designed to
provide a supportive atmosphere for novice researchers who
have an interest in self-directed learning. Finally, the papers
and publications stimulated by the symposia disseminate
research findings, concepts and theory to scholars and
practitioners who have an interest in the topic, but for whom
the interest is not central.

The symposium is truly an international event with
participation of scholars from numerous nations. Previous
symposia have included papers by scholars from Australia,

Canada, England, and Nigeria. Self-Directed Learning: Consensus and Conflict contains chapters written by authors from Canada and Nigeria as well as the United States. Participants who did not present papers have visited from other countries such as the Peoples Republic of China.

A new activity has been added annually. During the Fourth Symposium, we experimented with two "Think-Tank" sessions. One session focused on research and theory and the other was concerned with application. It is too early to ascertain the long-term impact of the activity, however, it was obvious at the time, that the sessions provided useful opportunities to discuss some of the areas of consensus and conflict.

The various symposia seem to be characterized by particular themes that emerge through the papers presented and the chapters later published. For instance, papers presented at the first symposium, conducted in 1987, emphasized the non-linear nature of self-directed learning and the issue of a priori objectives. In 1988, the papers presented at the second symposium frequently explicated a common theme, more or less new to the literature of self-directed learning: the idea of psychological control as an important conceptual element. The third symposium, conducted in 1989, moved into the area of models and extended the psychological control concepts. The fourth symposium introduced a greater concern for self-directed learning by professionals while continuing to address issues of conceptualization and theory. More is said about this in the first chapter.

Huey B. Long

PART ONE

CHAPTER ONE

SELF-DIRECTED LEARNING: CONSENSUS AND CONFLICT*

Huey B. Long

Research into self-directed learning has increased in quantity and quality over the past decade. Emerging from Allen Tough's (1965) interest in learning projects and Malcolm Knowles' (1971) philosophical propositions concerning the adult learner, self-directed learning research has gained a robustness associated with few topics in adult education research literature. This robustness has been accompanied by increasing research methodologies and research questions. All is not well, however, as both theory and practice have failed to receive the attention they deserve. At this time, the area of self-directed learning research is characterized by ad hoc propositions rather than by broad nomological frameworks. Of course, theory may be bottom-up as well as top down, e.g., developed from a variety of empirical investigations, or from a conceptual position that focuses the research in order to explain or test the theoretical propositions. The practice aspects of self-directed learning research also appears to remain underdeveloped. Adult and continuing educators are challenged to expand their interests to include application issues and problems.

     Consensus concerning definitional and conceptual properties of self-directed learning is at best in the

This research was supported by the Oklahoma Research Center for Continuing Professional and Higher Education, University of Oklahoma, Norman, Oklahoma.

"emerging" stage. As reported in the Preface, the Fourth International Symposium on Adult Self-Directed Learning included two think-tank working sessions to provide participants with the opportunity to wrestle with problems of theory and practice. These sessions generated much discussion, but only limited agreement. Thus, self-directed learning as a theoretical, research, and applied topic may be compared to a gangling adolescent whose physical growth has not been matched by social, emotional, and mental maturity. This observation, however, is not completely negative. Many research topics fail to survive infancy, thus, the current strength in the area is a source of encouragement for scholars interested in the topic.

Other sources of satisfaction include the increasing recognition that self-directed learning is not to be equated with independent learning. There is the possibility of an over-lapping of the two, and they may not always be mutually exclusive terms. But, to speak of them as being identical in all cases is incorrect. For example, some independent learning is based on the use of highly structured materials that limit the learner's range of responses and initiative (Long, 1984; Long, 1989). In contrast some group learning activities provide numerous opportunities for learners to take control and manage their learning. See chapter two for additional comments on conceptualizations of self-directed learning.

The range and diversity of self-directed learning research are demonstrated by the various publications based on the previous international symposia on self-directed learning (Long and Associates, 1988; Long and Associates, 1989; and Long and Associates, 1990). This publication extends the research reported at previous symposia. The following chapters are roughly grouped according to general concerns and treatments. Part One, in addition to this introduction, contains the more theoretical chapters: chapter two, Challenges in the Study and Practice of Self-Directed Learning by Long; chapter three, A Conceptual Model of Autodidactism, by Tremblay and Theil; chapter four, Functional and Dysfunctional Uses of Self-Directedness in

Adult Learning, by Bonham; Part Two contains chapters that are characterized as empirical research; chapter five, Relationships Between Scores on the Self-Directed Learning Readiness Scale, Oddi Continuing Learning Inventory and Participation in Continuing Professional Education, by West and Bentley; chapter six, Demographic and Personal Factors in Predicting Self-Directedness In Learning, by Adenuga; chapter seven, College Students' Self-Directed Learning Readiness and Educational Achievement, by Long; chapter eight, Human Behavior as a Construct for Assessing Guglielmino's Self-directed Learning Readiness Scale: Pragmatism Revisited, by Confessore; chapter nine, The Validity Generalization of Guglielmino's Self-Directed Learning Readiness Scale, by McCune and Guglielmino; chapter ten, Spark Gap to Space: A Study of Self-directed Learning, by Redding. Part three contains chapters that are more closely aligned with practice concerns: chapter eleven, Reflection on a Personal Self-Directed Independent Learning Activity, by Steele; chapter twelve, The Staged Self-Directed Learning Model, by Grow; chapter thirteen, Facilitating the Self-directed learning by Professionals, by Hill; chapter fourteen, Processes Involved with Developing Autonomous Learning Competences, by Baskett; chapter fifteen, The Future of Self-Directed Learning as Related to Continuing Professional Education, by Rountree, Lambert, Rice and Korhonen; and chapter sixteen, Adapting the Concept of Self-Directed Study to Islamic Educational Practice, by Kazeem.

The above paragraph and the Table of Contents reveal some thematic emphases of the current research in self-directed learning. For example, several of the authors write about self-directed learning of professionals. West bases his research on public school personnel while Baskett and Hill are concerned with a range of professional practitioners. The interest in self-directed learning in the lives of professionals is appropriate when one considers the rapid change in the information that impacts on the daily lives of professionals. For example, most professional practices are effected by changes associated with new scientific discoveries, such as DNA; new inventions that result in the introduction of new pharmaceuticals, machines and processes into the world of work and play, such as the "pill", fax machines, computers and robotics; new laws and regulations that effect professional practice, such as tax laws, accounting procedures based on them and so forth; changes in social patterns and morals, such as the sexual revolution following the "pill," social patterns associated with television and related entertainment media, and life-extending technologies; and personal changes that occur in each individual as a consequence of various aging trends such as occupying different positions in their career ladder, psychological changes associated with advancing life and physical changes associated with aging. Normally, it is expected that professionals, as a group, encounter change in a more rapid and intense fashion than other occupations. Even if this is not the case, professionals' performance often has direct impact on the lives of others in a more sensitive and profound manner than may be true of a range of occupations.

Greater attention to the learning of professionals is needed in the future. We need to discover and implement new ways of encouraging professionals to access and to learn of new developments in their areas of practice. It is apparent, that the new ways of delivering information to professionals must be discovered and used. It is equally clear that these new delivery mechanisms must go beyond the current inefficient methods that are based on high travel costs and face-to-face personal interactions. Discussions with physicians and others, also, indicate that we cannot expect the technology of computers, radio and television to automatically resolve the problem.

Professionals may ultimately provide a useful group of learners upon which to base models of self-directed learning for other occupational areas. The problem seems to be multi-faceted and complex, however. For example, the eventual model should provide for (1) the curriculum, or the information that is most useful; (2) criteria for determining the information to be delivered; (3) organization of the information; and (4) delivery of the selected information. But the problem is not resolved simply by the above. There needs to be a multi-media availability. Furthermore, the materials need to be based on greater knowledge of the self-directing behaviors of individual professionals. Without the latter, the materials, that is, information will likely take on the highly structured, but limiting programs of computer based instruction and some of the interactive video based materials currently available. The model should be based on some of the existing understandings as identified in the next paragraph.

Enough is now implied by the previous research in self-directed learning to identify several significant characteristics. First, as suggested by Spear and Mocker (1984) it appears that self-directed learning has a highly fortuitous aspect to it. That is, the learner is frequently constrained by the availability and accessibility of learning resources. They use what is easily available. Second, the issue of prior learning objectives is not clear. Contrary to the rational advance planning, based on apriori objectives, as noted by Tough (1967), it is occasionally implied that self-directed learning is mostly serendipitous Spear (1988). As in many things, it appears that the positions are extreme. Both may be true when applied to different people. For most people the truth is likely to be somewhere between the extremes. My hypothesis is that the self-directed learner often has a "global" goal that is gradually refined through the search and learning process. At the beginning of the learning effort the learner has only a vague idea of what he or she wishes to learn. It may be to learn to sketch, to paint, to use a computer and so forth. As the learner obtains more information the specifics gradually become clearer. The individual who wishes to learn to sketch, may determine that he or she needs to know how to present perspective, how to identify basic forms and draw them, and so forth. Experience with each step leads to the next. It may not always be precise and may reflect some trial and error. Learning as identified in the self-directed learning literature is not linear. This finding is supportive of the hypothesis concerning global goals. It is also suggested that self-directed learning depends, to a large degree, on important variables such as (a) personality, (b) attitudinal variables and (c) process skills such as awareness of learning processes (metacognition), positive attitudes toward learning (motivation) and skills such as reading, observation, sketching, and so forth. The process skills are those procedures by which an individual obtains information and integrates it with existing knowledge. Different individuals possess different skills, sometimes related to what Bonham discusses as learning styles. The point is that the self-directed learner must have some process skill. It is difficult to assert which skill is the most important, but in a literate society based on the written word, reading skills are obviously critical.

Scholars of self-directed learning are challenged to learn how the above findings and their implications can be applied in the development of programs designed to facilitate self-directed learning. Suggested examples include the development of a high quality, information rich environment. This step enhances the quality of the learning outcomes and is a responsibility shared by the professional and employers of the professionals. Second, the information must be readily and easily accessible. The utility of the information will be directly and positively associated with convenience and simplicity. Third, the concepts of non-linearity in learning and the global characteristics of learning goals must be understood and addressed. Fourth, and finally, educators must learn how to develop and positively exploit the variables of personality, attitude, interest, motivation and process skills.

The above also raises additional concerns. For example, how are the variables of personality, attitude and process skills developed? We seem to think that we have an acceptable level of understanding about the ways and means by which some process skills such as reading are developed, but we do not understand fully why some people enjoy reading more than others. What role does formal education activities play compared with informal social reinforcements that are derived from family and other activities? Longitudinal study of this problem is missing, but it, too, is gradually being accumulated in two ways: (a) longitudinal studies of school children (Eisenman, 1990) and biographical analysis (Long, 1989b, 1990).

Other continuing interests of researchers concerned with self-directed learning include the issue of identification and measurement of important personal characteristics, which are either associated with self-directed learning, or which cause it. Guglielmino's Self-Directed Learning Readiness Scale continues to be the foremost instrument available for this purpose. To a lesser degree, Oddi's Continuing Learning Inventory has been used for similar purposes. Chapters in this book reveal the continuing interest in the validity and reliability of these instruments. Despite the multitudes of investigations based on the above instruments all questions have not been answered. For example, how can the instruments best be used? Are they predictive of behavior? Are they primarily measures of attitude, if so, how directly does attitude effect behavior? Is performance on the these scales universal?, that is, will a person be equally self-directing in learning of various content or aptitude areas?

The controversies in self-directed learning are also revealed in the following chapters? For example, is self-directed learning to be defined by philosophical values. In chapter two, Long challenges this position as taken by Brookfield (1986) and Mezirow (1985). Two additional controversies are revealed in Bonham's chapter. For example, how important is motivation in defining and studying self-directed learning? Long (1989a) suggests that intrinsic motivation may provide a productive theoretical foundation for theoretical development. Bonham, in chapter four, seems to discount that proposition. She also challenges the position that encouraging or promoting self-directed learning is always functional.

Other productive concepts, challenges, issues and propositions are revealed in the various chapters not discussed. For example, Kazeem, addresses an interesting problem of cultural impacts on self-directed learning. As described in his chapter, Islamic education is extremely rigid and is based on a an authority structure that is in contrast to self-directed learning. Yet, he envisions the possibility of applying self-directed learning concepts to Islamic education. Grow provides an interesting model based on the problem of developing self-directed learning in students whose prior experiences may have inhibited its development. Tremblay and Theil provide a provocative possibility for theoretical exploration and development. McCune and Guglielmino provide additional research that is supportive of the generalizibility of Guglielmino's SDLRS.

SUMMARY

This chapter introduces Self-Directed Learning: Consensus and Conflict. As such it lists and identifies the 15 following chapters. Particular attention is focused on the importance of self-directed learning in the lives of professionals and some concepts that may be useful in devising conditions that contribute to professionals' self-directed learning. Some controversies touched upon in the following chapters are also discussed.

REFERENCES

Brookfield, S. (1986). Understanding and facilitating adult learning. San Francisco: Jossey-Bass.

Long, H. (1989a). Theoretical foundations for self-directed learning. A paper presented at the Commission of Professors of Adult Education Annual Meeting, Atlantic City, NJ.

Long, H. (1989b). Truth unguessed and yet to be discovered: A professional's self-directed learning. In H. Long and Associates, Self-directed learning: Emerging theory and practice. Norman, Oklahoma: Oklahoma Research Center for Continuing Professional and Higher Education, 125-135.

Long, H. (1990). Peter the Great: A social-historical analysis of self-education principles. 31st Annual Adult Education Research Conference Proceedings. Athens, GA: The University of Georgia, 130-134.

Mezirow, J. (1985). A critical theory of self-directed learning. In S. Brookfield, <u>Self-directed learning: From theory to practice</u>, (New Directions for Continuing Education Series, No. 25) San Francisco: Jossey-Bass, 17-30.

Spear, G. (1988). Beyond the organizing circumstances: A search for methodology for the study of self-directed learning. In H. Long and Associates, <u>Self-directed learning: Application and theory</u>. Athens, GA: Adult Education Dept., University of Georgia, 199-221.

Spear, G. and Mocker, D. (1984). The organizing circumstance: Environmental determinants in self-directed learning. <u>Adult Education Quarterly</u>, <u>35</u> (l), 1-10.

Tough, A. (1967). <u>Learning without a teacher</u>. (Educational Research Series No. 3) Toronto, Canada: The Ontario Institute for Studies in Education.

Consensus and Conflict

CHAPTER TWO

CHALLENGES IN THE STUDY AND PRACTICE OF SELF-DIRECTED LEARNING*

Huey B. Long

The Fourth International Symposium on Adult Self-Directed Learning is evidence of continuing widespread interest in self-directed learning. The posters and papers presented at the symposium, along with the chapters published in this book provide archival evidence of the challenges and opportunities for those interested in the study and practice of self-directed learning. The purpose of this chapter is to examine and discuss some of the challenges that reside in the concepts, definitions and theoretical dimensions of self-directed learning. The following discussion focuses on four topics. First a brief historical overview places the topic in time and identifies scholars who were early associated with adult self-directed learning. Second, some conceptual and definitional challenges are noted. Third, theoretical and procedural challenges are discussed. Fourth and finally, practice challenges are presented.

HISTORICAL OVERVIEW

The notion of self-directed learning captured the attention of educators of adults in the 1970s. Yet, the idea of self-directed learning and self-education is found in the recent literature as early as 1957. Paul Sheats described the ideal

* This research was supported by the Oklahoma Research Center for Continuing Professional and Higher Education.

11

role of adult education as being "symbolized in this view is that of the self-reliant and self-directing individual learner who knows what his educational goals are and proceeds to attain them, using institutional resources of adult education as they may be appropriate to his purposes" (italics mine) (Sheats, 1957, p.232). Cy Houle (1957) provides a description of the self-educated leader that is engaged in a complex process of selecting media, questioning and participating in formal education. It is likely that a thorough search of the literature would reveal earlier uses of the term. However, the point of this discussion is to indicate that while self-directed learning and self-education were not unknown terms prior to Allen Tough's (1965) research, they were not used as often as they have been in the recent decade.

Following the widely acclaimed work of Allen Tough (1965, 1967, 1971) with adults' learning projects and Malcolm Knowles' (1970, 1975, 1984) popularization of andragogy, adult educators increased their commitment to the study of self-directed learning. While some may challenge the point, it is likely that the greatest boost to the study of self-directed learning was provided by Lucy Guglielmino's Self-Directed Learning Readiness Scale (1977/78). Since the publication of the Guglielmino SDLRS numerous dissertations and research articles concerning self-directed learning have been conducted. Many of them based in some way on the SDLRS.

The SDLRS has been used to address questions concerning the relationship of self-directed learning attitudes and numerous other variables such as age, sex, education achievement level, and personality characteristics. Another area of research has focused on the scale itself. A number of investigators have examined issues of validity and reliability (Brockett, 1985; Long and Agyekum, 1983). The investigations have produced a range of results. Nevertheless, with one exception (Field, 1989) the body of research concerning the validity and reliability of the SDLRS has been supportive of the scale's validity and reliability. The validity of Field's (1989) conclusion was refuted by Guglielmino, Long and McCune (1989).

Despite the volume of research focused on self-directed learning a number of challenges to its study and practice remain. Some of the challenges to the study and practice of self-directed learning are addressed in the next few pages. First challenges to the study of self-directed learning are discussed. Then challenges to the practice of self-directed learning are noted.

CHALLENGES TO STUDY

Three challenges to the study of self-directed learning are (1) conceptual/definitional, (2) theoretical/procedural and (3) practical/application.

Conceptual/Definitional

It has been noted that the term self-directed learning has been used to refer to both a goal and to a process. Two goal conceptualizations as well as two process conceptualizations are noted. One goal conceptualization represents self-directed learning as the goal. In another instance, one writer has implied that since learning should be used as a noun a change in consciousness is the goal of self-directed learning. Hence, self-directed learning is equated with a change in consciousness (Brookfield, 1986). It should be self-evident to most sophisticated readers when the term refers to some desirable goal or consequence of development or instruction rather than to the result of self-directed learning. Thus, the alert individual should quickly recognize the difference between the two goal connotations.

There is no great problem in communication when we state that our goal is to stimulate or strengthen an individual's capacity to engage in self-directed learning. We are merely noting that we are interested in improving a process. Such a position is similar to stating that we are interested in developing improved reading ability. The ability to read is thus a goal, but reading is also a process.

The process connotation of self-directed learning seems to be of greatest utility. Yet, the use of the term self-directed learning to refer to a process opens the door to further uncertainty. One process based idea focuses on pedagogical procedures. In contrast a second use of the process idea emphasizes an internal personal psychological framework (Long, 1987b). The process of self-directed learning is often expanded beyond the idea of a psychological process to include pedagogical elements. Illustrations of some of these process concepts are discussed briefly. To avoid complex language, all of the following comments concern the process of self-directed learning unless otherwise noted.

Brookfield (1985), Knowles (1975), and Long (1987a) provide three definitions that illustrate different process conceptualizations. The three definitions are listed in their order of appearance in the literature.

Knowles (1975) provided the first definition some fifteen years ago. He defined self-directed learning as follows:

> In its broadest meaning "self-directed learning" describes a process in which individuals take the initiative, with or without the help of others, in diagnosing their learning needs, formulating learning goals, identifying human and material resources for learning, choosing and implementing appropriate learning strategies, and evaluating learning outcomes. (Knowles, 1975, p. 18)

Brookfield's (1985) definition, as reported below, follows his observation that self-directed learning is a process. He defines self-directed learning as an "internal change in the consciousness of an individual after he or she has engaged in a critical analysis of alternative possibilities..." (emphasis mine, p. 85). The restrictive phrase and the way Brookfield discusses "a change of consciousness" suggests that he is not really commenting upon a process, but upon the result of a process that involves "a critical analysis." If self-directed learning is a change in consciousness as defined in the quote from Brookfield self-directed learning is an outcome, hence not a process. If self-directed learning is merely a synonym for critical analysis of alternative possibilities the definition requires additional specification.

Long's (1987A) definition is as follows:

First, I'm of the opinion that we should speak of degrees of self-direction rather than to limit our concept to an all-or-nothing position. Accordingly, I believe that various degrees of self-direction are likely to be found in all kinds of teaching-learning activities. Therefore, I define self-directed learning as a <u>personally directed purposive mental process usually accompanied and supported by behavioral activities involved in the identification and searching out of information</u>. Information may be of several kinds: sensations, memory, imagination, written, oral and symbolic material. This position does not necessarily exclude serendipitous learning, it is primarily to focus on purposive mental activity (p. 3).

Note, while this definition does depend on individual <u>control</u> as reflected in the phrase "personally directed purposive mental activity ..." it is not dependent upon the pedagogical, physical or social independence or isolation of the learner. This conceptualization is not greatly different, in terms of its emphasis upon personal motivation, from Alexander and Hines' (1966) idea of independent study. They said "independent study is considered by us to be a learning activity largely motivated by the learner's own aims to learn and largely rewarded in terms of its intrinsic values" (p. 67). What is important in these ideas is the person of the learner, often discussed as the self.

A review of the definitions provided by Brookfield, Knowles and Long suggest that they may be discussing different things that may be associated, but which may not be identical. A summary presentation of their definitions follows:

(a)   A process of locating and accessing information (Knowles, 1975).

(b)   The result of the process, i.e. change of consciousness (Brookfield, 1985).

(c)   A process by which information is acted upon (Long, 1987a).

We are challenged to determine if we can define self-directed learning in terms of either of these uses, or if self-directed learning is a combination of them.

Other conceptual challenges are associated with several aspects of the term self-directed learning. Some of these challenges emerge from the very early development of the topic from the efforts to merge Tough's learning projects research and Knowles' andragogy. It is possible that the conceptual soup of self-directed learning has also been supplemented by a dash of Mezirow's (1985) perspective transformation and Brookfield's (1985, 1986, 1987) continuing efforts to re-define self-directed learning. More is said about these theoretical aspects in the next section.

Briefly stated, it appears that Tough and Knowles had two different concepts that are reflected in their terminology. While he does not exclude other kinds of learning, Tough's interest in learning projects suggests a greater interest in the independent learner engaged in informal learning. While Knowles (1975) does not ignore this possibility, his interest seems to focus on the learner engaged in some kind of formal learning in which others are directly engaged. The title of his 1975 book that includes the phrase, "a guide for learners and teachers" supports the assertion. Long (1987a) has referred to these two kinds of learning settings as "free learning" and pedagogical self-directed learning, respectively.

Papers presented at the first three North American Symposia on Adult Self-Directed Learning reveal investigators use the term self-directed learning in a range of ways. Generally, the conceptual problems have followed the positions of Tough and Knowles. They reflect three major conceptual properties: psychological, sociological and structural. To a lesser degree philosophical elements are also involved, especially in the positions reported by Brookfield (1985, 1986) and Mezirow (1985).

Psychological concepts are foremost in the work of those who relate self-directed learning to a cognitive activity and/or personality trait. Accordingly, cognitive processes such as executive functions, memory, divergent production, convergent production and evaluation are involved. This conceptual foundation also underlies the questions concerning self-directed learning as a cognitive style. When viewed from the personality perspective self-directed learning is represented as a reflection of one's general predisposition to be autonomous. Combinations of the cognitive and personality elements are also possible within the psychological framework.

Sociological conceptualizations focus upon (a) the interaction of the learner with others; (b) the nature of the interaction, i.e., as an equal or in a subordinate role to one or more people. According to the various applications of the first sociological concept self-directed learning occurs in splendid isolation. As a result the extreme suggestion is that the self-directed learner is a Lone Ranger or Robinson Crusoe type, and that any learning that involves other people cannot be self-directed. The second of the sociological conceptualizations deals with the issue of social relationships and social power. In the extreme form it may be suggested that self-directed learning does not occur when the learner is in a subordinate social role such as a student. Hence, the role of teacher has been supplanted by the role of facilitator. However, the validity of the need to remove the teacher from the process has not been confirmed.

Structural conceptualization is concerned with the pedagogical elements and the autonomy of the learner. Five common pedagogical elements are learning goals, content, resources, activities and evaluation. An extreme position suggests that self-directed learning cannot occur unless the learner has complete control over all of the pedagogical elements. Other structural or methodological concepts equate learning contracts with self-directed learning.

Philosophical concepts, also, are found in the literature. According to these positions content and purpose are critical to the identification of self-directed learning. Accordingly, it is implied that "real" self-directed learning has to do with major shifts of perspectives identified with a change in consciousness (Brookfield, 1985). In other words, what is labeled "self-directed learning" must be qualified by the outcome or result.

The above four conceptualizations generally seem to include 99% of the various ways of conceptualizing self-directed learning. It is apparent that they leave much to be desired when taken individually. Each one seems to exclude much of what others believe to be important. Considered in a singular fashion they also often appear to be self-contradictory. For example, computer assisted instruction meets the sociological requirements of independence and isolation. However, the way the CAI program is developed is inconsistent with structural requirements that specify the learner must be in <u>complete</u> control.

Long (1986, 1989) indicates that one difficulty with the conceptualizations of self-directed learning is that they tend to be overly simplistic. He calls for an interactionist concept. Such concepts have been presented by Garrison (1989), Jarvis (1990) and Long (1989b). The schemes devised by Garrison and Long are preferred over the one presented by Jarvis. Space prevents a robust explication of the interaction concepts developed by Garrison, Long and Jarvis, it is sufficient to note, however, that they each differ while some areas of common agreement may be identified.

The previous discussion of conceptualizations of self-directed learning indicates that students of self-directed learning are faced with an important challenge. That challenge seems to be, how do we conceptualize self-directed learning to adequately account for the critical characteristics that distinguish self-directed learning? The problem is illustrated by the suggestion that learning can be used as a noun (Brookfield, 1987). When learning is used as a noun as opposed to its use as a verb the results are significant. Learning as a noun connotes the results or product of some activity. Learning as a verb connotes the process that leads to some modification of one's knowledge, skills or attitudes and emotions. It has been noted elsewhere that to conceptualize learning as a noun reflects behaviorism (Long, 1987b). The difficulty in conceptual development of self-directed learning is further illustrated by some who prefer to represent self-directed learning as an all-or-none phenomenon. Finally, the issue is further confused by tendencies to equate self-directed learning with one other kind of cognitive activity or procedure such as critical reflection (Brookfield, 1986), learning projects (Brookfield, 1986) and andragogy. Brookfield (1986) implies that there are two levels of self-directed learning; one is low and the other is high. The classification into lower and higher levels is based on a combination of (a) content or purpose, and (b) degree of personal transformation.

The definitional problems of self-directed learning seem to be sufficient without introducing the philosophical issue. It would appear that the process is not dependent upon concensus about the goodness of its outcomes.

It should be apparent by now that the current literature on self-directed learning contains sufficient conceptual diversity to make it possible for two different writers to use the term while discussing significantly different ideas. It is important to narrow the conceptual range so that we are reasonably confident that we are talking and writing about the same thing.

Theoretical

As expected, theoretical and procedural challenges in self-directed learning are associated with some of the conceptualizations discussed above.

Tough's (1965) research was the first major research in adult education identified with what we now refer to as self-directed learning. Knowles' philosophical ideas labeled andragogy, which emphasizes self-directed behavior, followed closely on the heels of Tough's work. It was not difficult for graduate students and others who replicated Tough's learning project research to slide over to employ Knowles' term self-directed learning. It appears, however, that no one took the time to ask the question about differences between the two topics. Tough did not use the term self-directed learning in his earliest publications. He used such terms as self-instruction, learning without a teacher, and so forth. But he did not use self-directed learning. Furthermore,

Tough's learning project activity as identified by his subjects frequently included independence in learning, or the isolated learner. From a review of his early work, it seems as if Tough was concerned most with the individual learner who learned through informal means. Finally, it appears that Tough may have derived some of his ideas from the literature of therapy. A review of his references indicated that the term self-directed was used to refer to self-directed therapy such as Berzon & Solomon (1964) "The self-directed therapeutic group:...." more often than to self-directed education. Usually there is a distinction between therapy and education, some possible exceptions will be noted later. Therapy usually refers to some kind of curative activity (Chaplin, 1968). In contrast education is usually conceived of as development, knowledge, attitudes and behavior as the result of instruction (Chaplin, 1968).

Knowles' views of self-directed learning appear to have been sufficiently different to serve as a warning to those seeking to use the two concepts of self-directed learning and learning projects interchangeably. While Knowles writes about the self-directed learner, he leaves little doubt that he is usually concerned with the group learner -- the individual who has chosen to enroll in some formal learning group. Knowles was also influenced by some of the same individuals that may have influenced Tough, such as Carl Rogers, nevertheless the educative purpose seems to dominate the therapeutic dimensions in Knowles' concepts of self-directed learning.

Thus, it appears the two individuals who are often most directly identified with self-directed learning in the 1970s were writing about different things. In summary they differed in (1) learning settings; (2) theory base; and (3) emphasis as illustrated below:

	Tough	Knowles
learning setting	independent/ informal	group/formal
theory base	humanistic psychology	humanistic education
emphasis	educative	educative

Following Tough and Knowles others have added to the literature. Brookfield and Mezirow present views that differ from those of Tough and Knowles. For example, Mezirow's perspective transformation and his use of the term self-reflective learning as a synonym for self-directed learning, as described in 1985, is Freudian in nature as he draws from psychoanalytic therapy, e.g. a system designed to understand, prevent and cure mental illness, and refers to "traumatic childhood events" (p.21). Brookfield's (1985) positions on self-directed learning have varied across a range of concepts including self-directed learning as a "goal" and as a "method" (1985,p.6). He also identifies it as an "internal change in consciousness..." (1985, p.15). Later Brookfield, apparently influenced by Mezirow defined self-directed learning as "an internal change in the consciousness of an individual after he or she has engaged in a critical analysis of alternative possibilities..." (emphasis mine, p. 85). Thus, Brookfield and Mezirow have overlaid self-directed learning with a veneer of critical theory.

As indicated in the discussion of concepts some have turned to other disciplines for assistance. Long (1986, 1987a) has turned to different schools of psychology. For example, he believes that cognitive psychology, especially meta-cognition and intrinsic motivation may be important in the eventual development of a sound theory of self-directed learning. There is also the possibility that self-theory may make significant contributions to the study and practice of self-directed learning.

It is important that the theoretical framework developed for self-directed learning be an interactionist theory that provides for a multiple variables. One such idea is represented by Long's (1989b) suggestion that an interaction between pedagogical control and psychological control determines the degree to which a learner engages in self-directed learning. Figure 2.1 provides an illustration of this position.

Figure 2.1: **An Illustration of the Relationship Between Pedagogical and Psychological Control in Self-Directed Learning.**

High Psychological Control

Quadrate I	Quadrate II

Low Pedagogical Control		High Pedagogical Control

Quadrate IV	Quadrate III

Low Psychological Control

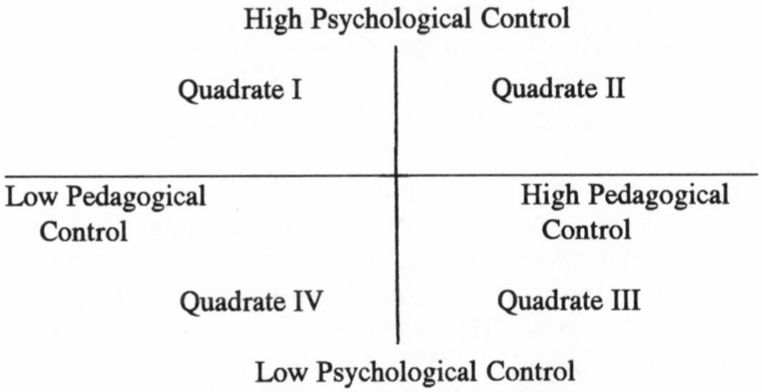

The knowledge base in self-directed learning is perceived to be sufficient for theoreticians and researchers to continue to enrich the research methodology and model building activities. Few longitudinal studies are available to help answer questions concerning the developmental aspects of psychological control as it relates to self-directed learning. In lieu of longitudinal studies a few biographical studies are available (Long, 1989a). While we are developing longitudinal investigations we are challenged to increase our biographical information. Furthermore, even though there is a need for biographical, historical and other forms of qualitative research we also need some experimental studies to determine the impact of different environments.

Mocker and Spear (1984) speculate on the usefulness of Lewin's force-field theory in the study of self-directed learning. Long and Ross (1986) report a set of five heuristic models for engaging in self-directed learning. The models all contain the same variables: (a) contextual, (b) situational, (c) social and (d) personality. The contextual model appears in Figure 2.2. Other heuristic models change the relationships among the four categories of variables. For example one model provides for interaction among the variable classes as shown in Figure 2.3.

Figure 2.2: The Contextual Model for Analysis of Interacting Variable Categories in Self-Directed Learning.

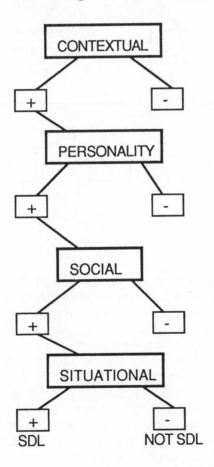

Figure 2.3:   **An Interaction Model for Analysis of Interacting Variable Categories in Self-Directed Learning.**

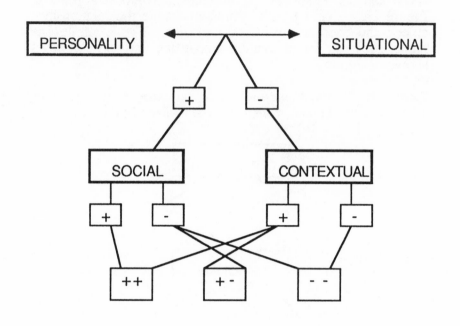

        Each of the remaining models in the set contain the same variables, however, the initiating variables are changed. The current literature fails to indicate the path of the forces. Research is needed to determine if the sequence varies or if uniform which sequence is persistent.

        In summary, challenges to the theoretical dimensions of self-directed learning are closely related to the conceptual challenges. They differ in that they are related more directly to the content and procedures questions, e.g. what are the questions we need to be asking to obtain a better explanation of self-directed learning? and, what is the best way to obtain answers to the questions once posed?

CHALLENGES TO PRACTICE

The practice dimension of self-directed learning presents as many challenges as does the study dimension. It could be briefly stated that the practice, that is, the use of self-directed learning in formal and informal learning transactions appears to be limited. It has been noted that adult educators who desire to stimulate self-directed learning are negatively influenced by the absence of documented procedures. Those familiar with the best relationship between theory and practice should not be surprised by such an assertion. Practice, as research, should be based on some kind of theoretical and conceptual base. Given the confusion about what qualifies as self-directed learning it is not difficult to imagine how professors and teachers are confused about what supports and stimulates self-directed learning.

Aware that practical issues cannot be frozen in time until the conceptual and theoretical issues are resolved it is imperative that scholars and practitioners begin to address some of the fundamental problems. Some of these basic practice problems are briefly noted in the following comments:

1. What kind of learning environments are most conducive to self-directed learning?

2. What kind of teacher behaviors are most supportive of self-directed learning?

3. What kinds of evaluation procedures are most appropriate and useful to assess the consequences of self-directed learning?

4. How does the teacher develop and/or strengthen attitudes favorable to self-directed learning?

5.   How do the kinds of support activities differ according to learning environment, e.g., solitary learning and group learning, informal learning and formal learning?

6.   How does recognition for intrinsically motivated learning affect the strength of such motivation?

7.   How can teachers employ differential learning conditions for learners with differing levels of self-directed learning motivation?

There are at least another seven or perhaps seven times seven challenges to the practice of self-directed learning that may be identified. However, the above list of challenges may help to organize our thinking and discussion of the challenges in self-directed learning.

SUMMARY

This chapter contains three major topical sub-divisions. The first is a brief historical overview of the emergence and development of self-directed learning. The second is a discussion of challenges to the study of self-directed learning. The third consists of comments about challenges to practice of self-directed learning.

It is noted that research and practice have both improved in recent years, however, important challenges concerning the above topics remain.

REFERENCES

Alexander, W. and Hines, V. (1966). Independent study in secondary school. Washington, D.C.: Office of Education, USDHEW.

Berzon, B. and Solomon, L. (1964). The self-directed therapeutic group: An exploratory study. International Journal of Group Psychotherapy, 14, 366-369.

Brockett, R. (1985).   Methodological and substantive issues in the measurement of self-directed learning readiness. Adult Education Quarterly, 36, 15-24.

Brookfield, S. (1986).   Understanding and facilitating adult learning. San Francisco: Jossey-Bass.

Brookfield, S. (1988).   Conceptual, methodological and practical ambiguities in self-directed learning.   In H. Long and Associates, Self-directed learning: Application and Theory. Athens, Georgia: Adult Education Dept., University of Georgia, 11-37.

Chaplin, J. (1968).   Dictionary of Psychology.   New York: Dell Publishing Co.

Field, L. (1989).   An investigation into the structure, validity and reliability of Guglielmino's Self-Directed Learning Readiness Scale. Adult Education Quarterly, 39, 125-139.

Garrison, D. (1989).   Facilitating self-directed learning: Not a contradiction in terms.   In H. Long and Associates, Self-directed learning: Emerging theory and practice. Norman, OK: Oklahoma Research Center for Continuing Professional and Higher Education, University of Oklahoma, 53-62.

Guglielmino, L. (1977/78) Development of the self-directed learning readiness scale. Doctoral dissertation, University of Georgia, 1977. Dissertation Abstracts International, 38, 6467A.

Guglielmino, L., Long, H. and McCune, S. (1989).   Reactions to Field's investigation into the SDLRS. Adult Education Quarterly, 39, 236-247.

Houle, C. (1957).   Education for adult leadership. Adult Education, VIII (1), 3-17.

Jarvis, P. (1990).   Self-directed learning and the theory of adult education. In H. Long and Associates, Advances in Research and Practice in Self-Directed Learning.   Norman, OK: Oklahoma Research Center for Continuing Professional and Higher Education, 47-66.

Knowles, M. (1970).   The modern practice of adult education.   New York: Association Press.

Knowles, M. (1975).   Self-directed learning. Chicago: Follett Publishing Co.

Knowles, M. (1984).   Andragogy in action. San Francisco: Jossey-Bass.

Long, H. (1986).   Self-direction in learning: Conceptual difficulties. Lifelong Learning Forum, III (1), 1-2.

Long, H. (1987a). Self-directed learning and learning theory. Unpublished paper presented at Commission of Professors Conference, Washington, D.C.

Long, H. (1987b). Self-directed learning reconsidered. In H. Long and Associates, Self-directed learning: Application and theory. Athens, GA: Adult Education Dept., University of Georgia, 1-9.

Long, H. (1989a). Biography and history in the study of adult self-directed learning. Commission of Professors of Adult Education Proceedings of the 1988 Annual Conference, 115-119.

Long, H. (1989b). Self-directed learning: Emerging theory and practice. In H. Long and Associates, Self-directed learning: Emerging theory and practice. Norman, OK: Oklahoma Research Center for Continuing Professional and Higher Education, 1-12.

Long, H. (1990). Psychological control in self-directed learning. International Journal of Lifelong Education, 9 (4), 331-338.

Long, H. and Agyekum, S. (1983). Guglielmino's self-directed learning readiness scale: A validation study. Higher Education, 12, 77-87.

Long, H. and Ross, J. (1986). Forces for self-direction in learning. Unpublished paper.

Mezirow, J. (1985). A critical theory of self-directed learning. In S. Brookfield, Self-directed learning: From theory to practice, (New Directions for Continuing Education Series, No. 25). San Francisco: Jossey-Bass, 17-30.

Sheats, P. (1957). A middle way in adult education. Adult Education, VII (4), 231-233.

Spear, G. and Mocker, D. (1984). The organizing circumstances: Environmental determinants in self-directed learning. Adult Education Quarterly, 1, 1-10.

Tough, A. (1967). Learning without a teacher. Educational Research Series, No. 3. Toronto, Canada: The Ontario Institute for Studies in Education.

Tough, A. (1971). The adults learning projects: A fresh approach to theory and practice in adult learning. Toronto: Ontario Institute for Studies in Education.

CHAPTER THREE

A CONCEPTUAL MODEL OF AUTODIDACTISM

N.A. Tremblay
with the collaboration of J.P. Theil

The concept of self-direction in learning can take on various meanings, depending on the general context within which it is used. The research we have done deals specifically with self-directed learning in an autodidactic context, i.e. in "learning whichis accomplished by an individual without benefit ot either an institution (Legendre, 1988) or of any other formal educational agent (Tremblay, 1981)".

The nature of this definition of autodidactism is due less to the fact that, in this type of situation, learners learn on their own (in the sense in which learning = internal process) than to the fact that they can acquire knowledge resulting from a learning endeavour in which no-one intervenes as an instructor. Autodidactism is defined here in opposition to learning in a formal instructional environment. As Spear and Mocker (1984) point out:

> "Because SDL occurs in a natural environment dominated by chance elements and is in contrast to the artificial and controlled elements which characterize formal instructional environments, it seems useful to investigate the possibility of differing effects of the natural environments on the learning process". (Spear and Mocker, 1984, p. 9)

This definition must be borne in mind when studying autodidactism as a specific aspect of self-directed learning. Moreover, the study of autodidactism as learning in a natural setting offers a new perspective in the theoretical development of the SDL current of thought, wich surrounds SDL in adult education.

SOME CONSIDERATION

This part of the chapter deals with the concept of self-direction in learning as it has developed through the literature of the past few decades. As well, actual models of autodidactism proposed by different authors are presented. It seems important to take into account the theoretical context now prevailing in SDL in order that the model presented in a later section of this chapter be considered in light of its general contribution toward the furthering of SDL theory.

Development of the Concept
The emergence of the SDL issue in adult education owes much to TOUGH'S discovery (1967, 1971), of the importance and preponderance of self-planned learning among adults. Thus, he speaks of self-planned and self-directed learning projects, as he calls these successful learning endeavours initiated outside the educational system. Tough's discovery made adult learning in the educational system appear residual and like the tip of an iceberg of which the submerged part is situated in a context not intentionally structured to be educational. As Long puts it:

> ... self-direction in learning must be simplistically conceptually limited to (a) complete independance of the learner from a teacher or institution (b) an all-or-nothing condition (c) self-directed learning as an educational, method, technique or delivery procedure and (d) self-directed learning as a personality characteristic... (p. 1)

When we consider the typology of the research subjects dealing with SDL, it becomes apparent that we have moved from a problem of autodidactism as learning free from the educational context to a problem of autodidactism as learning within the context of the educational system. Incorporated into the conceptual field of SDL, autonomy became the attribute of certain adults, of some of their ways of learning, of certain ways of teaching them - indeed, the attributes characterising the essence of a certain conceptions of adult education. If we refer to Tough's work, however, we see that another factor apart from autonomy might constitute the intermediary variable which explains the correlation between autonomy as understood by Tough and quality of learning, namely the <u>matching</u> of a learning strategy with the learning context in which it is situated.

<u>Some Models of SDL</u>
Retrospectively, it is surprising to think that the role of the learning context, as an element to be considered in order to understand autodidactism and SDL, has been so greatly under-estimated. As Spear puts it (1988):

> To understand self-directed learning without reference to environment ignores both important research and common-sense. (p. 207)

Autodidactism thus initiates a movement which seeks to consider such questions as the place of the learning context, its characteristics, the extent to which it influences the nature of the learning process, the extent to which this eventual influence limits and/or encourages autodidactism. A number of authors now subscribe to this new approach to autodidactism as a type of experiential learning. These are, among others, Spear (1988), Peters and Lazarra (1988), Candy (1990), Theil (1989) and Tremblay (1989)[1]. In their view, the problem of autodidactism may be addressed from new bases.
Considering the place of the context in autodidactism, Spear (1988) tries to describe the nature of the interaction constituted by this special learning technique. The author

---

[1]Theil's and Tremblay's research follows the work done by Danis and Tremblay (1985) and GRAAME (Groupe de recherche sur les apprentissages autodidactiques) since 1982.

hypothesizes that the reciprocal determination of the environment and a subject does not mean that individuals are merely objects manipulated by the environment nor that they can do whatever they please in it.

The interest of this approach is to conceive the effectiveness of autodidactic learning skills as the matching of a group of directed, exploratory, fortuitous actions with the state of the context encountered at each moment of the learning process (consistent or fortuitous environment). It should be noted here that as early as 1978, Penland seemed to have grasped the essentials of the nature of the situation:

> In the process, new competencies are acquired by observing and receiving "instructions" from environmental imperatives, by making trial performance before adjusting to feedback, and by growing more flexible and independent. (p. 12)

Peters and Lazarra (1988) have studied the learning process in an informal setting from a specific angle: the ability to solve problems. Their present research (1988) models autodidactic learning as being the application by an individual of rules of production similar to those "used" by an expert system to solve a problem. They note that in studies concerning the functioning of thought, two new trends may be observed:

> One trend is the increasing realization that much of what people do is determined by the peculiarities and particularities of the situations or contexts in which they find themselves. Another trend is found in studies of reasoning and thinking that place greater emphasis on what learners know as opposed to the process by which they learn what they know. (1988, p.240)

The interest of these authors' work lies in the fact that autodidactic learning skill is seen as expertise, i.e. a group of skills that are context-sensitive while being content-free insofar as they are the result of a transfer of knowledge that an autodidact has developed in another field but which presents the same contextual particularities.

The self-instruction model proposed by Martin (1984) also involves an analogy with systems theory. The autodidact is presented in it as an "information-processing system" one of whose critical tasks is to create an information structure, a task usually left to the instructor in an educational context.

Also noteworthy are the studies of Candy (1989) who proposes a constructivist model taking into consideration the random nature of the context in autodidactism:

> constructivism is subsumed under the root-metaphor of contextualism, which emphasizes constant change and novelty. Events are in constant flux, and the conditions of one event alter the context of a future event. In view of the way in which self-directed learning activities often unfold an approach which emphasises and allows for the ebb and flow of circumstances would seem to be preferable to one which presumes a simple linearity. (p. 98)

The random character of the context of an autodidactic situation is also considered by Theil (1989). Following a study of various authors in the self-organization field (Atlan, 1986; Moreno, 1986, and Varela, 1988), he notes that the logic of the functioning of a system constitutes its sole system of reference even though it can only function by being open to an environment. In particular, it needs to know and re-know this environment constantly in order to be able to function within it viably and thus predictably. But the autodidactic environment is usually the place where randomly occur unpredictable, ambiguous and complex events that the system must recognize as becoming or ceasing to be vital (information), non-pertinent (noise) or as non "processable" by its present logical data processing apparatus (interferences). Theil's model is based on data processing as an important function of a cognitive process; it conceives autodidactism as the space of interaction of a learning system that tries to transform the random events that are present in its learning context into learning experiences.

A MODEL OF AUTODIDACTISM

The following presents the general methodology used first in identifying to identify the concept of autodidactism, and then in elaborating a model.

General Methodology
This particular study is the last part of a long term research project conducted by Danis and Tremblay; which aims at describing, with particular concern for theory building, the phenomenon of autodidactism from the perspective of self-taught adults.

During the years 1982 to 1985, the research focused on the educational practices among adults. The results indicated the importance of the SDL current and a conceptual wavering among the authors consulted. Consequently, it was decided to study fully self-directed learners in a natural setting to make it possible to overcome the wavering observed.

During the years 1985 to 1988, the strategies used by self-taught adults were studied. The content analysis of the narratives of 20 self-taught adults that have succeeded in their domain have been analyzed, and they provided 14 propositions that corresponded to the characteristics observed.

For the past two years, the research was mainly concerned with the theoretical aspects of the phenomenon. If the characteristics can describe the elements observed in autodidactism, it lacked to explain the nature of what is going on. It became obvious that it would be of great interest to find the concepts strategy that permits descript in the nature of the observed phenomenon. (Tremblay, 1989).

The Concepts of Autodidactism
The concepts have been extracted from the 14 descriptors (characteristics) identified in a previous research (Danis et Tremblay, 1985a). A concept is here defined as a mental representation that can characterize in some general manner a reality that has been described. According to the specific

characteristics observed in autodidactic settings, four concepts emerged. Since these concepts are named here for the first time, the reader is asked to excuse the audaciousness in the choice of terms. The first concept has to do with the random aspects of the process and is called **Non-algorithmic Syntaxes**. A second one is designed to represent the fact that many functions and roles usually assumed by different persons and resources are here assumed in the same unit; it has been called **Ubiquity in Functions and Roles**. The third concept had previously been identified and named by Spear and concerns the effect of circumstances on strategies and means; Spear named this concept **Organizing Circumstances**. The last concept has been identified by Danis and Tremblay in 1984 in a study of meta-learning experiences in autodidactism and has been called **Internalization of Rules and Operations**.

Non-Algorithmic Syntaxes
The terms used here are meant to indicate that an autodidactic process presents an order ("taxis" - syntax) which does not evolve in a linear manner. An algorithm allows the group of actions necessary for a task to be presented sequentially and predictably. The autodidactic process appears to operate differently, suggesting operations of the autodidactic situation - representations established in relation to a problem-management or problem-solving process. Several researches having utilized Tough's operational framework finally succeeded in classifying the elements observed under dimensions borrowed from management (planning, organization, content acquisition, choice of resources, evaluation). If this metaphorical organization of the data suits a static level, it does not take into account the dynamics of the operational process. Indeed, autodidactic processes operate around intentions which take shape without any prior consideration. The objectives are constantly readjusted depending on personal tastes and wishes and circumstances. The process is characterized by its heuristic, iterative and contextual aspects:

> The study of autodidactic learning processes reveals rather multiple processes which do not correspond with the unidirectional representations predominant in the authors' work. (Danis & Tremblay, 1985, p. 435)

The concept of the "non-analgorithmic" syntax is here significant as a characteristic element of autodidactism because it refers to a situation in which an adult learns in a natural setting and because this setting corresponds with a random context. However, it questions once more the extension that may have been given to permit the inclusion of certain formal educational practices (education by contract, computer-assisted learning, etc.) sometimes creating confusion between the primary nature of the term (learning by oneself) and its derived nature (accounting for the learner in learning). The above considerations differ from the model widely accepted among the theorists in which needs precede learning and in which the evaluation would complete the process and reactivate it. Autodidacts, according to all the evidence, speak another language and act differently.

Ubiquity in Functions and Roles
This concept accounts for the fact that in autodidactism there exist normally dichotomized functions which are reconciled in the same place or time. Thus, action/reflection, practice/theory, learning/teaching can emerge in the same unit. Autodidactism might thus be defined as an eminently experiential method, in that action and reflection share the same space, thus agreeing with Freire's notion of "praxis". The same is true for theory which, as can be observed in autodidactic practices, may emerge from the act under way and which can be developed from action and in later confrontation with existing theories if the nature of the learning project lends itself to it. There seems to exist a form of refusal to dissociate the application and theoretical input that may emerge from the action.

Moreover, the self-taught adult is both learner and teacher, according to a contract that is not pre-established. Here again we find united in a same place two functions that are often dichotomized in more formal settings. And it would be false to believe that the various resources consulted by the autodidact suffice to satisfy the teaching aspect. The persons consulted provide varied help but no more than 20% of the help required to acquire the content, find the resources, decide what strategies to adopt: 80% of the decisions to be taken and tasks to be accomplished are assumed by the autodidact (Tough, 1978; Tremblay, 1981).

Organizing Circumstances and Strategies or Means (Spear's Concept)
This concept is undoubtedly the one which, up to now, is the most clearly defined and which has been verified concurrently in the various research projects.

Spear observed that the autodidacts, in their search for information and resources, was dependent on the elements available in their immediate environment and that they articulated their project by taking this variable into account. He thus stressed the importance of the environment in the study of learning in autodidactism and underlined the random component. This concept thus shatters a certain image of the autodidact directing his whole process at will, to insist rather on the impact of the availability of the resources in the environment. This concept is verified in the research of Tremblay (1981), Danis & Tremblay (1985) and Tsala (1990). The concept has shed new light on a group of phenomena observed by Tremblay (1981) concerning the criteria which guide autodidacts in the choice of a resource. It was observed that in 75% of cases, the autodidacts questioned had not planned to use the resource consulted and that this had been chosen by chance or quite simply because it had come to hand. A later observation of the learning experiences of autodidacts, moreover, enabled Danis and Tremblay to formulate a principle which takes into account the role in autodidactism of the resources available in the environment, namely that "self-taught adults seize every opportunity that chance may offer them to learn". The remarks made by various autodidacts questioned during these studies demonstrate the pertinence of this concept. Finally, research by Tsala among participants in Cameroon eshuans (autonomous self-help groups) highlights the fact that the choice of means utilized by these groups is largely dependent on the resources immediately available and that they condition the strategies adopted.

Internalization of Rules and Operations

This concept is intended to take into account the unique, individual and interior nature of an autodidactic process. It refers to characteristics of meta-learning which have been observed in autodidactism and to the self-referential element which often governs the choices made by the autodidact.

When analyzing the educational accounts given by autodidacts (Danis & Tremblay, 1984), it was noted that these adults spontaneously formulated a group of rules and principles respecting their field of study, certain traits of their personality, and what the fact of learning implies. Even though the account then used as a research method constitutes a useful technique for reflection on self and on one's experience, these autodidacts nonetheless showed a rare ability to transcend their own experience; it had then been agreed to classify all these phenomena under the heading of meta-learning and to propose this definition: "what encompasses and exceeds the various dimensions of the educational process in the sense of an understanding of its reality by the autodidact himself" (1984, p. 10). The confrontation of the principles later traced from the study of autodidactic experiences and the learning principles proposed by educational theorists has merely strengthened these first observations to indicate a more global and integrated acceptance of the very notion of learning and to question, with other authors, the possible existence of a stage going beyond the formal operational stage which would be characteristic of the adult, especially the autodidact adult.

The existence of rules and principles which govern learning in the autodidact might also suggest the existence of a sort of personal grammar in which behaviours would be encoded as their pertinence is verified in relation to the educational situation. The criteria which govern the various choices to be made would probably be previously identified by the individual. Without denying the impact that circumstances can have on the organization of the process, certain phenomena observed nonetheless indicate that the operations occur in relation to certain codes developed by the autodidact and apparently known only to him. This concept would explain in a certain way the numerous differences which exist in the educational career of autodidacts, beyond a situation which is common to all. The rates of learning differ for one particular individual and for the whole group, projects may be subdivided, branch out, the project may be interrupted and resumed. But, it is mainly at the evaluation level that it has been possible to observe a clear illustration of the present concept. Autodidacts often try out their competence by considering the tangible results they obtain and by trusting to an inner feeling that tells him he has succeeded (Danis & Tremblay, 1985, p. 430).

Enaction as an Analogue
Since the inductive method such as that used by the authors and the group of research (GRAAME) did not permit the formulation of a theory capable of explaining the concepts in question, it was decided to look to theoretical frameworks proposed in other fields so as to:

> suddenly (after eventual hesitations) and globally recognize an essential resemblance (i.e. as regards the pertinent dimensions within the context created by the problem). (Andler; 1986, p. 69)

Four specific theoretical frameworks have been studied: the New Communication (Bateson, 1984) the Cognitive Psychology (Weinstein, 1988), the societal aspect of Self-organisation (Morin, 1986) and the Epistemology of sciences (Varela, 1989). The theory of enaction of Varela (1989) emerged as a pertinent analogue regarding the concepts of autodidactism. This theory will be explained briefly here since it is new and therefore little known.

A proper understanding of the theory of enaction proposed by Varela (1989a, 1989b) requires a lengthy look at the evolution of the sciences of cognition. Indeed, his theory was formulated in reaction to certain problems identified in the models that have emerged from the main scientific current of this century.

The sciences and techniques of cognition now offer a fundamental as well as an applied corpus as indicated by the various fields which belong to it: artificial intelligence, linguistics, epistemology, neuro sciences, cognitive psychology. These fields have developed up to the present along two main axes according to the particular manner of defining cognition. These axes are called "Representationism" and "Connexionism". The main characteristics of the currents can be summarized and criticized as follow:

1. Only a pre defined world can be known
2. What is to be known must be predictable and organized in a linear manner.
3. The act of knowing is defined in terms of solutions to be found.

As Varela pointed out, the common sense seemed to have been evacuated, so he addressed theorists the following questions: "What is going on when I create or ask questions? What is going on when I try to learn in my everyday experiences?"

A return to the action of knowing is the means by which Varela moves away from the usual propositions regarding cognition and tries to posit premises of a more pertinent model. First, he notes that knowledge is not only defined in terms of solutions to be found but also in terms of questions to be asked, and the order of these questions cannot be pre-defined. Moreover, these questions, the sources of knowledge, are enacted in that they come both from action and from the actor involved in them. Cognition can be defined, according to Varela, as the ability to effect viable operations in a world in which the endogenous and exogenous are mutually defined throughout their history.

> The use of cognition which follows is not the solving of problems or means of representations, but rather the creative causing to emerge of a world, on the sole condition of being operational: it must assure the durability of the system in question. (1989 a, p. 112)

The theory of enaction suggested by Varela is intended to go beyond certain limits of the Representationist and Connexionist schools. The characteristic elements of the model in question are described as follows:

From (Representationism) (Connexionnism)	To (Enaction)
Task dedicated	Creative
Problem solving	Problem definition
Abstract, symbolic	Historical, incarnate
Universal	Contextual
Centralized	Distributed
Sequential, hierarchical	Parallel
Pre-defined world	Enacted world
Representation	Productive action
Development by concept	Development by evolutionist strategies
	Varela, 19.., p. 110)

Enaction, as a theoretical construct, is based on three concepts. Varela presents his theory as the culmination of his reflection as a neurobiologist on the principle characteristics of living systems and in doing so isolates the concepts of **autopoeis, emergence,** and **structural coupling.**

Autopoeis refers to the ability of living systems, unlike machines and other non-living systems, to produce their own constitutive elements and to modify their structure without loss of identity.

Emergence refers to the manner in which reality, in living systems, is defined without the constraint of arrested finality [-ies]. In other words, reality is defined without prior condition, in a random context.

Structural coupling refers to the manner in which, cognition, in living systems, is related to the history of what has been experienced in the course of interaction between a system and its environment. Thus, differenmt sets [bodies] of knowledge concerning a supposedly identical reality may be viable and pertinent.

The key concepts of enaction as defined by Varela present a number of analogies with the key concepts of autodidactism as extracted through analysis of the experiences of self-taught adults.

Linking Enaction and Autodidactism

How may the utilization of a theoretical analogue developed in relation to the cognitive aspect in an autodidactic context be justified? In the present case, the evolution of the research seems to invite an attempt to explain phenomena observed at different levels and by different investigators so as to introduce greater coherence. Furthermore, the evolution of the sciences of cognition presents analogies with the evolution of research on autodidactism. The representationist current and the preliminary studies in autodidactism, for example, have served to describe elements present in the situations studied. On the basis of these first current and first researches, studies have been undertaken concerning particular aspects and a start has been made to analyze the elements described. It is also on the basis of grounded theory that certain investigators try to define the dynamics of the phenomenon of autodidactism and that Varela proposes his theory.

A second analogy is worth establishing between the historical perspective and the temporal dimension introduced by Varela and the utilization of the personal account as a popular methodological tool in the study of autodidactism. From the very beginning, research in autodidactism was developed around the notion of a project (cf. Tough's definition) inviting the numerous investigators who were inspired by this referential framework to study this phenomenon globally rather than fragmentarily. Moreover, the educational account has been widely used as a strategy, which has permitted a coherent comparison of the results and a collection of special elements within a global framework. As suggested by Varela, it would be through their own historical career that the phenomena observed in cognition matters can be explained. The notion of time is thus also considered through the theory of Enaction and the methodological choices adopted in autodidactism.

The very concept of Enaction proves a powerful analogue in relation to autodidactism. It indicates the eminently experiential character of the act of knowing, replacing the actor/learner and action/learning in a dynamic which aligns the relationship of the action and the actor, as pointed out by Theil (1989) in speaking of the theory of enaction.

> Information does not lie in teaching as if that was a sort of "ecothèque" but must be produced by the system from events/meetings. (p. 5)

At most, autodidactism might represent the privileged relationship of experiential-type learning as indicated by the nature of the projects listed during research and surveys. As the syntheses of the research of Tough (1978) and Coolican (1973) have shown, as well as the survey of the Study Commission on Adult Education in Quebec (1982), most autodidactic projects are related to problems encountered by a person in the course of daily life as parent, spouse, worker, member of society, etc.

How can both concepts be articulated in such a manner that the theory of Enaction can make evidence for autodidactism. It appears that autodidactism and living systems share the same mystery. How can we explain that there is maintenance of a system in a random context? How can we explain that a learner produce an educational activity in a context not intended to be educational? The paradigm of enaction may suggest a new comprehension of the dynamic that occurs in such a context.

1.   According to the concept of autopoeis, the system would be maintained because it can produce constitutive elements and can modify its structure without loss of identity. This notion of autopoeis seems to correspond to the concept of internalization of rules and operations that have been proposed for autodidactism. This concept has been defined in relation to the ability of self-taught adults to encompass and exceed the various dimensions of the educational process in the sense of understanding of its reality by the self-taught adult himself/herself (Danis et Tremblay, 1984). These notions of autopoeis and meta-learning could also explain the ability of a self-taught adult to assume generally dichotomized functions and roles that are encoded here in the same unit (the learner himself). Those conceptual elements (autopoeis, meta-learning and ubiquity in the functions and roles) could explain the maintenance of the system.

2.   The concept of emergence must be understood in relationship to enaction as it has just been considered. Unlike the representationist and connexionist views in which reality may be represented a priori, enaction proposes a different version in which reality is defined through the evolution of a system and different interrelationships. While an a priori understanding of reality makes possible an algorithmic representation, the realization of the random nature of the context is an invitation to reconsider this type of representation. The study of the different paths in autodidactism shows that the syntax of a process is defined as it takes place. It is also possible to see that the goals and objectives of learning are defined and redefined constantly and without prior considerations (Danis & Tremblay, 1985a). Considered as a system, the autodidact possesses the ability to extract information and means that prove pertinent to the realization of his project. This characteristic has, moreover, enabled the questioning of certain models which represent autodidactism as a problem-solving or managerial process (Danis, 1988). Even though functions specific to management or to problem-solving (diagnosis, evaluation) can

be observed in autodidactism, it is important to distinguish between the function involved and the dynamics of the process of which it is a part.

3.   The concept of coupling presents a close link with that of emergence. It is in fact through an uninterrupted sequence (history) of couplings (interactions) that knowledge probably emerges. The study of cognition in the past decades often lied between two poles: one states that the external world comprises fixed rules, and the other that the world is created according to the internal laws of an organism. From the viewpoint of enaction, however, it seems more accurate to consider both the endogenous and exogenous aspects in question. This consideration has been taken into account by Spear in the formulation of his "Organizing Circumstances" concept as indicated by this citation of Bandura that he reports:

> Reciprocal determinants mean that people are not powerless objects controlled by environmental forces nor are they entirely free agents who can do whatever they please. (1978, p. 357)

This reciprocal determination can be observed in autodidactism in relation to the choice of resources, for example. On the one hand, the order of available resources influences the choices made and the organization of the process (influence of the exogenous over the endogenous) and, on the other, the autodidact, through the use he makes of it, may confer an educational character to a ressource.

The concepts of enaction (autopoeis, emergence and structural coupling) can be linked to the concepts of autodidatism (internalization of rules, ubiquity in functions, non-algorithmic syntaxes and organizing circumstances). Nevertheless, how can enaction sheds new light on autodidactism?

Figure 3.1: Model of Autodidactism (Tremblay, 1990).

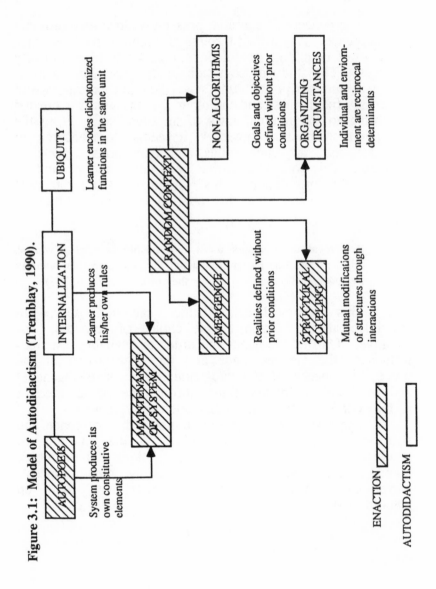

A model of autodidactism
The theory of enaction, here use as an analog, introduces more coherence regarding the concept of autodidactism. When the question of "how a system can be maintained in a random context" is addressed, the conceptual elements of autodidactism receive better understanding, as illustrated in Figure 3.1.

The illustration summarizes the main analogies established between the theory of enaction and the situation of autodidactism and may be considered as a first theoretical proposition. The key concepts identified following the study of the phenomenon of autodidactism are placed in a logical relationship as a first theoretical proposition. The key concepts identified following the study of phenomenon of autodidactism are placed in a logical relationship to each other with respect to the question of the logic of maintaining of system in a random context. The random context characteristic of an autodidactic situation would explain special characteristics with regard to the process syntax (non-algorithmic syntaxes) and the environment (organizing circumstances). On the other hand, the internalization of the rules of functioning and the ubiquity in the functions and roles assumed by the autodidact might explain the logic of the maintenance of this system in a random context.

CONCLUSION

This first theoretical proposition must be critically examined, however. Care must be taken first of all to ensure, with the help of a pertinent methodology, that the chosen analysis has not introduced unacceptable distortions into the formulated proposition. Care must also be taken to ensure that the concepts are specific to an autodidactic situation; a comparative study of the characteristic elements of autodidactism in relation to other forms of didactic situations would be necessary. Lastly, care must be taken to ensure that the essential concepts in autodidactism have been recognized and announced and to have them identified for various populations, in various regions and for various kinds of educational projects. These last considerations should indicate paths for further research in a critical, theory-building perspective.

Despite the above considerations, this model of autodidactism could inspire a general definition of autodidactism. The parameters of the model could serve as criteria in a specific definition on the nature of an educational situation where self-direction in learning operates in an informal, natural context.

> The logic of functioning in autodidactism would have to do with the ability to produce inner rules or operations and to assume generally dichotomized educational functions through a set of organizing circumstances and a process evolving without prior considerations.

This definition attempts to distinguishs autodidactism from other educational situation in which the concept of self-direction is taken into account.

REFERENCES

Andler, D. (1986). Le cognitivisme orthodoxe en question, in Cognition et Complexité, Cahier du CREA no 9, Centre de recherche épistémologie et autonomie, École Polytechnique, Paris, 45-126.

Atlan, H. (1986). Créativité biologique et auto-création de sens, in Cognition et complexité, Cahier du CREA no 9, Centre de recherche épistémologie et autonomie, École Polytechnique, Paris, 145-190.

Bateson, G. (1984). La nature et la pensée, Paris: Seuil.

Caffarella, R.S., O'Donnell, J.M. (1987). Self-directed adult learning: a paradigm revisited, Adult Education Quarterly, 37 (4), 199-211.

Candy, P.C. (1989). Constructivism and the study of self-direction in adult learning. Studies in the Education of Adults, 21 (2), 17-38.

Coolican, P. (1974). Self-planned learning: implications for the future of adult education. Unpublished paper, Syracuse, Syracuse University Research Corporation.

Danis, C. (1988). Revision of self-directed models in Transatlantic dialogue: a research exchange, Leeds, England, CASAE/ACEEA, 120-125.

Danis, C., Tremblay, N.A. (1984). Manifestations de méta-apprentissage en situation d'autodidaxie, Proceedings of the Third Annual Conference of the Canadian Association for the Study of Adult Education. Montréal, Université de Montréal, 151-166.

Danis, C., Tremblay, N.A. (1985a). Critical analysis of adult learning principles from a self-directed learner's perspective. Proceedings of the Twenty-sixth Annual Adult Education Research Conference, March 22-24, 1985, Tempe, Arizona State University, 138-143.

Danis, C., Tremblay, N.A. (1985b). The self-directed learning experience: Major recurrent tasks to deal with. Proceedings of the Fourth Annual Conference of the Canadian Association for the Study of Adult Education, May 28-30, Montreal, University of Montreal, 283-301.

Danis, C. et al., (1989). Analyse interdisciplinaire des principales caractéristiques de la situation d'autodidaxie - Symposium. Proceedings of the 8th Annual Conference of Canadian Association for the Study of Adult Education, René Bédard Éd., Cornwall, University of Ottawa, 100-195.

Freire, P. (1970). Pedagogy of the oppressed. New York: The Seabury Press.

Legendre, R. (1988). Dictionnaire actuel de l'éducation, Montréal: Larousse Éd.

Long, H.B. (1990). Changing concepts of self-direction in learning in H.B. Long and Associates, Advances in research and practice in self-directed learning. Oklahoma Research Center for Continuing Professional and Higher Education of the University of Oklahoma, 1-8.

Martin, J. (1984). Toward a cognitive schemata theory of self instruction, Instructional Sciences, 13, 159-180.

Moreno, A. (1986). Épistémologie des modes de représentation in Cognition et complexité, Cahier du CREA no 9, Centre de recherche épistémologie et autonomie, École Polytechnique, Paris, 191-222.

Morin, E. (1986). La connaissance de la connaissance. Paris: Seuil.

Penland, P. (1978). Individual self-planned learning, Washington, D.C., Office of Education.

Peters, J.M., LAZARRA, P.J. (1988). A knowledge acquisition method for building expert system: studying adult reasoning and thinking. Proceedings of Adult Education Research Conference, Calgary, Canada, 240-245.

(QUÉBEC) Commission d'étude sur la formation des adultes, Apprendre: une action volontaire et responsable, Ministère de l'éducation du Québec, Éditeur officiel, 1982.

Spear, G.E., Mocker, D.W. (1984). The organizing circumstance: environmental determinants in self-directed learning. Adult Education Quarterly, 35 (1), 110.

Spear, G.E. (1988). Beyond the organizing circumstances: a search for methodology for the study of self-directed learning in H.B. Long and Associates: Self-directed learning: application and theory, Georgia, Adult Education Department on Lifelong Learning, 199-221.

Theil, J.P. (1989). La situation autodidactique comme situation d'auto-éco-organisation, Actes du 8e Congrès de l'Association canadienne pour l'étude de l'éducation des adultes, René Bédard Éd., Cornwall, Université d'Ottawa, Ont., 304-309.

Tough, A. (1967). Learning without a teacher: a study of tasks and assistance during adult self-teaching projects, Toronto: Ontario Institute for Studies in Education.

Tough, A. (1971). The adult's Learning Projects, Toronto: Ontario Institute for Studies in Education.

Tremblay, N.A. (1981). L'aide à l'apprentissage en situation d'autodidaxie, Doctoral dissertation (Ph.D.), section d'andragogie, Faculté des sciences de l'éducation, Université de Montréal.

Tremblay, N.A. (1989). Quelques concepts-clés en autodidaxie. Actes du 2e Congrès des sciences de l'éducation de langue française du Canada, Sherbrooke (Québec), Université de Sherbrooke.

Tremblay, N.A. (1990). Le concept d'enaction et la syntaxe autodidactique. Actes du 9e Congrès annuel de l'Association canadienne pour l'étude de l'éducation des adultes, Victoria, B.C., University of Victoria, 407-412.

Tsala-Mvilongo, A. (1990). Étude du mode d'intervention éducative caractérisant l'Eshuan camerounien. Doctoral dissertation, département de psychopédagogie et d'andragogie, Faculté des sciences de l'éducation, Université de Montréal.

Varela, F.J. (1989a). Connaître les sciences cognitives: tendances et perspectives. Paris, Seuil.

VARELA, F.J. (1989b). <u>Autonomie et connaissance: essai sur le vivant</u>. Paris, Seuil.

Weinstein, C.E. et al. (1988). <u>Learning and Study Strategies - Issues in Assessment, Instruction and Evaluation</u>, San Diego, CA: Academic Press. Inc.

Autodidactism

CHAPTER FOUR

FUNCTIONAL AND DYSFUNCTIONAL USES OF SELF-DIRECTEDNESS IN ADULT LEARNING

L. Adrianne Bonham

In earlier papers, suggestions have been made that it might be helpful to think of self-directed learning as a set of learning styles (Bonham, 1989a, 1989b). This chapter goes a step further, exploring ways and contexts in which each style element may be functional and dysfunctional.

BACKGROUND

First, let us review the groundwork. It includes (1) a definition of self-directedness in learning, (2) an identification of what should be added to our understanding in order to see self-directedness as a learning style, and (3) definitions of possible elements or styles.

A Definition of Self-Directed Learning
While there are many definitions of self-directed learning, the most useful are the ones that deal with the circumstances of learning. When persons choose their own learning goals, their own learning methods, and the content and process resources they will use, they are being self-directed learners.

I do not see intrinsic motivation as a definition of self-directedness. In some writing about self-directed learning and in much of the everyday talk about it, people call learners self-directed if they are interested in what the teacher wants them to learn, if they are eager to do the assignments laid out by the teacher. This is not a helpful definition, for several reasons.

A chief reason is that people can want to learn a certain thing -- can be motivated to learn it -- but want a teacher to tell them how to learn. In other words, motivation is not a characteristic that separates self-directed learning from other kinds of learning. It separates learning from not-learning.

A second reason that motivation is not a useful definition is that the self-directedness issues we usually should be concerned about are not issues of motivation but issues of process. A person who approaches someone for help with a specific learning need is expressing motivation. That is usually the only person that a teacher has a chance to help. The unmotivated is beyond the teacher's reach, in any context where participation is voluntary. Furthermore, if the teacher helps the motivated person learn the process of being self-directed, he/she can be even more self-directed the next time there is a recognized need for learning.

This is not meant to imply that motivation is not an issue in adult education -- only that it is not the issue in identifying self-directed learners. In this paper, I would like to consider only motivated learners and then try to decide which of them is self-directed, and how.

Needs of a Learning Style Theory

There is at least as much diversity in the definitions of "learning style" as in the definitions of "self-directed learning." There are some points of agreement, however, about what is needed in order to describe a learning style theory. Justification for the characteristics given here is that they are a distillation from earlier research, a study of the theory underlying the field of cognitive and learning styles as well as theories underlying individual instruments (Bonham, 1988). There seem to be at least three ways in which we need to expand our thinking on self-directed learning in order to consider it as a learning style construct.

First, we need to define multiple style elements. Existing instruments, such as the Guglielmino and Oddi questionnaires (Guglielmino, 1978; Oddi, 1985), measure more or less of one characteristic. Learning style theories, however, identify several styles. The two existing instruments imply that increase of self-directedness means lessening of something else. The questionnaire items themselves -- and much of what is written about the instruments and done with them in research -- seem to say that the "something else" is non-learning and lack of motivation. Thus, we are back to the earlier discussion of motivation.

Second, in defining the multiple styles, we need to define positively valued styles, ones that are useful in at least some contexts. This need is another reason for eliminating "non-learner" and "unmotivated" as opposites to "self-directed." If we can identify several positive dimensions in relation to self-directed learning, we can help adults appreciate and use their learning strengths -- and then recognize the weakness of always using the same approach.

A third need is to decide on the purpose or use of style information. I prefer a two-step use. First, the teacher/facilitator/counselor helps learners understand their styles and the strengths and weaknesses of various styles. Second, learners gain skill in choosing a style that is suitable for a given task.

A style-information use that should be strongly resisted is that of matching a teaching method with the learner's style. That solution is shortsighted, in that it opts for immediate accomplishment of short-term goals related to learning content but does not aim at making the learner a more resourceful learner for the future. Furthermore, research indicates that matching does not consistently do a better job of accomplishing even the short-term, content-related goals (Bonham, 1988).

POSSIBLE STYLES

Against this background, it seems possible to define three styles which might be called other-directedness, linear self-directedness, and holistic self-directedness.

Other-directed learners are motivated to learn. (We often make the mistake of assuming that they are not motivated and that being other-directed is the same as not learning.) These persons, however, want or need for the teacher to say how the learning should take place. Such learners may lack skill in identifying specific learning goals or available resources or appropriate relationships; but they do want to learn.

Persons who take a linear approach to being self-directed are also motivated. They tend to plan life in detail, so that is the way they plan their learning. They emphasize clear but limited objectives, discrete steps taken in a predetermined sequence, and frequent checks on accomplishment of the objectives. While formal education develops skills in this sort of planning, what we need to remember here is that some people tend to see life this way. It is interesting to speculate if Allen Tough sees life this way and if that is why his model of self-directed learning ended up with 13 discrete planning steps (Tough, 1979).

Holistic self-directed learner. If there is any truth to this idea that the theorist lives his own theory, George Spear and Donald Mocker (1984) are living examples of the third style: the holistic self-directed learner. Persons with this style have only loosely defined learning goals -- usually focused on long-range learning projects. They make up their learning plans as they go, being strongly influenced by what is available in their environment. Perhaps they go for long periods, gathering seemingly random pieces of information, then suddenly have the pieces fall into place.

EXAMPLES OF FUNCTIONAL AND
DYSFUNCTIONAL USES OF THE THREE STYLES

This paper examines learning in three contexts: (1) graduate courses in adult education, (2) courses or classes not for academic credit, and (3) learning in life. "Learning in life" is defined as an on-going process made up of many learning episodes related to the same broadly defined interest or need. The first context is important to some either because we teach in such an adult education graduate program or because we learn in one. The second is important because it composes probably the bulk of adult education. The third is important becauses -- based on the findings of Tough and many others (e.g., Tough, 1966, 1978) -- it composes the bulk of adult learning.

These three contexts will be viewed from the standpoint of an other-directed learner, a linear self-directed learner, and a holistic self-directed learner. These portraits of learners are overstated but will serve to sharpen our awareness of the issues involved. The question is, When is each style functional, and when is it dysfunctional?

Let us acknowledge in passing that, when any one style is demanded by a teacher, it is functional for the student to be able to use that style. Our intention as teachers, though, is to be more sensitive to times when one style is more functional in terms of either the content or the context or both.

The Other-Directed Learner
Tom entered the doctoral program in adult education last fall, with high GRE scores, a high grade point average, and a strong motivation to learn all he can about adult education. He was not long in choosing a chair for his advisory committee, a faculty member known to be more content-centered than process-centered. Tom consults with his chair frequently about what courses he should take and about how he is doing on the problems course he is taking this semester. The chair is already anticipating that Tom will hang on to him tightly when Tom begins preparing the dissertation proposal

and doing that research. Therefore, the chair is pushing Tom to develop skills in defining his own objectives and finding resources and methodology.

Tom and his chair have had frequent conferences about an adult education faculty member who, Tom feels, does not do his job well. This professor likes to facilitate while students plan the course, choose resources, and determine their learning methods. Tom feels this is a cop-out, and he feels lost and resentful in classes taught by that professor.

On the other hand, Tom is doing well -- better than most -- in his statistics class. The teacher is precise about learning objectives and provides detailed instruction that will accomplish the objectives. Tom approaches the extensive homework assignments with a sense of comfortable interest, confident that the teacher has laid the groundwork for Tom to be able to work the problems. He feels comfortable going to the teacher for help, and can usually state clearly what he does not understand.

Tom regrets that the adult education faculty dislikes programmed instruction. In his undergraduate studies, he took some classes that majored on this format, and he always made good grades. Furthermore, he remembered much of what he had learned. He appreciated the orderliness of the thinking involved and the amount of effort that had gone into the teacher's development and testing of the learning materials.

Even while a graduate student, Tom has continued an interest in duck carving. That interest began when Tom saw what fun a neighbor was having in a duck-carving class. Tom signed up for the next available class and takes a class every time one is offered through the continuing education program at the community college. He appreciates the expertise of the instructor and often asks for evaluation and suggestions. When the instructor mentions a new book on carving or one that provides useful pictures of various species of ducks, Tom gets the book. He has won prizes for his duck carvings, and is known especially for the accuracy of detail in the carving and painting.

While Tom has always been pleased with the duck-carving classes, he only lasted through one class period when he took a continuing education course in how to trace one's family history. He felt totally lost because everyone else had specific questions -- about how to find service records for the War of 1812 or exactly when the deeds burned in the county courthouse. Actually, Tom was lost because the teacher was willing to follow wherever students' questions led. Tom thought the teacher had an obligation to organize the content and give an overview of the process of finding family history. When the teacher did not do that, Tom quit the class and got a book that would teach him in an organized manner.

He soon lost interest in digging out family history, however. It was just too confusing and disjointed, finding a fact here about one family member and a fact there about someone from another branch of the family in another century -- not to mention finding contradictory evidence or no evidence at all.

When Tom has to learn things in everyday life, he tends to look for a class or a how-to book. He asks a friend for information -- if he is sure the friend will have the answer. He has trouble, though, if he has a complicated problem that he cannot define clearly or that will require his getting pieces of information from several sources. His biggest problem is when he has to put together the pieces and come up with some new information.

A case in point is the do-it-yourself remodeling of his back porch. "It would have been easier to build it from scratch," Tom mutters to himself as he sifts through four how-to books, trying to decide the order in which he should take out old paneling, jack up part of the foundation, install new windows, and put in the insulation and electrical outlets. He thinks longingly about the deck kit he saw at the hardware store -- complete with step-by-step directions.

Even the remodeling seems easy, compared to the time Tom was trying to learn to understand his teen-age son. Tom could not even figure out what the questions were, let alone the answers. It was frightening to him that he felt more comfortable when he knew the question: "How do I deal with a kid on drugs?" At least then he knew who to consult for answers.

The Linear Self-Directed Learner

Dick also entered the adult education doctoral program last fall, with credentials as strong as Tom's. He went immediately to his temporary advisor and asked for a detailed run-down of the steps he must take in getting through his doctoral program. When they got to the part about filing a degree plan, Dick pulled out the list he had made of all the courses he wanted to take. He asked for the advisor's ideas about the value of courses in question but went away to make his own decisions. When Dick did choose a committee chair (at the time designated in the process), he laid out his detailed plans for completing coursework and finalizing a dissertation topic.

Dick consults regularly -- but perhaps less frequently than Tom -- with his chair. When Dick makes an appointment, he has a clearly defined purpose, and it usually includes getting some detailed information or the professor's reaction to a specific question. Dick is always thinking ahead, so his questions are asked well before he needs to know the answers.

One of the first things Dick did on campus was to arrange a guided tour of the library, with its various computerized data retrieval systems. He caught on fast to this library's system because he always takes this proactive approach in getting to know learning resources and methods.

Dick has put on his degree plan a number of problems courses. He likes the feeling of control he has in laying out his learning goals (tailored to his needs, as they cannot always be in a class) and the plans by which he will accomplish those goals. He has never gotten an "incomplete" in a problems course -- except the one time when he and the faculty member agreed in advance that he would take two semesters to complete some out-of-town interviews.

Despite liking problems courses best, Dick thinks a close next-best is the professor whom Tom dislikes for being only a facilitator. One difference in Dick and Tom's approaches is that Dick deliberately uses the professor as one of his information and planning sources, making appointments on a regular basis and being prepared to lead the discussion to meet his needs. Dick can tell he is on the same wave length as the professor, who likes to use learning contracts and, thus, likes for students to make detailed plans at the beginning of the semester.

Before he got to the doctoral program, Dick dealt with a problem that had originally kept him from getting maximum profit from this kind of self-planned learning experience. Dick used to get frustrated when he laid out a learning plan and something went wrong -- needed books were missing from library shelves or a teacher had to delay a scheduled conference. Then Dick learned to stop himself and make a wholly new plan.

It was at such times that Dick thought of his younger brother. They are much alike in the organized way they go about everything, including learning. The brother, however, has much less formal schooling. He lacks some of the planning skills Dick has developed; and his range of known resources is often more limited than Dick's. Even so, Dick can see that their natural learning patterns are similar.

Dick knows, for instance, that he and his brother would have the same reaction to that statistics class. Dick appreciates the work the teacher has done in preparing the class presentations and homework assignments. At least, he appreciates those things now that he has thought through the course syllabus for himself and seen how it makes sense. Dick wishes, though, that each person could determine when he has worked enough problems in order to understand a concept.

Dick, like Tom, does duck carving and wins prizes for his excellent detail. He took several classes when he was beginning to learn the basics; but half-way through the third class, he got restless because the teacher did not know about the species Dick wanted to carve. Dick took charge of his own learning then, deciding on a mix of individual consultation with master carvers, attendance at short workshops, and the building of a library of basic resources.

He even taught a class or two when time permitted. At first, he had short-term goals, like mastering the carving of a new species. Later, he planned his activities for several years, leading up to a try for the state championship in decoy carving. When he placed second, he felt his goal had been relatively well accomplished, and he decided to shift his spare-time attention to the study of family history.

Dick was in the genealogy class that was so frustrating to Tom. Dick was frustrated too, but he solved his problem differently. He laid out a six-month plan by which he would learn the basics of genealogical research, using a combination of books and friends as his sources. For that six months, he saw the actual family research as practice to help him learn the basic research methods. Then he re-enrolled in the class, with a long list of specific questions. When discussions got into areas unrelated to his immediate interests, he had no hesitation about turning them off or even leaving for the night.

Dick developed a plan for how he would bring order to what is, by its nature, a disordered process of finding clues about many people in many places at many times. He set up an extensive but expandable filing system. He would choose a particular family line and work on it until he had gone back at least two generations; then he would write up that material, choose another line, and repeat the process. When he serendipitously came across information related to other family lines or earlier centuries, he carefully filed it away for later reference. Such information helped him at the point of choosing and planning the next research component.

Coincidentally, Dick was also like Tom in having a porch that needed remodeling. His actions and reactions were different, however. The most fun for Dick was getting the how-to books and planning the project. He spent six months pouring over the books, standing on the porch with a notepad, and making extensive lists; all the things that he wanted to add or change, the order in which those things should be done, materials and equipment needed for each, where he could buy the materials and borrow or rent the equipment, and the anticipated cost of each. When he was ready to start building, Dick proudly taped his lists to the porch wall and hung nearby a pencil he would use in checking off each step.

Unlike Tom, Dick has no children. He does work with teenagers in his church and has done so for several years. When he was enlisted to teach a Bible study class -- with no experience in relating to teens -- he was nervous, especially because they wanted him to start teaching the next Sunday. He went immediately to the youth minister, who helped him lay out a plan for learning about teenagers, informal counseling, and Bible teaching. As soon as he had the plan, he felt better. Even if he didn't have all the knowledge and skills he needed that first Sunday -- or that first year -- he did have a plan for getting those things.

If Dick seems the perfect self-directed learner, you need to know that several adult education faculty members have some poorly defined uneasiness about what Dick is learning. There seems to be a shallowness to some of his self-planned learning. He fails to get below the surface, seldom seeing that he needs to refine learning objectives as he discovers more about a topic. He sees each problems course or class as a separate topic and sometimes fails to link his understandings into a pattern. Furthermore, he is usually content to discover what others think, rather than using that research as a basis for new ideas of his own. Specifically, Dick's chair wonders about two graduate-school hurdles that Dick must encounter. Will Dick perform well on the written and oral preliminary exams, in which the emphasis is on synthesizing for oneself and on original thinking? Second, what will happen if the hypotheses are not supported when Dick does his dissertation research? Will he be able to discover and evaluate alternative explanations for the findings, or will he simply report that the theory is faulty?

The Holistic Self-Directed Learner
Harry is further along in his program than are Tom and Dick. In fact, he has been working on his dissertation for two years -- after working on his proposal for a whole year. Harry's chair knows that this ongoing problem is not Harry's failure to start on a project; the problem is getting so involved that

he does not stop researching and start writing in time to meet a deadline.

Having worked with Harry on several problems courses, the chair analyzes the stumbling block as lack of focus. Harry used to come in with only a vague idea of what he wanted to do in the course, and he would resist the professor's efforts to have Harry sharpen the objective and make firm plans about how to accomplish it. Half-way through a semester, Harry would have done enough reading or interviewing to satisfy the professor; but Harry would still be asking himself new questions and struggling to find a shape for his ideas. A semester late, he would come in with a paper long enough to be a dissertation. The A he got, though, was for the original thinking that went beyond all that he had read. He would have pulled together seemingly unrelated ideas and produced a well-defined Gestalt. Sometimes the Gestalt jolted the professor and prompted arguments with Harry; but it was always clear that Harry had either thought through the issues the professor named or that he set about to do so on the spot.

Discussions with Harry were always interesting, in an uncomfortable way. They were long and seemed to lack focus, and Harry rarely had a well-formed purpose when he asked for a conference. On the other hand, he was obviously engrossed in his subject and had intriguing ideas. That was an evaluation that Harry's committee also gave to his written and oral prelims, despite the fact that (as they thought back later) Harry had not given much detailed recall information in his answers.

Another irritating habit of Harry's was that, while he was doing his coursework, the professor would not see Harry outside of class for a month and then would be asked for four conferences in a 10-day period. Harry said that was because his ideas had suddenly come together. The professor's concern now is that, knowing Harry's style of self-directedness, the professor should not have turned Harry loose on the qualitative data collection and analysis without an agreement about when and how often they would talk. What if Harry goes on forever with his data collection?

It is no wonder, given Harry's interest in qualitative research, that he did not like the statistics courses required on his degree plan. He also disliked, however, the manner in which they were taught. He felt frustrated when a teacher would not deviate from the stated topic (usually the derivation of formulas) to discuss a question that had just come into Harry's mind about how the statistic should be used. Sometimes he tried to find the answer outside of class; but after continually being frustrated in class -- and not caring much for statistics, anyway -- he began to ignore his own questions and learn just what was needed for an adequate grade.

Outside of graduate studies, Harry has a habit of developing long-term interests. He never got into duck carving, as Tom and Dick did. That was much too detailed and tedious to appeal to Harry as a leisure time activity. He did take several sculpture classes, however, one for woodcarving and one for stonecarving. He liked to begin with a block of walnut or marble and chip away until he began to see a form emerging from the material itself. Teachers who took that approach to their own sculpting liked Harry's initial attempts and wanted him to go on with his efforts. That wasn't practical for Harry, given the time, space, and equipment required for the kind of attention he would have wanted to give this interest.

Harry was, however, left with an interest in sculpture. Over the years, he developed a small but choice set of books on the subject, attended lectures by visiting sculptors, helped to secure sculpture exhibits for the local art museum, and became friends with several professional sculptors. Those friends considered Harry enough of an expert -- though self-taught -- that they asked for his ideas when considering new approaches to their work.

An even greater interest of Harry's is genealogy. He drifted into study of family history through renewed contact with some cousins he had known in childhood. They got him started with a textbook on family history research, but he soon branched in many directions, making a conscious effort to learn research processes along with getting details about his family. Harry does not share with his cousins an interest in joining patriotic organizations, which require proof of ancestry. He is intrigued with tracking down clues and gaining new insights about his ancestors' relationships to historical events.

The cousins are horrified at the way Harry does his research and keeps records on it. He actually seems to enjoy being unsystematic! He tends to get sidetracked, too, chasing records on some distant relative or studying 19th century westward migration patterns. When those side trips sometimes result in unexpected finds about ancestors or interesting explanations for their actions, the cousins grumble about luck or wasted motion.

They don't know what frustrates Harry about himself: Because he does not keep an organized record of what he has found, he sometimes loses track of valuable information, only to stumble over it again months later. Or he has a moment of fresh understanding about a family event but loses it because he does not write it down. "The material got cold, and I could never recall what I found so revealing about it," he says.

One reason Harry has this problem -- with genealogy or graduate study -- is that he is unusually aware of information he runs into in daily life. Almost everything he experiences seems related to other things he knows about. While his brain is not an errorless filing system, he does seem able to hold a multitude of information at the ready and to cross-sort it with incoming information. He seems able to use so many kinds of resources and to see so many everyday things for their value in his learning.

Those capabilities make Harry a good learner when there is no class to teach him what he wants to know. They help him to create new knowledge as he processes incoming information along with what he already knows.

Harry sometimes creates problems for himself, though, by delaying decisions about exactly what he needs to know. His porch remodeling project is a case in point. He didn't think through the whole set of steps, so he had the new paneling up before he decided he would like to have a telephone jack on the porch. Then he had to take time to learn how to wire the jack before he could read the directions on how to lay the vinyl flooring. In the meantime, the weather turned cold, and he had to wait for warmer weather before staining the paneling, because he had just read the label on the can of stain.

Harry decided the porch project was one of those cases where being a self-directed learner got him in trouble. It would have been much simpler to take a class in home remodeling and adapt those general ideas to his specific needs. Even better, he could have asked for advice from his neighbor who had just remodeled his own porch. "Sometimes, reinventing the porch can be an inefficient way to learn," says Harry.

ABSTRACTING MEANING FROM THE EXAMPLES

Graduate programs in adult education seem to value most highly the learning style of Dick, the person who likes to plan his own learning and who will do that planning in a detailed, linear way. Such planning shows the initiative of the student in a way that the teacher can evaluate and assist from the beginning. There is also the assumption that learning is greater when the learner has this kind of involvement in planning and conducting the learning activities. The learner is seen somehow to be more adult when he/she is like Dick.

Perhaps it is time these adult education programs take a look at some other learning styles and at their functional and dysfunctional uses in graduate programs, in voluntary non-credit adult education, and in the everyday informal learning of adults.

An other-directed learner like Tom has the advantage when the learning task is simple and when the need is to transmit existing knowledge in the most efficient way. Tom is advantaged when he needs to learn something simple in a hurry; he will follow the lead of the teacher, who has planned the most effective way for the learner to operate.

Tom is at a disadvantage when there is no person, book, or other appropriate teacher to tell him how to learn something. Tom also tends not to recognize help when he accidentally comes upon it in his daily life. Tom's need for guidance is especially a problem when he must create new knowledge, as he is expected to do in certain parts of his doctoral program and as everyone often has to do in everyday life.

The strengths of Dick (the darling of adult educators) are his ability to plan in detail -- and his liking for the actual process of planning. In fact, Dick sometimes seems to get greater satisfaction from the successful execution of his plan than from the knowledge he acquires as a result. His approach is functional when he knows enough about a subject to be able to form a precise learning objective and when he knows enough about learning resources and methods to work out a plan for accomplishing his objective. Like Tom, Dick is most successful when the learning task is the discovery of existing information, rather than the creating of new information.

A dysfunctional aspect of Dick's style is that, when the information does already exist, discovering it for himself may not be as efficient as Tom's way of letting the teacher tell him how to learn it. Dick can have a problem planning his learning when he knows little about the subject or the needed resources. He may be so committed to his planning that he has trouble changing plans or taking advantage of resources that he stumbles upon. Dick may also tend to see learning as isolated episodes and be slow to see the relationship among the episodes. Thus, he may not get maximum cumulative benefit from his learning.

Harry's approach is most functional when he needs to bring together information from different perspectives in order to form new ideas. His plan is to begin with a general idea, gather information as it becomes available, and reshape both his plan for learning and the content of his learning. This style may be the most productive over a lifetime of learning about the same subject, because Harry tends to see learning as one long, evolving process. It is the process of learning, not the process of planning, that gives Harry the greatest pleasure.

On the other hand, Harry's learning is not efficient. He may disdain predigested information and such structured learning methods as programmed instruction, even when these would be adequate for learning certain content. He may not choose the most helpful resources, because he responds to all resources that he recognizes rather than selecting them purposefully. Because he values the gaining of sudden insights over the incremental accumulation of knowledge, he may be frustrated for long periods while he accumulates the knowledge on which his insight will be based. Insights may not always come by the time a paper is due, so that the most significant learning will be aborted or the paper will be late.

USING INFORMATION ABOUT STYLE

The purpose of this chapter is to suggest possible functional and dysfunctional aspects of several styles of self-directed learning. I would like to conclude, however, with a few ideas about how this knowledge could be useful.

Teachers would do well to think about different learning tasks as perhaps calling for different approaches in terms of the kind and amount of self-directedness. Such distinctions even suggest that there are times when it is not helpful to be self-directed! Teachers may need to give up the assumption that all self-directed learning should be defined by the same kind of learning contract, always written during the first week of the semester.

It may be helpful, when teaching people to learn in everyday life, to concentrate less on a detailed planning process and to emphasize instead an openness to resources available in the environment. The ability to delay learning gratification may be a skill worth teaching adult learners; it is sometimes necessary to hold onto isolated bits of information long enough to work through frustration and come to moments of insight.

In short, learning can be enhanced -- through the use of style information and beyond the person's original style -- for every Tom, Dick, and Harry.

REFERENCES

Bonham, L.A. (1988). Theoretical and practical differences and similarities among selected cognitive and learning styles of adults: An analysis of the literature (Doctoral Dissertation, University of Georgia, 1987). Dissertation Abstracts International, 48, 2788A. (University Microfilms No. 88-00255)

Bonham, L.A. (1989a). Self-directed orientation toward learning: A learning style? In H. B. Long and Associates, Self-directed learning: Emerging theory and practice (p. 13-42). Norman, OK: Oklahoma Research Center for Continuing Professional and Higher Education of the University of Oklahoma.

Bonham, L.A. (1989b, October). What if self-directedness in learning is a learning style? Paper presented at the meeting of the Commission of Professors of Adult Education, Atlantic City, NJ.

Guglielmino, L.M. (1978). Development of the Self-Directed Learning Readiness Scale (Doctoral Dissertation, University of Georgia, 1977). Dissertation Abstracts International, 38, 6467A.

Oddi, L.F. (1985). Development of an instrument to measure self-directed continuing learning (Doctoral Dissertation, Northern Illinois University, 1984). Dissertation Abstracts International, 46, 49A-50A.

Spear, G.E., & Mocker, D.W. (1984). The organizing circumstance: Environmental determinants in self-directed learning. Adult Education Quarterly, 35, 1-10.

Tough, A. (1966). The assistance obtained by adult self-teachers. Adult Education, 17, 30-37.

Tough, A. (1978). Major learning efforts: Recent research and future directions. Adult Education, 28, 250-263.

Tough, A. (1979). The adult's learning projects: A fresh approach to theory and practice in adult education. Toronto: The Ontario Institute for Studies in Education.

PART TWO

CHAPTER FIVE

RELATIONSHIPS BETWEEN SCORES ON THE SELF-DIRECTED LEARNING READINESS SCALE, ODDI CONTINUING LEARNING INVENTORY AND PARTICIPATION IN CONTINUING PROFESSIONAL EDUCATION

Russell F. West
Ernest L. Bentley, Jr.

Over the past ten years a great deal has been written about the concept of self-directed adult learning. Researchers in the field of adult education have found this to be an attractive area of investigation (Caffarella, R. & O'Donnell, J., 1987). Research efforts in the area of adult self-directed learning have continued to expand. According to Long (1989), there has been a movement in the field toward a more comprehensive view of self-directed learning which includes not only issues of sociological and pedagogical control, but also the critical issue of psychological control and the interrelationships between these three dimensions. Recently Bonham (1989) suggested that self-directed learning is really a learning style, termed a self-directed orientation toward learning (SDOL), and identified future research needs in the area. While new directions are being forged on the self-directed learning front, the two most widely used measurement tools for assessing an individual's tendency to be self-directed in learning remain the Self-directed Learning Readiness Scale (Guglielmino, 1978) and the Oddi Continuing Learning Inventory (Oddi, 1985). While the psychometric properties of these instruments have been assessed individually in previous studies, there is no empirical evidence documenting the relationship between scores on these two inventories and the predictive capabilities of the two assessment tools have not been directly compared within a single sample. The purpose of the present study was to determine the extent of relationship between scores on the Self-Directed Learning Readiness Scale (SDLRS) and the Oddi Continuing Learning Inventory (OCLI) and to determine which instrument could be used most effectively in making predictions about participation in self-directed learning activities.

The SDLRS was developed through a three-round delphi process in which 14 leaders in adult education were asked to define the characteristics of a self-directed learner. In her study, Guglielmino (1978) described self-direction in learning as follows:

> It is the author's assumption that self-direction in learning exits along a continuum; it is present in each person to some degree. In addition, it is assumed that self-direction in learning can occur in a wide variety of situations, ranging from a teacher directed classroom to self-planned and self-conducted learning projects. Although certain learning situations are more conducive to self-direction in learning than others, it is the personal characteristics of the learner--including his attitudes, values and his abilities--which ultimately determine whether self-directed learning will take place in a given learning situation. The self-directed learner more often chooses or influences the learning objectives, activities, resources, priorities and levels of energy expenditure than does the other-directed learner (p.34).

The initial question posed to the expert panel was written as follows:

> What do you judge to be the characteristics of the highly self-directing learner which are the most closely related to his self-directed learning behavior? Personality characteristics, attitudes, values and abilities of the self-directing learner might be included, as well as any other factor you feel is important (p. 93).

As the result of the delphi process, Guglielmino constructed a 41 item instrument that contained 8 orthogonal factors identified through a factor analysis. The instrument has been revised and the more recent version contains 58 items which measure these eight factors. Respondents on the SDLRS indicate the extent to which they agree with statements describing their feelings about learning using the following modified Likert-type rating scale:

1) Almost never true of me; I hardly ever feel this way,
2) Not often true of me; I feel this way less than half the time,
3) Sometimes true of me; I feel this way about half the time,
4) Usually true of me; I feel this way more than half the time, and
5) Almost always true of me; there are very few times when I don't feel this way.

Examples of items on the scale are "I love to learn," "I try to relate learning to my long term goals," or "I learn several new things on my own each year." While the SDLRS was initially developed to measure eight factors that represented "readiness for self-directed learning," recent research efforts have demonstrated the presence of one general factor (e.g., West & Bentley, 1989; Field, 1989). Bonham (1989) has argued that the SDLRS is really measuring enthusiasm for learning, in general, and not specifically self-directed adult learning. The reliability of the SDLRS has been established in several studies. Internal consistency reliabilities of .87 (Guglielmino, 1978), .89 (Field, 1989), .88 (Wang, West & Bentley, 1989) and .87 (Brockett, 1985) have been reported. The validity of the scale has also been examined by looking at the relationship between SDLRS scores and various criterion measures. For example, Crook (1985) found low, but statistically significant relationships between SDLRS scores and first year final nursing grades ($r=.28$) among 63 nursing students. The SDLRS scores were also related to overall peer nominations of students' self-directedness ($r=.26$). Torrance and Mourad (1978a) found an abbreviated SDLRS to correlate with fluency ($r=.28$) and originality ($r=.56$) scores among 274 gifted students. Torrance and Mourad (1978b) also found SDLRS scores to be significantly related to creativity, originality and right hemispheric dominance scores. Sabbaghian (1979) found a significant relationship between SDLRS scores and self-concept. Validation studies have shown the SDLRS to be related to other criterion measures. For example, Long & Agyekum (1983), found no relationship between SDLRS scores and faculty ratings of student self-directedness, although SDLRS scores were related to the learner's age and educational level. Other studies by these researchers have yielded similar results (Long & Agyekum, 1984a; Long & Agyekum, 1984b). McCune and Garcia (1989) completed a meta-analytic investigation of research on the link between SDLRS scores and measures of psychological well-being. These researchers found an overall effect (ES) of .24, which they considered to be a moderate effect. Researchers have also investigated the linkage between SDLRS scores and participation in self-directed learning activities. Hassan (1981) found those with higher SDLRS scores to have completed more self-directed learning projects, thus supporting the validity of the SDLRS. In recent meta-analysis involving five individual studies, McCune, Guglielmino & Garcia (1990) found an overall effect size (ES) of .27 between SDLRS scores and degree of involvement in self-directed learning activity. These researchers operationalized self-directed learning activity as number of learning projects, number of hours spent in self-directed learning or degree of participation in extension education. They concluded that there was a moderate relationship between SDLRS scores and participation in self-directed learning activity. In general, the literature has shown weak to moderate relationships between SDLRS scores and the various criterion measures. Field (1989) has recently challenged many of these validation efforts on the basis of what he termed the inconclusive findings.

The Oddi Continuing Learning Inventory (OCLI) was developed, in part, as a reaction to the SDLRS. According to Oddi (1986 & 1987), the OCLI was developed to measure the personality dimensions that characterize the self-directed adult learner. These items were developed after reviewing the literature on the types of personality characteristics of adult self-directed learners. According to Oddi (1986):

The perspective adopted in the present study, therefore, focused on the personality characteristics of individuals whose learning behavior is characterized by initiative and persistence in learning over time through a variety of learning modes, such as the modes of inquiry, instruction and performance proposed by Houle (p. 98).

The OCLI is a 24 item self-report scale, to which an individual records the extent of agreement along a 7-point Likert scale. The response categories on the scale are arranged as follows: 1) Strongly Disagree 2) Moderately Disagree 3) Slightly Disagree 4) Undecided 5) Slightly Agree 6) Moderately Agree and 7) Strongly Agree. The 24 items are summed to obtain a score that reflects the extent to which an individual's personality characteristics lead him or her to "initiate and persist in learning through various modes (p. 105)". The OCLI was originally developed to measure three bipolar psychological dimensions; proactive drive versus reactive drive, cognitive openness versus cognitive defensiveness and Commitment to Learning versus Aversion to learning. A subsequent factor analysis by Oddi, however, revealed three different factors; A General Factor, Ability to be Self-regulating and Avidity of Reading. Results from the work of Oddi (1984), Six (1989) and McCoy and Langenbach (1989) demonstrated full-scale internal consistency coefficients of .85, .77, and .79, respectfully. There has not been a great deal of research conducted on the validity of the OCLI. Oddi (1986) found the instrument to have both convergent and discriminant validity and described moderate relationships with several psychological outcome measures. Recently, Six (1989) found that the three factors identified by Oddi remained consistent across study samples. McCoy and Langenbach (1989) failed to find differences in OCLI scores between those who felt they were required to participate in self-directed learning activities and those who did not. Likewise, there was no relationship between OCLI scores and the number of learning activities in which individuals engaged, a fact which led McCoy and Langenbach to conclude that:

One could question if the OCLI provides a valid measurement of self-directed continuing learning. At least it appears to have failed to demonstrate concurrent validity in this study. It is possible that there is a need for additional items on the OCLI that would provide a more thorough definition of the self-directed learner (p.84).

Recent factor analyses of the OCLI (Six, 1989) suggests the presence of one dominant factor which reflects a general positive orientation to self-directed learning. The following are examples of items on the scale: "After I read a book or see a play or film, I talk to others to see what they think about it" or "I regularly read professional journals".

Research suggests that both the SDLRS and OCLI measure one general factor. There is some evidence to suggest that the dominant factor on the SDLRS is an enthusiasm or excitement for learning. The general factor found on the OCLI suggests a proactive approach to learning. These two instruments represent the most widely used measures employed in the field to identify self-directed continuing learners. It is expected that the two instruments are measuring traits which have a great deal in common and that the overlap between them would be significant.

As a result of a review of the literature, it was hypothesized that there would be a positive correlation between scores on the SDLRS and OCLI. Likewise, it was hypothesized that both OCLI scores and SDLRS scores could be used successfully to predict self-reports of participation in self-directed learning activities.

METHODS

Subjects
During the Spring, 1989 semester, a survey instrument was sent to all public schools that participated in the TN LEAD administrative development program during the 1987-88 school year (Cycle 1 schools) and the 1988-89 school year

(Cycle 2 schools). This represented a follow-up to a Fall, 1988 survey for the Cycle 2 schools. The total number of participating schools was 30. This included all 16 Cycle 2 schools and 14 schools from Cycle 1. Seven of the Cycle 1 schools did not return their survey materials, although follow-up letters and phone calls were made. The surveys were distributed by principals in the schools, with all teachers and administrators at each of the schools being asked to complete the survey. The median response rate from the schools was 85%, while the lowest response was 39%. A total of 810 surveys were returned, although not all contained responses to all items. Seventy-nine percent of the respondents were female, while 44% of the respondents were working at the elementary school level. The demographic characteristics of the sample are shown in Table 5.1.

Twenty-seven percent of the valid responses came from high school staff, while 26% worked at the middle school level. Most respondents (92%) were teachers and the majority were White (88%). The average respondent was 41 years of age and had 11-12 years of teaching experience.

Measurement of Variables
The Oddi Continuing Learning Inventory (OCLI) and Self-directed Learning Readiness Scale (SDLRS) were both administered to the sample as part of the larger survey. In addition, respondents were asked to complete a questionnaire in which they indicated the extent to which they participated in certain self-directed learning activities.

Scores

Table 5.1.:   Descriptive Profile of Individuals Responding to the
               TN LEAD Survey During Spring 1989

SPRING 1989	f	%
Gender:		
Male	163	21
Female	<u>610</u>	<u>79</u>
Total	773	100
Age:		
< 30	71	9
30-39	257	34
40-49	281	37
50-59	112	15
> 59	<u>36</u>	<u>5</u>
Total	757	100
Race:		
White	689	88
Black	75	10
Other	<u>19</u>	<u>2</u>
Total	783	100
School Type:		
Elementary	341	44
Junior/Middle	204	26
High School	214	27
Other	<u>23</u>	<u>3</u>
Total	782	100
Years of Experience:		
< 5	82	11
5-8	78	10
9-12	143	19
13-16	167	22
> 16	<u>296</u>	<u>39</u>
Total	766	100

These questions were modified from a series of questions
used in a previous study (Peters & Gordon, 1974). In addition
to the SDLRS and the OCLI, respondents also completed a
Demographic Information Sheet which asked for information

pertaining to gender, race, type of school, position in the school and years of experience.[1]

Data Collection Procedures

The instruments were administered to every teacher and administrator in the 30 participating schools. Principals were sent directions on administering the surveys to the teachers in their schools. All surveys were administered during the same two week period and then returned to the TN LEAD office.

Data Analysis

Simple descriptive statistics were used to describe scores on the SDLRS and OCLI, by age, sex and type of school subgroups.

One-way analysis of variance was used to test the significance of group differences. Frequency distributions were also used to describe the respondents' level of participation in self-directed learning activities. To address the relationship between SDLRS and OCLI scores, Pearson product moment correlation coefficients were calculated between scores on the SDLRS and OCLI. These correlations were then examined within subgroups based on age of the respondent, sex of the respondent and school type.

The SDLRS and OCLI scores were then broken down into 5 categories in an effort to look at the SDLRS and OCLI relationship using ordinal level statistics. The categories were formed by breaking the distribution of scores into fifths so that there would be approximately equal sized groups. The categories were assigned as follows:

---

1 For the purposes of this research, a royalty-free copyright license for the use of the OCLI was granted by Lorys Oddi.

Scores

	Score Range	Category Code
SDLRS		
	85-223	1 = Lowest
	224-238	2
	239-251	3
	252-264	4
	265-290	5 = Highest
OCLI		
	42-126	1 = Lowest
	127-134	2
	135-140	3
	141-147	4
	148-168	5 = Highest

The age variable was also collapsed into categories so that comparisons could be made between age groups. These categories are shown below:

	Age Range	Category Code
AGE		
	20-29	1 = Youngest
	30-39	2
	40-49	3
	50-59	4
	60 and Above	5 = Highest

Gamma and tau-b represented the two ordinal measures of association used to assess the relationships between SDLRS and OCLI score categories. The relationships between SDLRS and OCLI scores and levels of participation in self-directed learning activities were also assessed using the Pearson product moment correlation coefficient, gamma and tau-b. In order to use the Pearson product moment correlation coefficient, midpoints of the self-directed learning activity variables were correlated with actual SDLRS and OCLI scores. Gamma and Tau-B were used to look for associations between the ordered categories. Finally, multiple regression analysis was used to determine if SDLRS and OCLI scores could be used to predict an overall level of participation in self-directed learning activities. Data were analyzed using the SPSS/PC+ microcomputer analysis package (Norusis, 1988).

Results
The respondents' scores on the SDLRS and OCLI are presented in Table 5.2 along with the results of the analysis of variance.

Table 5.2: **Means and Standard Deviations on the Self-Directed Learning Readiness Scale (SDLRS) and Oddi Continuing Learning Inventory (OCLI), by Age, Sex and Type of School in Which Employed**

	SDLRS				OCLI			
	n	M	SD	F	n	M	SD	F
Total	657	241.8	28.0		690	135.0	17.3	
Age:								
20-29	57	242.2	29.4	.3	62	133.6	13.7	2.1
30-39	216	240.3	24.4		223	132.7	18.8	
40-49	230	243.0	28.3		245	136.1	16.8	
50-59	91	241.5	30.4		89	138.0	16.0	
60+	25	240.8	41.5		29	132.9	19.1	
Sex:								
Males	135	233.2	33.5	16.5	139	131.5	15.5	6.5
Females	501	244.0	25.6		520	135.7	17.8	
Type of School:								
Elem.	276	243.1	27.4	1.2	288	36.1	16.1	2.2
Middle	167	243.6	27.0		187	132.7	21.2	
High	179	239.6	27.0		176	135.5	15.2	

*p < .05

As shown in the table, there was a statistically significant difference between the scores of males (M=233.2) and females (M=244.0). There were, however, no differences between the age groups nor differences between

81

elementary, middle and high school teachers. The scores on the two scales were quite high.

Table 5.3.:   Frequency Distribution of Responses to the Questions Pertaining to Amount of Self-Directed Learning Activity in the Previous Year (Magazines Read, Courses Taken, Colleague Discussion & Trips).

Self-Directed Activity	f	%
Magazines/Journals Read:		
never	13	2
0-2 hours per week	412	58
3-5 hours per week	216	30
6-8 hours per week	44	6
over 8 hours per week	32	4
Total	717	100
Courses Taken at an Agency/Institution:		
none	325	45
1 course	213	30
2-3 courses	104	15
4-5 courses	21	3
over 5 courses	53	7
Total	716	100
Met With Colleagues For Discussion:		
never	67	9
1-2 times per month	403	56
3-4 times per month	127	18
5-6 times per month	49	7
over 6 times per month	71	10
Total	717	100
Trips Taken for Professional Development:		
none	79	11
1 trip	244	34
2 trips	186	26
3 trips	80	11
over 3 trips	130	18
Total	719	100

The frequency distributions of responses to the questions pertaining to the amount of self-directed learning activity are presented in Table 5.3 and Table 5.4.

Table 5.4.: Frequency Distribution of Responses to the Questions Pertaining to Amount of Self-Directed Learning Activity in the Previous Year (Correspondence Courses, Inservice, Meetings & Books Read)

Self-Directed Activity	f	%
Correspondence Courses:		
none	670	94
1 course	28	4
2 courses	10	1
3 courses	2	<1
over 3 courses	6	≤1
Total	716	100
Inservice Programs Attended:		
none	3	<1
1	24	3
2	74	10
3	94	13
over 3	522	73
Total	718	100
Professional Meetings Attended:		
none	116	16
1-2 times per month	520	73
3-4 times per month	56	8
5-6 times per month	8	1
over 6 times per month	10	2
Total	710	100
Professional Books Read:		
none	89	12
1-3 books	397	56
4-6 books	108	15
7-9 books	51	7
10 or more books	69	10
Total	714	100

As shown in Table 5.3, the majority of the respondents read journals or magazines for a total of 0 to 2 hours per week (58%) and a small percentage (10%) read for more than 5 hours per week. Most (45%) of the respondents had not taken an agency or institutionally sponsored course within the previous year, while 30% had taken one such course. Nine percent of the respondents suggested that they had never met with colleagues to discuss professional issues, while the majority (56%) reported having such discussions 1-2 times per month. While 11% of the respondents reported taking no trips for professional development purposes, 18% made over 3 such trips. Few (6%) of the respondents had taken any correspondence courses. Seventy-three percent of the respondents had participated in more than three inservice programs during the previous year. While 12% of the respondents reported that they had not read any professional books over the previous year, 56% had read between 1 to 3 books.

To examine the initial relationship between SDLRS and OCLI scores, Pearson product moment correlations, gamma coefficients and tau-b coefficients were calculated for the total group and for the subgroups. These correlations are shown in Table 5.5.

The total group correlation between the two measures was $r=.38$ ($n=572$, $p<.01$), indicating that only 15% of the variability in one scale could be explained by its relationship with the other. The SDLRS/OCLI correlation was higher in the male subgroup ($r=.55$) than it was in the female subgroup ($r=.32$).

Table 5.5:   Pearson Product Moment Correlation Coefficients, Gamma Coefficients and Tau-B Coefficients Expressing the Relationship Between SDLRS and OCLI Scores, By Sex, Age and Type of School

	r	n	p	Gamma	Tau-B
Total Group	.38	572	<.01	.51	.42
Sex:					
Males	.55	118	<.01	.54	.43
Females	.32	436	<.01	.49	.40
Age:					
< 30	.31	50	ns	.46	.37
30-39	.30	191	<.01	.45	.37
40-49	.38	208	<.01	.55	.44
50-59	.33	74	<.01	.52	42
> 59	.92	20	<.01	.77	65
School Type:					
Elementary School	.40	235	<.01	.47	.38
Middle School	.31	157	<.01	.48	.39
High School	.48	154	<.01	.59	.49

There did not appear to be any differences in the size of the correlations between the age groups, except for the older age category, where the correlation was ($r=.92$). While the patterns of relationship were similar for the ordinal measures of relationship, the ordinal measures were slightly higher than the corresponding Pearson product moment correlations.

The relationships between SDLRS, OCLI and participation scores are shown in Table 5.6.

Table 5.6.: Pearson Product Moment Correlation Coefficients Expressing the Relationship Between SDLRS Score, OCLI Score and Degree of Participation in Self-Directed Learning Activities

Pearson Product Moment Correlations

	Q1	Q2	Q3	Q4	Q5	Q6	Q7	Q8
SDLRS	.14*	.05	.11*	.11*	-.03	.05	.05	.09
OCLI	.22*	.05	.10	.17*	-.04	.06	.07	.06

Gamma Coefficients

	Q1	Q2	Q3	Q4	Q5	Q6	Q7	Q8
SDLRS	.21	.12	.16	.18	-.10	.13	.16	.15
OCLI	.32	.10	.19	.22	-.10	.04	.21	.18

Tau-B Coefficients

	Q1	Q2	Q3	Q4	Q5	Q6	Q7	Q8
SDLRS	.15	.09	.11	.14	-.03	.08	.09	.11
OCLI	.22	.07	.13	.17	-.03	.02	.13	.13

Key: Q1=Magazines/Journals Read, Q2=Courses Taken at Agency or Institution, Q3=Colleague Discussion, Q4=Trips for Professional Development, Q5=Correspondence Courses, Q6=Inservice Programs, Q7=Professional Meetings, Q8=Professional Books Read, SDLRS= Self-Directed Learning Readiness Score, OCLI=Oddi Continuing Learning Inventory.

The strongest measures of relationship occurred between the OCLI score and number of journals read (r=.22, G=.32, tau-b=.22). The next highest relationship occurred between the OCLI and number of trips taken for professional development (r=.17, G=.22, tau-b=.17). The slight negative relationship between the OCLI, SDLRS and the number of correspondence courses taken was probably due to the extreme skew in the distribution of scores on the correspondence school measure, since very few of the respondents had taken any correspondence courses. As shown in the table, most of the relationships between the participation measures and the OCLI/SDLRS scores were very low.

The results of the stepwise multiple regression analyses are shown in Table 5.7. The dependent variables in the analyses consisted of the mid-points of the categories of the participation variables.

As shown in the table, there was very little predictive power in the equations. In fact, only predictions of the number of journals read, discussions with colleagues, professional development trips and professional books read, reached statistical significance. None of the equations, however, were useful in explaining variability in the participation variables. The highest R-square value was found in predicting the number of journals/magazines read from OCLI scores (R-Square=6%). The total participation variable was calculated by summing the responses to the individual participation items. Only 3% of the variability in Total Participation could be predicted by the OCLI.

Based on these findings, it did not appear that either the OCLI or SDLRS could be used to predict participation in self-directed learning activities, as measured on the TN LEAD evaluation instrument. While the differences were slight, it appeared that the much shorter OCLI was at least as effective as the SDLRS in predicting participation in those activities.

Table 5.7: Summary of Stepwise Multiple Regression Analysis for Predicting Self-Directed Learning Activity Scores and Total Self-Directed Learning Activity Score From SDLRS and OCLI Scores

Dependent Variable	First Predictor	R-Square
Q1:Magazines/Journals Read	OCLI	.06
Q2:Courses Taken		
Q3:Discussion With Colleagues	SDLRS	.01
Q4:Professional Development Trips	OCLI	.03
Q5:Correspondence Courses		
Q6:Inservice Attended		
Q7:Professional Meetings Attended		
Q8:Professional Books Read	SDLRS	.01
Total Participation	OCLI	.03

DISCUSSION

An major purpose of this study was to assess the extent of relationship between OCLI and SDLRS scores. This type of analysis represented a new look at the concurrent validity of these two widely used instruments. The findings of the study indicated the relationship between the two measures was low; lower than would have been expected if the two scales measured a general factor associated with self-directed learning activities. Even given the conceptual distinctions between the instruments, as defined by those who developed them, the total group correlation of r=.38 suggested the measures did not have a great deal in common. These correlations were stronger when the scales were broken into five ordered categories and ordinal level measures of association were calculated. The magnitude of these coefficients was dependent, in part, on the manner in which the cumulative distribution of responses was broken into quintiles. In this particular study, the categories were formed with the intention of obtaining groups that were close in size. In most cases, however, the tau-b coefficients were similar in magnitude to the Pearson coefficients.

There did appear to be differences in the magnitude of the relationship between males and females, with the relationship being stronger among males. Perhaps this suggests that females responded to the survey in a more discriminating way than the males and were able to make more effective discriminations between the conceptual foundations undergirding the two instruments. It also appeared that high school teachers (r=.48) were not as discriminating as the middle school teachers (r=.31) or the elementary school teachers (r=.40).

The results also suggest that neither the SDLRS nor the OCLI were very useful in explaining participation in self-directed learning activities, as measured as a series of responses to questions about the frequency of participation over the previous year. Most of the correlations were close to zero, when both Pearson product moment correlations and the ordinal measures of association were calculated. While the measurement of participation in self-directed learning activities was limited to the particular variables used in this study, a stronger relationship was expected. Based on these results, it does not appear that either the SDLRS or the OCLI are very helpful in predicting those who would participate in a greater number of self-directed learning activities. Neither instrument would appear to serve as a powerful screening tool to detect individuals who engage in self-directed learning activity.

Finally, the weak results make it very difficult to determine if the SDLRS or the OCLI is a better predictor of self-directed learning behavior. Since the 24 item OCLI correlated with the criterion measures, at least as well as the longer SDLRS, the more parsimonious instrument would perhaps be preferred. Given these findings of a weak relationship between the OCLI and SDLRS, coupled with the inability to predict these criterion variables, it is not recommended that either of these instruments be used as screening tools for self-directed learning programs. Furthermore, it does not appear that the two instruments are measuring the same or strongly related concepts. Further work is need with different criterion measures to assess the link between these instruments and participation in self-directed learning.

REFERENCES

Bonham, L. A. (1989). Self-directed orientation toward learning: A learning style. In H.B. Long & Associates (Eds.), Self-Directed Learning: Theory & Practice, (pp. 13-42)Norman: Oklahoma Research Center for Continuing Professional and Higher Education, University of Oklahoma.

Brockett, R. G. (1985). Methodological and substantive issues in the measurement of self-directed learning readiness. Adult Education Quarterly, 36, 15-24.

Caffarella, R. S. & O'Donnell, J. M. (1987). Self-directed learning: A critical paradigm revisited. Adult Education Quarterly, 37, 199-211.

Crook, J. (1985). A validation study of a self-directed learning readiness scale. Journal of Nursing Education, 24, 274-279.

Field, L. (1989). An investigation into the structure, validity, and reliability of Guglielmino's self-directed learning scale. Adult Education Quarterly, 39, 125-139.

Guglielmino, L.M. (1978). Development of the self-directed learning readiness scale. (Doctoral dissertation, University of Georgia, 1977). Dissertation Abstracts International, 38, 6467A.

Hassan, A. M. (1981). An investigation of the learning projects among adults of high and low readiness for self-directed learning. (Doctoral dissertation, Iowa State University, 1981). Dissertation Abstracts International, 42, 3838A.

Long, H. B. (1989). Self-directed learning: Emerging theory and practice. In H.B. Long & Associates (Eds.), Self-Directed Learning: Theory & Practice, (pp. 1-11) Norman: Oklahoma Research Center for Continuing Professional and Higher Education, University of Oklahoma.

Long, H.B. & Agyekum, S.K. (1984a). Multi-trait-multi-method validation of Guglielmino's self-directed learning readiness scale. Proceedings of the 25th Annual Adult Education Research Conference, 194-198.

Long, H. B. & Agyekum, S. K. (1984b). Teacher ratings in the validation of Guglielmino's self-directed learning readiness scale. Higher Education, 13, 709-715.

Long, H.B. & Agyekum, S.K. (1983). Guglielmino's self-directed learning readiness scale: A validation study. Higher Education, 72(1), 77-87.

McCoy, C. & Langenbach, M. (1989). Self-directed learning among clinical laboratory scientists: A closer look at the OCLI. In H.B. Long & Associates (Eds.), Self-Directed Learning: Theory & Practice, (pp. 77-85). Norman: Oklahoma Research Center for Continuing Professional and Higher Education, University of Oklahoma.

McCune, S. K. & Garcia, G. Jr. (1989). A meta-analytic study of the relationship between adult self-direction in learning and psychological well-being: A review of the research from 1977 to 1987. In H.B. Long & Associates (Eds.), Self-Directed Learning: Theory & Practice, (pp. 87-97) Norman: Oklahoma Research Center for Continuing Professional and Higher Education, University of Oklahoma.

Norusis, M. J. (1988). SPSS/PC+ V2.0 Base Manual. Chicago: SPSS.Oddi, L.G. (1987). Perspectives on self-directed learning. Adult Education Quarterly, 38, 21-31.

Oddi, L. F. (1986). Development and validation of an instrument to identify self-directed continuing learners. Adult Education Quarterly, 36, 97-107.

Oddi, L. F. (1985). Development of an instrument to measure self-directed continuing learning (Doctoral dissertation, Northern Illinois University, 1984). Dissertation Abstracts International, 46, 49A.

Peters, J.M. & Gordon, S. (1974). Adult learning projects: A study of adult learning in urban and rural Tennessee. Knoxville: University of Tennessee (ERIC Document Reproduction Service No. 102 431).

Sabbaghion, Z.S. (1979). Adult self-directedness and self concept. An exploration of relationships (Doctoral dissertation, Iowa State University, 1979). Dissertation Abstracts International, 40, 3701A.

Scores

Six, J. E. (1989). The generality of the underlying dimensions of the Oddi Continuing Learning Inventory. Adult Education Quarterly, 40, 43-51.

Torrance, E.P. & Mourad, S. (1978a). Self-directed learning readiness skills of gifted students and their relationship to thinking creatively about the future. The Gifted Child Quarterly, 22, 180-186.

Torrance, E.P. & Mourad, S. (1978b). Some creativity and style of learning and thinking correlates of Guglielmino's self-directed learning readiness scale. Psychological Reports, 43, 1167-1171.

Wang, X., West, R. & Bentley, E. (1989, November). Factor structure of the Self-Directed Learning Readiness Scale. A Paper presented at the Mid-South Educational Research Conference, Little Rock, AK.

West, R.F. & Bentley, E.L. (1989, February). Structural analysis of the self-directed learning readiness scale: A confirmatory factor analysis using LISREL modeling. North American Symposium on Adult Self-Directed Learning. Oklahoma Research Center for Continuing Professional and Higher Education. Norman: University of Oklahoma.

CHAPTER SIX

DEMOGRAPHIC AND PERSONAL FACTORS IN PREDICTING SELF-DIRECTEDNESS IN LEARNING

Tunde Adenuga

The quest for knowledge about factors that are critical to adult self-directed learning is evident from the volume of literature and enthusiasm for research on this subject in the last two decades. Different aspects of self-directed learning have been explored for relationships with various demographic and personality variables. Learning style, which refers to a person's typical way of receiving and processing information, has been suggested to play a notable role in an adult's decisions to engage in self-planned learning (Hebron, 1983; Pratt, 1984; Theil, 1984; Brookfield, 1984, 1986). However, a dearth of empirical support coupled with a divergence of many of the conceptually derived proposals (for facilitating self-directedness in learning) has limited the use of learning style information in adult self-directed learning. Therefore, more empirical studies relating self-directedness to learning styles are needed to clarify their relationship. Such a clarification would upgrade professional understanding, and facilitate the identification and matching of individual predispositions with appropriate strategies for increased effectiveness.

This ex post facto study explored the predictive capabilities of demographic and learning style measures for self-directedness in learning. Kolb's (1984) learning style model was adopted for this study because of its adult orientation and relatively well-developed theory base (experiential learning); and compatibility with the conceptual underpinnings of the self-directed learning paradigm.

Hypotheses - It was hypothesized that:

1. The transformation dimension (AE-RO scores) will be significantly ($P < 0.05$) more predictive of readiness for self-directed learning (SDLRS scores) than the prehension or taking-in of information dimension (AC-CE scores).
2. After nationality and program are accounted for, none of the demographic variables will contribute significantly ($P < 0.05$) to the variance associated with subject's readiness for self-directed learning (SDLRS scores).
3. A combination of demographic and learning style measures will be more predictive ($p < 0.05$) of SDLRS scores than either alone.

Rationale for hypotheses
Involvement in self-directed learning requires individuals to take initiative, with or without the help of others, and be actively involved in the entire process of planning, implementing, and evaluating the learning effort (Knowles, 1975). Highly self-directed individuals (with high SDLRS score) carry out more self-planned learning projects (Hassan, 1981; Hall-Johnsen, 1985) than less self-directed individuals. Practice ranks highest (above reading and discussion) as the most commonly used method in self-directed learning projects (Coolican 1974, 1975). Based on these revelations and the descriptions of characteristics associated with the different learning styles (Kolb, 1984), it was conjectured that regardless of the preferred mode of taking-in information, persons who have a preference for an active style of transforming information (as indicated by high AE-RO scores) will be significantly more ready for self-directed learning than those with a preference for a reflective style (low AE-RO scores). Hypothesis 1 addresses this conjecture.

The second hypothesis is based on past research which indicates that level of formal education is the only demographic variable that is significantly associated with readiness for self-directed learning (Sabbaghian, 1979; Hassan, 1981; Brockett, 1983). Nationality is given additional emphasis in this study to reflect current professional concerns about cross-cultural generalizability of self-directed learning research (Tough, 1978; Long and Agyekum, 1984; Brookfield, 1985). The emphasis was intended to provide some insights on the role of socio-cultural and cross-national influences on self-directed learning readiness. The third hypothesis further explores the relative contribution of the independent variables to the prediction of self-directed learning readiness.

METHODOLOGY

The dependent variable of the study is self-directed learning readiness (SDLR), as measured by the total score of subjects on Guglielmino and Guglielmino's (1982) self-directed learning readiness scale (SDLRS). The independent variables include: learning orientation/style, as measured by Kolb's (1985) learning style inventory (LSI); and demographic variables - age, gender, nationality, program of study (master's vs. doctorate), academic major (physical vs. social science), and work experience (total years).

The SDLRS instrument is a 58-item, 5-point Likert-type scale which scores an individual on 8 factors deemed to define attitudes, values, and abilities of learners associated with preparedness or readiness for self-directed learning. The range of total score on this scale represents an inner-outer directedness continuum along which an individual's readiness for self-direction in learning can be located. A high SDLRS total score indicates a high level of readiness for self-directed learning. Like most attitudinal measures, some aspects of the self-directed learning readiness scale have been criticized (Brockett, 1985; Field, 1989; West and Bently, Jr., 1990). However, the SDLRS remains, as Field (1989) put it, "the only widely accepted means of quantifying an individual's readiness for self-directed learning" (p. 125). Support for its validity and reliability have been well documented (Torrance and Mourad, 1978; Sabbaghian, 1979; Hassan, 1981; Brockett, 1985; Long and Agyekum, 1983; Hall-Johnsen, 1985; Guglielmino et al., 1989; West and Bently Jr., 1990).

Kolb's (1985) LSI is a twelve-item self-description questionnaire which measures the subject's preference for four learning modes or abilities--AC (abstract conceptualization), CE (concrete experience), AE (active experimentation) and RO (reflective observation) which underlie learning from experience. The learning orientation combination scores, namely, AC-CE (abstract-concrete) and AE-RO (active-reflective), are derived from scores on the four modes. These scores are indicative of the subject's prehension and transformation styles respectively; that is, the extent to which he/she prefers abstractness over concreteness (AC minus CE scores), and action over reflection (AE minus RO scores) in the context of learning. Kolb's learning styles inventory is a popular instrument for identifying predominant learning styles of individuals, and has been applied to many different populations and situations. Questions of reliability and validity have also been addressed (Kolb, 1976, 1984; Bonham, 1988).

Data Collection Procedures - Based on a comprehensive list of 3,669 graduate students registered at Iowa State University in spring 1989, a stratified random sample of 300 subjects - 75 males and 75 females was selected from each of two nationality categories. The nationality categories, included American students, and foreign students from less developed countries (LDCs). A third category, foreign students from more developed countries (MDCs) was deleted due to inadequate representation in the population studied. The foreign categories were based on the United Nations (1986) classification. According to this classification, MDCs include all of Europe and North America; Australia, New Zealand, Japan and the USSR. The rest of the world is classified as LDCs.

The data collection was done through a mail survey consisting of the current versions of the SDLRS and LSI instruments and a subsection consisting of questions that elicit information about the demographic variables of interest to the study.

Data Analysis - The data were analyzed using the mainframe computer version of the Statistical Package for Social Sciences (SPSS-X). The hypotheses of the study were evaluated based on the results of Pearson product-moment correlations, and multiple regression analyses and procedures. Hypothesis 1 was evaluated using the procedures and formula for testing the null hypothesis that there is no difference between two population correlation coefficients based on dependent samples (Hinkle et al., 1988). Hypotheses 2 and 3 were evaluated based on the results of two multiple regression models - full model and demographic models. The full model involved a regression of the criterion variable (SDLRS) on all the six demographic variables (age, gender, nationality, academic major, program of study, work experience), and learning style (AC-CE, AE-RO) scores; and the demographic model involved a regression of SDLRS scores on all the six demographic variables.

RESULTS

A total of 178 (59.3%) questionnaires were returned. Seventy-seven (43.3%) of the respondents were males and 101 (56.7%) were females; 81 (46.6%) subjects were Americans and 93 (52.2%) were foreign students from developing countries. Four individuals did not indicate their nationality. Ages for all subjects, ranged from 21 to 62 years with a mean of 30.5 (median = 29.0 and mode = 25; n = 177). Fifty-eight percent (103) of the respondents were in a master's degree program while forty percent (71) were pursuing a doctorate degree. Eighty-two (47.4%) students were majoring in social sciences and 89 (51.4%) were in the physical sciences.

97

Respondents' total SDLRS scores ranged from 170.9 to 286 with a mean score of 230.8 and a standard deviation of 22.3 (median = 232.5 and mode = 208). The mean SDLRS score of 230.8 obtained for this sample is greater than the normative average (214) reported by Guglielmino and Guglielmino (1982). Table 6.1 summarizes subjects' readiness scores by the different demographic variables.

Scores on the abstract-concrete (AC-CE) or taking-in of information dimension ranged from a minimum of -36 to a maximum of 34 with a mean of 9.9, mode of 18 and a standard deviation of 14.6. The active reflective (AE-RO) or transformation dimension scores ranged from -25 to 32.0 with a mean of 3.8, mode of 0.0 and a standard deviation of 11.2. On the average, abstract conceptualization is the dominant style of taking-in information while active experimentation is the dominant transformation style for the entire sample.

The results of pearson correlation (Table 6.2) indicate that the AC-CE ($r = 0.15$, $p < 0.05$) and AE-RO ($r = 0.25$, $p < 0.01$) scores are each positively correlated with SDLRS scores beyond 0.05 and 0.01 significance levels respectively. A statistical comparison of the indices of correlation produced a t-value of 0.97 (df = 167) which was less than the table t-value of 1.96 at the 0.05 level of significance. Therefore, hypothesis 1 was not supported; the null hypothesis was retained. In addition, the results of a 2-predictor variable case multiple linear regression of SDLRS on AC-CE and AE-RO scores indicated that both AC-CE and AE-RO contribute significantly to the prediction of subject's SDLRS scores (F = 7.68, df = 176, $p < 0.01$). A total of 8% of the variance in SDLRS scores was explained by a combination of the LSI scores. The regression equation based on the LSI scores was:

$$SDLRS = 0.50 \text{ AE-RO} + 0.23 \text{ AC-CE} + 226.56.$$

Table 6.1: **Means and Standard Deviations (SD) of SDLRS Scores by Selected Demographic Variables.**

Demographic Variables	Self-Directed Learning Readiness (SDLRS)		
	Ns	mean	SD
Gender			
Male	77	229.10	20.61
Female	99	232.07	23.48
Nationality			
American	79	238.64	18.14
Foreign	93	223.82	23.50
Major			
Social Sci.	80	228.56	24.17
Physical Sci.	89	231.32	20.17
Program			
Master's	102	226.76	22.64
Doctorate	71	236.21	20.96
All Subjects	176	230.77	22.26

Table 6.2: **Correlation Coefficients Between Demographic Variables, LSI Scores and SDLRS Scores**

Variables	Total SDLRS scores	Number of Subjects (n)
AC-CE	.15*	167
AE-RO	.25**	167
Gender	.07	176
Nationality	-.33**	172
Major	.06	169
Program	.20**	173
Age	.08	175
Work Experience (Total years)	.13	169

* Significant at > 0.05.

** Significant at > 0.01.

Table 6.3 contains a summary of the results of the two regression models. The result of the demographic model indicates that only nationality (R = -0.32) and program (R = 0.16), out of six variables, contributed significantly to the prediction of subjects' SDLRS scores (F = 21.05, p < 0.01). This result provides support for hypothesis 2; that is, after nationality and program are accounted for, none of the other demographic variables is significantly predictive of subjects' SDLRS scores.

In the full model, both of the LSI scores (AC-CE, AE-RO) were significant predictors of the SDLRS scores. The demographic model accounted for 14% (R = 0.38, p < .05) while the full model accounted for 21% (R = 0.46, p < .05) of the variance in SDLRS scores.

The regression equations for the two models are:

1. Full model--SDLRS = 0.24 AC-CE + 0.39 AE-RO + 7.40 PROGRAM -14.16 NATIONAL + 234.38; and
2. Demo model--SDLRS = -14.36 NATIONAL + 8.98 PROGRAM + 240.16.

A test of the R square increment of 0.07 (Table 6.3) obtained between the demographic and full models was found to be significant (p < 0.05). The third hypothesis was supported. That is, a combination of demographic and learning style measures (R = 0.46, p < 0.01) is more predictive of SDLRS scores than either alone.

DISCUSSION

Results of the bi-variate correlation analysis indicated that a statistically significant proportion of the variance in SDLRS scores is explained by the variance in each and both of the learning style scores. Although, in this sample, the transformation dimension appears to be a stronger predictor of subjects' SDLRS scores than the prehension dimension, statistical tests indicated that they are not significantly different in their predictive capability in the population.

Table 6.3: **Summary of Multiple Linear Regression Models for the Analysis of SDLRS Scores Variance.**

Model/ Variables in equation	R	Multiple R square	B	Beta	F Value
1 Full_.46	.21				10.85**
AC-CE			.24	.15*	
AE-RO			.39	.19**	
Program			7.40	.16*	
Nationality			-14.16	-.32**	
Constant			234.38		
2 Demo	.38	.14			21.05**
Nationality			-14.36	-.32**	
Program			8.98	.20**	
Constant			240.16		

* Significant > 0.05.
** Significant > 0.01.

As expected from theory (Kolb, 1976, 1984), the two dimensions of the experiential learning orientations are not significantly correlated ($r = -0.04$, $p < 0.05$). This fact complements the findings that they are individually positively correlated with SDLRS scores to support that as individuals increase their preference for each or a combination of active and abstract experiential learning abilities, they increase their readiness for self-directed learning. While these revelations are in support of activity as an index of self-directedness in learning, the positive correlation of SDLRS scores with AC-CE scores (abstract-concrete dimension) is contrary to the suggestion by Theil (1984) and Brookfield (1986) that abstract conceptualization abilities are inconsequential or unnecessary for self-directed learning. The findings also support Kolb's (1984) criticism of Piaget's overemphasis on the transformation dimension; and support the contention that the two styles are equally important for experiential learning.

The relationship obtained between the SDLRS scores and nationality variable implies that the American students in the population studied were significantly more ready for self-directed learning than their counterparts from less developed nations (Table 6.1). This finding seems to lend support to Brookfield's (1985) speculation that less self-directed learners are presumably more prevalent in less democratic societies with emphasis on "role definition, social control, and respect for authority" (p. 8). However, given the way nationality is operationalized in this study, this result seems to be only suggestive of some underlying socio-cultural variables rather than nationality per se. More studies involving a wider variety of social/cultural variables and adult learners from more developed nations are needed to further identify the specific factors. Also, it is unclear whether there are differences in subjects' perception or interpretation of the term "learning" in a manner that systematically affects their responses to the SDLRS questionnaire. To prevent this possible bias, particularly when dealing with culturally diverse groups, the SDLRS instrument may need to provide a guiding definition that better reflects the broader usage of the term "learning" in the context of self-directed learning.

Similarly, subjects pursuing a doctorate program were significantly more ready for self-directed learning than those in a master's program. This result is consistent with previous findings that level of education is significantly related to self-directed learning readiness (Sabbaghian, 1979; Hassan, 1981; Brockett, 1983).

Age, gender, academic major and years of work experience show no predictive capability for self-directed learning readiness. These results are similar to those of prior studies (Hassan, 1981; Hall-Johnsen 1985).

CONCLUSIONS

A general conclusion to be made from the findings of this study is that formal education, learning style preferences and socio-cultural variables play a significant role in an adult's propensity to be self-directing in the context of learning.

A person's style of taking-in information is as indicative of his/her level of readiness for self-directed learning as is his/her style of transforming or processing information. While it seems tenable to infer, based on above findings and the experiential learning theory, that a balance of preference for both active and abstract learning abilities are enhansive of self-directedness in learning, additional studies will be needed to identify what levels of activity and abstractness are optimal for effective self-directed learning.

Whether one is an American student or a foreign student from a developing nation; and whether one is pursuing a master's or doctorate degree are significantly predictive of one's propensity to engage in self-planned learning. Predicting a person's level of preparedness for self-directed learning from these factors is improved significantly by additional information about preference for experiential learning styles.

Although, the magnitude of variance in self-directedness explained by these variables is not large enough to justify definite recommendations for practice, the relationships unveiled by the study, if corroborated by further studies, could greatly enhance the use of learning style information for academic advising, individualized instruction and independent study. In addition to its potential for optimizing learner-resource transactions, these findings can contribute significantly toward the unification and integration of professional efforts related to two traditions of experience-based learning (self-directed and learning styles) research.

Finally, because learning style is a relatively more amenable trait of the individual, these findings can improve the practical utility of models and principles for facilitating self-directedness in learning.

REFERENCES

Bonham, L. A. (1988). Learning style instruments: Let the buyers beware. Lifelong Learning, 11(6), 12-16.

Brockett, R. G. (1983). Self-directed learning and hard-to-reach adults. Life-long Learning: The Adult Years, 6(8), 16-18.

Brockett, R. G. (1985). Methodological and substantive issues in the measurement of self-directed learning readiness. Adult Education Quarterly, 36(1), 15-24.

Brookfield, S. D. (1984). Self-directed learning: A critical paradigm. Adult Education Quarterly, 35(2), 59-71.

Brookfield, S. D. (1985). Self-directed learning: A critical review of research. In Brookfield, S. D. (Ed.). Self-directed learning: From theory to practice (p. 1-16). New Directions for Continuing Education, (25). San Francisco: Jossey-Bass Inc.

Brookfield, S. D. (1986). Understanding and facilitating adult learning. San Francisco: Jossey-Bass.

Coolican, P. M. (1974). Self-planned learning: Implications for future of adult education. Syracuse, N.Y.: Educational Policy Research Corporation.

Coolican, P. M. (1975). Self-planned learning: Implications for future of adult education. An addendum to 1974 paper. Washington, D.C.: Division of Adult Education, US Office of Education.

Field, L. (1989). An investigation into the structure validity, and reliability of Guglielmino's self-directed learning readiness scale. Adult Education Quarterly, 39(3), 125-129.

Guglielmino, L. M. & Guglielmino, P. J. (1982). Learning style assessment. (Self-directed learning readiness scale). Boca Raton, Florida: Guglielmino and Associates.

Guglielmino, L. M., Long, H. B, & McCune, S. K. (1989). Adult Education Quarterly, 39(4), 236-246.

Hall-Johnsen, K. J. (1985). The relationship between readiness for, and involvement in self-directed learning. (Unpublished doctoral dissertation, Iowa State University).

Hassan, A. M. (1981). An investigation of the learning projects among adults of high and low readiness for self-direction in learning. (Unpublished doctoral dissertation, Iowa State University).

Hebron, C. W. (1983). Can we make sense of learning theory? Higher Education 12, 443-462.

Hinkle, D. E., Wiersma, W. & Jurs, S. G. (1988). Applied Statistics for the Behavioral Sciences. Boston: Houghton Mifflin Company.

Knowles, M. S. (1975). Self-directed learning: A guide for learners and teachers. New York: Association Press.

Kolb, D. A. (1976). Learning style inventory technical manual. Boston: McBer and Company.

Kolb, D. A. (1984). Experiential learning: Experience as a source of learning and development. Englewood Cliffs, New Jersey: Prentice-Hall, Inc.

Kolb, D. A. (1985). Learning style inventory. Boston: McBer and Company.

Long, H. B. & Agyekum, S. K. (1983). Guglielmino self-directed learning readiness scale: A validity study. Higher Education, 12, 77-87.

Long, H. B. & Agyekum, S. K. (1984). Multi-trait-method validation of Guglielmino's self-directed learning readiness scale. In Proceedings of the 1984 Twenty-Fifth Annual Adult Education Research Conference, Raleigh NC. Raleigh: North Carolina State University, 272-277.

Mourad, S. A., & Torrance, E. P. (1979). Construct validity of the self-directed learning readiness scale. Journal for the Education of Gifted, 3(2), 93-104.

Pratt, Daniel D. (1984). Andragogical assumptions: Some counter-intuitive logic. In Proceedings of the 1984 Twenty-Fifth Annual Adult Education Research Conference, Raleigh NC. Raleigh: North Carolina State University, 147-153.

Sabbaghian, Z. (1979). Adult self-directedness and self-concept: An exploration of relationship. (Unpublished doctoral dissertation, Iowa State University).

Theil, J. (1984). Successful self-directed learners' learning styles. In Proceedings of the 1984 Twenty-Fifth Annual Adult Education Research Conference, Raleigh NC. Raleigh: North Carolina State University, 237-242.

Torrance, E. P. & Mourad, S. A. (1978). Some creativity and style of learning and thinking correlates of Guglielmino's self-directed learning readiness scale. Psychological Reports, 43, 1167-1171.

Tough, Allen. (1978). Major learning efforts: Recent research and future directions. Adult Education, 28(4), 250-263.

United Nations. (1986). In World Population Data Sheet. Washington, D.C.: Population Reference Bureau, Inc.

West, R. F. & Bently, E. B., Jr. (1990). Structural analysis of the self-directed learning readiness scale: A confirmatory factor analysis using lisrel modeling. In Long, H. B. and Associates (Eds.). Advances in research and practice in self-directed learning. Norman: Oklahoma Research Center for Continuing Education of the University of Oklahoma, 157-180.

CHAPTER SEVEN

COLLEGE STUDENTS' SELF-DIRECTED LEARNING READINESS AND EDUCATIONAL ACHIEVEMENT*

Huey B. Long

Self-Directed Learning Readiness and achievement is a complex topic. We know little about the various factors that cause or influence persistence in educational activities (Long, 1983). Also, little is known with certainty about the variables associated with mastery of a body of knowledge or skill (Long, 1983; Knox, 1977). Long (1983) and Knox (1977) among others, have identified some of the variables including health and intelligence. Intelligence is perhaps the one variable most often identified with educational performance defined in terms of course grades. But, those familiar with the work of Guilford (1967) know that intelligence itself is a complex concept that seems to include numerous sub-elements.

Thus, it is no surprise that educators of adults are concerned with ways and means of explaining and predicting educational achievement of at least two kinds: level of achievement (quantity) and educational performance (quality). The problem for adult educators is further complicated by the recognition of three kinds or types of learning modes: (a) learning that is guided or directed by a teacher, (b) learning that, to a large degree, is primarily the responsibility of the learner and (c) learning that integrates (a) and (b) within traditional frameworks (Hiemstra, 1987).

---

* This research was supported by the Oklahoma Research Center for Continuing Professional and Higher Education, University of Oklahoma, Norman, Oklahoma.

The search for predictors and consequences of educational activity generates some interesting questions for the adult educator. For example, we are primarily concerned here with the question of the relationship between self-directed learning readiness (SDLR) as measured by Guglielmino's (1977/78) Self-Directed Learning Readiness Scale (SDLRS) and the two kinds of educational achievement (quantity and quality) noted above.

Even though numerous studies based on Guglielmino's scale have been conducted since 1977 (Brockett 1985a, 1985b, Caffarella and O'Donnell 1987, Long 1986) the question of how SDLR and educational achievement may be related has not been adequately addressed. Only one study (Savoie, 1979/ 1980) has been located that was designed to study the relationship between SDLRS scores and course performance. Six studies including educational achievement level (years of schooling completed) have been identified and reviewed (Brockett 1985a, Finestone 1984, Hassan 1981/1982, Long and Agyekum 1983, 1984, Zemke 1982).

The theoretical foundations of SDLR are assumed to be related to two important educational variables: (a) achievement level, i.e., the amount of education one has completed and (b) grade point average, i.e., a qualitative measure of educational performance. If SDLR is a learned attitude, or more specifically, a consequence of education, a positive correlation between educational achievement level and SDLR should exist. Furthermore, if SDLR is a learned attitude, or more specifically, a consequence of education, a positive correlation between educational achievement level and SDLR should exist. Furthermore, if SDLR is a reflection of one's ability to learn, or if it indicates a tendency towards mastery of knowledge or skill, or if people who have it self-select themselves up the educational ladder, then a similar positive correlation should exist between SDLR and grade point average (gpa).

Support for the assumptions of associations between SDLR and the two educational variables is suggested by most of the eight factors Guglielmino identified with SDLR.

Specifically she reported the following factors, among others, underlie the SDLRS: (a) openness to learning; (b) self-concept as an effective learner; (c) initiative and independence in learning; tolerance of risk, ambiguity and complexity in learning; (d) acceptance of responsibility for one's own learning (e) the love of learning; (f) creativity, (g) future orientation and (h) ability to use basic study skills and problem stating skills (Guglielmino, 1977/78). The factors underlying the SDLRS are further described below:

Factor 1:
Openness to Learning Opportunities indicates a high interest in learning, a love of learning that incorporates an anticipation for maintaining a learning mind set, an affinity for sources of knowledge, a tolerance of ambiguity, the capacity to constructively use criticism, intellectual accountability, and an awareness of personal responsibility for learning.

Factor 2:
Self-concept as an Effective Learner embraces assurance in self-learning, skill in organizing personal time for learning, self-discipline, awareness of needs and resources, and self-perception as an inquisitive individual.

Factor 3:
Initiative/Independence in learning includes the energetic pursuit of difficult questions, acknowledgment of the desire for learning, preference for personal involvement in planning learning experiences, faith in the ability to work alone, love of learning, satisfaction with reading comprehension ability, skill in planning personal work, and initiative in starting new learning projects.

Factor 4:
Informed Acceptance of Responsibility for One's Own Learning includes a self-perception as average or above average in intelligence, willingness for serious study in subjects of interest, giving credence to the exploratory nature of education, desire for an active role in planning personal learning, willingness to should responsibility

for personal learning, and skill in evaluating personal learning progress.

Factor 5:   Love of Learning shows a high regard for others who are continuously learning, exhibits an intense desire to learn, and possess a pleasure for systematic investigation.

Factor 6:   Creativity implies risk-taking, skill in designing atypical solutions, and ability to conceive of multiple approaches to a topic.

Factor 7:   Future Orientation includes a self-perception as a lifelong learner, pleasure when reflecting on future events, and the ability to see difficult situations as challenges not problems.

Factor 8:   Problem Solving Skills relate to possessing skills for study and problem solving.

Literature Review

Course grades as indicators of educational achievement have received very little attention from investigators. Savoie (1979/1980) reported a positive correlation between SDLR and achievement in one course. We have been unable to identify and locate any studies of the relationship between SDLR and students' overall gpa.

Long and Agyekum (1987b) identify three studies (Long and Agyekum, 1983, 1984) and Finestone (1984) that report no correlation between educational achievement level (years of school) and SDLR. Hassan (1981) also reports no relationship. Of studies reviewed, only Brockett's (1985a) study of 64 older adults reports a significant (.05 level) correlation between SDLR and educational level.

Contrasting inferences can be drawn based on the above factors. One could perhaps argue that these specific factors could be associated with the rejection of schooling as reflected by a measure of educational achievement in years. According to this view, schooling may stifle or diminish self-direction in learning. A negative significant correlation (between SDLRS and educational achievement level) would support this position. Another argument is that the identified factors would interact with years of schooling and become progressively stronger with achievement level (years of school). A positive significant correlation between SDLRS and educational achievement level would support this argument. A similar debate could conceivably exist concerning gpa. On one hand, students scoring high on Guglielmino's SDLRS could be expected to have high gpas because of the strength of the above factors, if one assumes the above factors and schooling are positively associated. The counter argument suggests the contrary: a negative correlation between SDLRS and gpa based on the belief that gpa is a result of teacher rewarded behavior that is negatively associated with SDLRS, e.g. the teacher rewards passive dependent behavior and punishes active independent learner behavior. The absence of any significant correlation between the variables would raise questions about the theory of the SDLRS and the sample.

The current literature generally is silent or ambivalent on the above positions. Therefore the purpose of this study was to determine the association between SDLR and the two selected measures of educational achievement: (a) gpa and (b) level of education.

The major contribution of this research resides in the extension of knowledge concerning the relationship between SDLR and gpa. A secondary contribution is derived from the additional findings concerning SDLR and educational level. The latter contribution is also potentially strengthened by the use of a wider mathematical range in educational achievement, i.e., achievement measured in both years and quarter hours completed. Previous studies have used an extremely narrow numerical range based on years of educational achievement. While one hypothesis examined in this investigation is also based on a narrow range in terms of years the corollary use of quarter hours completed to test another hypothesis provides a wider mathematical range for calculating correlations. It is not believed this additional research design feature substantively reduces the effects of the veridically narrow education achievement level range. Yet, it is believed it addresses a technical issue associated with the mathematical artifact emerging from a situation where the lowest and highest subjects may be separated by as little as 4 years. While this design element does not address the substantive issue it should be instructive in suggesting the relative importance of the design question and the substantial question.

Methodology
Ninety-three full-time and part-time college students, ranging from freshmen to graduate students, at two Georgia colleges were selected as subjects for this study. One subject was dropped from the study because of incomplete information As a result 92 students were included in the final sample. The sample was a fortuitous one as students in six classes (three classes at each of two different colleges) were selected on the basis of instructor cooperation. While it cannot be suggested that the sample is a true random one, there is little reason to believe the sample is radically different from other students attending the two colleges. Partial results of this continuing study have been reported previously (Long and Agyekum, 1984). However, additional information, such as grade point averages and quarter hours completed, was obtained specifically for this study. Readers interested in the findings related to other questions and hypotheses are referred to the earlier source (Long and Agyekum, 1984).

Limitations
Because of the fortuitous nature of the sample used in this study generalizations to a larger population should be made with caution. Comments concerning findings and conclusions are limited to the sample studied unless otherwise noted.

Assumptions
It was assumed that the SDLRS is a valid and reliable measure of self-directed learning readiness. In addition it was assumed the subjects provided accurate and candid responses to the SDLRS items and to the question concerning years of

school completed. It was also assumed the gpa is a valid measure of quality of educational achievement, i.e., a high gpa indicated greater mastery of subject matter content, understanding and academic skills than a low gpa.

Instrumentation
The total study included the use of Rokeach's Dogmatism Scale (Rokeach, 1960), Couch and Kenniston's Agreement Response Set instrument (1960), Duttweiler's Internal Control Index (1981) and Guglielmino's Self-Directed Learning Readiness Scale (1977). Discussion of additional findings is found in Long and Agyekum (1984). Each subject also completed a personal information form that solicited information concerning age, sex, race, and educational achievement level (in terms of years of school completed). Later the Registrars of the two colleges provided information on grade point average and quarter hours completed.

Guglielmino's SDLRS. Guglielmino's SDLRS is a 58 item Likert type scale developed to determine the extent to which individuals perceive themselves to possess skills and attitudes often associated with self-directed learning readiness (Guglielmino, 1977/78). Several studies have reported on the reliability and validity of the SDLRS. Guglielmino estimated the reliability to be .87, as did Brockett (1985). Hassan (1981/1982) reported the internal and predictive validity of the scale as "being high". Others (Finestone, 1984 and Long and Agyekum 1983, 1984) have reported findings that support the scale's construct validity.
     The most troublesome questions concerning the reliability and validity of the SDLRS have been raised by Brockett (1985a, 1985b), Field (1989) and Long and Agyekum (1983, 1984, 1987b). Long and Agyekum (1983) were not satisfied with their findings concerning racial differences on the several instruments. However, they indicated until additional data are available they believe the SDLRS to be valid. Brockett (1985a) questions the appropriateness of the scale when used with subjects not engaged in institutionally sponsored education and with

subjects of low reading ability. As neither of these conditions were believed to apply in the current study Brockett's concerns were not perceived to be critical to the results. Reviewers intented in Field's comments should also read the response by Guglielmino, McCune and Long (1989).

Hypotheses
Five major hypotheses were tested in this study using an alpha level of .05 for rejection of the null-hypothesis. The hypotheses, stated in the null form, are as follows:

1. There is no significant correlation between SDLRS scores and college grade point average.
2. There is no significant correlation between gpa and education achievement level, defined in terms of years of school completed.
3. There is no significant correlation between gpa and scores and educational achievement level, defined in terms of quarter hours completed.
4. There is no significant correlation between SDLRS scores and educational achievement level, defined in terms of years of school completed.
5. There is no significant correlation between SDLRS scores and educational achievement level, defined in terms of quarter hours completed.

Data Analysis
The data for all hypothesis were analyzed through the use of the SAS statistical package as described in the SAS Users' Guide: Basics, 1982 Edition to obtain the Pearson Product Moment correlations. Due to the nature of the hypotheses and data analyzed the zero order correlation was believed to be the most appropriate statistical analysis. After the initial treatment a series of partial correlation analyses (using the SPSSX statistical package) were completed to identify the effects of holding selected variables constant.

Findings

Findings generated by this investigation are reported below in two divisions. First, general descriptive information concerning the study is provided in Table 7.1. Second, findings concerning the five major hypotheses are reported in narrative form.

Table 7.1: **Descriptive Data for 93 College Students**

Variable	N	Mean	Std Dev	Sum	Minimum	Maximum
Age	93	26.40	7.89	2455.000	17.00	51.00
Ed. Years	93	15.59	1.91	1450.000	13.00	19.00
Qts. Hrs.	93	58.49	57.67	5440.000	0.00	229.00
GPA	93	2.47	1.13	2294.90	0.00	4.00
SDLRS	92	229.90	21.71	21151.00	170.000	289.000

Hypotheses

Hypothesis one concerning the relationship between SDLRS scores and grade point average was rejected. A correlation of 0.22, significant at the 0.04 level was generated by the analysis. Hence, the alternate hypothesis of a correlation between the SDLRS and gpa was supported. Additional analysis through partial correlation reveals the association between SDLRS and gpa cannot be explained by the effects of age. The influence of age, however, is more problematic as the significance level for SDLRS and gpa when age is controlled was just beyond the region for rejecting the hypothesis of no relationship. See Table 7.2 for partial correlations.

Hypothesis two concerning correlations of importance emerging of the relationship between educational level (years of school completed) and grade point average was rejected. A correlation of 0.50, significant at the 0.0001 was noted. Additional analysis controlling for the effects of age leads to the conclusion that the correlation between educational level and gpa cannot be explained by age of the subject.

Table 7.2: **Partial Correlations: SDLRS, Age, Educational Level and GPA**

Variable 1	Variable 2	Controlled Variable	Co-efficient	Degrees of Freedom	Probability
SDLRS	GPA	AGE	.168	89	.056
SDLRS	GPA	Ed. Lev.	.187	89	.038
SDLRS	AGE	Ed. Lev.	.179	89	.044
SDLRS	Ed. Lev.	AGE	- .020	89	.424
Ed. Lev.	GPA	AGE	.419	90	.0001

Hypothesis three was also rejected as once again the alternate hypothesis of a correlation between educational level, in terms of quarter hours of college, and grade point average was accepted. A significant correlation between grade point average and quarter hours completed was also noted. A coefficient of 0.32, significant at the of 0.002 level, was produced by the analysis. Therefore, the alternate hypotheses of a correlation between educational level, in quarter hours of college completed, and grade point average was supported.

The fourth hypothesis concerning the relationship between SDLRS and educational achievement level, defined in terms of years of school completed, was not rejected. A correlation coefficient of 0.12, significant at the alpha level of 0.26, was generated by the data analysis.

Hypothesis five, concerning the relationship between SDLRS and education achievement level, defined in terms of quarter hours of college work completed, was not rejected. A coefficient of 0.07, significant at the alpha level of 0.50 was identified.

Discussion
Findings concerning the first three hypotheses are supportive of the argument that SDLR and educational achievement in terms of grades are related. The results can be used to infer the factors identified by Guglielmino enumerated earlier in

this report, do in fact interact with educational performance; or as more specifically stated, performance in school coursework.

The findings concerning the relationship between SDLR and gpa and the two different measures of educational achievement level present several interesting implications: (a) Guglielmino's SDLRS may be a useful general predictor of school performance; (b) the factors that underlie the SDLRS may be more strongly associated with group learning as experienced in schools than previously indicated; and (c) attitudes toward learning as measured by the SDLRS positively interact with quality of performance (defined by gpa in school).

The absence of a relationship between SDLRS and educational achievement level, defined in quantitative terms (years of schooling), suggests mere persistence in school activities is not a prediction of SDLR. In other words, the evidence implies that readiness for self-directed learning is more closely associated with quality of performance rather than quantity. Speculatively, based on the limited educational range available for study, it may be suggested that the composite factors that underlie SDLR are not directly, nor solely, the product of school enrollment.

This study confirms the previous research that reports no association between SDLRS and educational achievement measured in terms of hours completed or years of schooling. The testing of the relationship between SDLRS and education achievement measured in terms of quarter hours of college work completed partially addresses the question of a mathematical factor in computing the association. The number of quarter hours completed by the subjects in this study ranges from 0 to 220. Thus, accounting for the absence of a correlation based on a limited range of responses such as in years of school completed does not seem to be a sufficient explanation.

The failure to note a relationship between years of education (and quarter hours) completed and SDLRS suggests that schooling alone is not associated with SDLRS. In other words, SDLRS does not necessarily increase with the amount of one's schooling completed. Such a finding, if confirmed by other investigators, is additional grist for the charges that schooling may have no <u>effect</u> upon self-directed learning readiness. Furthermore, it could be hypothesized that schooling may have little or no effects upon the origins and development of SDLR. Alternative explanations are also available. One alternate explanation concerns the self-selection process and how it affects the relationship between SDLRS and educational achievement level. One argument, as noted at the beginning of this paper, concerns the possibility that students high in SDLR may drop out of school for a number of reasons. Another related, but different, explanation concerns external forces, i.e., pressure exerted by employers and others on some students to continue in school despite a low SDLR score. If both of these conditions were to apply students with low SDLRS scores may ultimately dominate the school population. The findings of no significant correlation may be the result of contrasting conditions: (a) some students high in SDLR do continue in school, but the mathematical effects of this group on the correlation coefficient are cancelled out by the effects of a group of students with low SDLRS scores who are in school because of external pressures. If this condition applies it is obvious that it is difficult to draw correct inferences concerning the association of SDLRS and educational achievement for individuals.

Three variables that appear to be connected in various complex ways are examined in this study: age, educational level and SDLRS. As implied in the introduction the relationships between and among the three are unclear. It is commonplace to argue that educational achievement level should be positively associated with the ages of subjects included in this study. Conversely, the relationship between age and gpa and gpa and SDLRS are more equivocal. The results of the analysis of correlation coefficients when the effects of the different variables are controlled reveal complex association.

Two sets of findings concerning relationships among the different variables examined in this study are particularly interesting. The two data sets include (a) age, educational level, and gpa and (b) age, gpa and SDLRS. Logically, the relationship between age and educational level, and educational level and gpa would suggest a relationship between age and gpa. Similarly, the relationship between age and SDLRS and gpa and SDLRS would imply also a relationship between age and gpa. Such is not the case, however, age and gpa are independent when examined by both correlation approaches. More importantly, age and gpa are significantly associated with both educational level and SDLRS. Yet, educational level and SDLRS are not significantly correlated. These findings indicate, that while older students (as examined in this study) have completed more years of education and have higher SDLRS scores one cannot predict high SDLRS scores or high gpas based on the age of the students. In fact, the partial correlation reported in Table 7.2 indicates the association between SDLRS and educational achievement level is almost non-existent when the effects of age are controlled. Conversely, students with high SDLRS are likely to have high gpas. Thus, SDLRS and educational achievement levels are independent while SDLRS and gpas are interdependent.

<u>Additional Research</u>
Several interesting questions are suggested by the above implications. First, do the factors underlying SDLRS apply equally to all modes or methods of education, i.e., group (course structured) education and less structured independent inquiry? Secondly, do individuals who prefer to learn alone score lower on the SDLRS than individuals who enroll in college courses? Third, does SDLRS predict performance equally well in credit and non-credit educational activities? If gpa serves as an accurate and valid measure of performance in school learning, and if the SDLRS is a valid reflection of the performance, will the SDLRS serve equally well to indicate quality of individual learning?

CONCLUSIONS

Based on the data obtained for this study and the results of the statistical analyses, the following conclusions were drawn:

1. There is a significant correlation between gpa and educational achievement level, defined in terms of years of school completed. However, when the effects of age are controlled, the correlation is not significant.
2. There is a significant correlation between gpa and educational achievement level, defined in terms of years of school completed.
3. There is a significant correlation between gpa and educational achievement level, defined in terms of quarter hours of school completed.
4. There is no association between SDLRS and education achievement level, defined in terms of years of schooling completed.
5. There is no association between SDLRS and education achievement level, defined in terms of quarter hours of college work completed.
6. There is a significant correlation between SDLRS and age when the effects of educational achievement level are controlled.
7. There is a significant correlation between SDLRS and gpa when the effects of educational level are controlled.

REFERENCES

Brockett, R. (1985a). The relationship between self-directed learning readiness and life satisfaction among older adults. Adult Education Quarterly, 35, 194-209.
Brockett, R. (1985b). Methodological and substantive issues in the measurement of self-directed learning readiness. Adult Education Quarterly, 36, 15-24.

Couch, A. and Kenniston, K. (1960). Yeasayers and nay-sayers: Agreeing response set as a personality variable. Journal of Abnormal and Social Psychology, 2, 151-171.

Duttweiler, P. (1981). Development of a new measure of locus of control in adults: The internal control index. (Doctoral dissertation, Athens, Georgia: University of Georgia).

Field, L. (1989). An investigation into the structure, validity, and reliability of the Guglielmino Self-Directed Learning Readiness Scale. Adult Education Quarterly, 39 (3), 125-39.

Finestone, P. (1984). A construct validation of the self-directed learning readiness scale with labour education participants. Unpublished doctoral dissertation, Toronto: University of Toronto.

Guglielmino, L. (1977/1978). Development of the self-directed learning readiness scale. (Doctoral dissertation, University of Georgia) 1977. Dissertation Abstracts International, 38, 6467A.

Guglielmino, L.; Long, H. and McCune, S. (1989). Reactions to Field's investigation into the SDLRS. Adult Education Quarterly, 39 (4), 236-246.

Guilford, J. (1967). The nature of human intelligence. New York: McGraw-Hill.

Hassan, A. (1981/1982). An investigation of the learning projects among adults of high and low readiness for self-direction in learning. (Doctoral dissertation, Iowa State University, 1981). Dissertation Abstracts International, 42, 3838A.

Houston, V. (1987). "An examination of research performed using Guglielmino's Self-Directed Learning Readiness Scale." Unpublished paper.

Knox, A. (1977). Adult development and learning. San Francisco: Jossey-Bass.

Long, H. (1983). Adult learning: Research and practice. New York: Cambridge Book.

Long, H. and Agyekum S. (1983). Guglielmino's self-directed learning readiness scale: A validation study. Higher Education, 12, 77-87.

Long, H. and Agyekum, S. (1984). Teacher ratings in the validation of Guglielmino's self-directed learning readiness scale. Higher Education, 709-715.

Long, H. and Agyekum, S. (1987). Self-directed learning: Assessment and validation. In H. Long and Associates, Self-directed learning: Application and theory. Athens, Ga.: Adult Education Department, University of Georgia.

Rokeach, M., et. al, (1960). The open and closed mind. New York: Basic Books.

Savoie, M. (1979/1980). Continuing education for nurses: Predictors of success in courses requiring a degree of learner self-direction. (Doctoral dissertation, University of Toronto, 1979). Dissertation Abstracts International, 40, 6114A.

Zemke, R. (1982). Self-directed learning: A must skill in the information age. Training HRD, August, 28-30.

CHAPTER EIGHT

HUMAN BEHAVIOR AS A CONSTRUCT FOR ASSESSING GUGLIELMINO'S SELF-DIRECTED LEARNING READINESS SCALE: PRAGMATISM REVISITED*

Gary J. Confessore

This is the report of a project in which Guglielmino's Self-Directed Learning Readiness Scale (SDLRS-A) was administered to a population consisting exclusively of persons judged to have a high degree of motivation to pursue a specific area of learning, and who were also judged to have an established record of 1) habitually taking the initiative in setting their own learning goals, 2) exhibiting imaginative and aggressive pursuit of the resources needed to achieve their learning goals, and 3) exhibiting a high degree of persistence in completing self-assigned learning projects.

The project was designed to determine whether the mean and distribution of scores on the SDLRS-A for this population differs significantly from the normative data reported in the materials which accompany the instrument.

Selected demographic data were also gathered in an effort to learn whether the population fits within certain limitations of the instrument described by Guglielmino (1977) in her original work on the SDLRS-A.

Following a model suggested by Whitehead and Russell (1910), this study seeks, by way of pragmatism, to learn whether a population judged to have habitually set their own learning goals, imaginatively and aggressively pursued the resources needed to achieve their learning goals, and to be persistent in completing learning projects they set for

* This research was supported by the Oklahoma Research Center for Continuing Professional and Higher Education, University of Oklahoma, Norman, Oklahoma.

themselves, will score significantly above the mean on Guglielmino's SDLRS-A. If this is determined to be a "true consequence," the proposition that the SDLRS-A is a valid and reliable instrument for identification of "readiness for self-directed learning" will also be judged to be a "true premise."

The determination that the members of the population meet the three criteria noted above was initially made in the spring of 1981 and was reconfirmed by survey in 1989. The SDLRS-A and a demographic survey of activities and developments in the lives of the survey population during the intervening eight years, were administered in the fall of 1989. The population selection model and the demographics are discussed with an eye toward establishing whether they form a reasonable basis for assigning the descriptor "self-directed" to members the population. Finally, SDLRS-A scores for this population are compared to Guglielmino's report of the expected distribution and percentile rank of scores, which accompanies the instrument.

REVIEW OF THE LITERATURE

In her original work on this topic, Guglielmino (1977) states that her purpose was:

> to obtain consensus from a panel of experts on the most important personality characteristics of highly self-directed learners, and to develop an instrument for assessing an individual's readiness for self-direction in learning." (p. 3-4)

The panel of fourteen experts, who agreed to use the Delphi technique in an attempt to reach the consensus Guglielmino sought, included such persons as Arthur Chickering, Cyril Houle, Malcolm Knowles, and Allen Tough. (p. 32)

Review, revision, field testing, and subsequent revision of the items given a median rating of "desirable" or better by the panel of experts, yielded an instrument, known as the SDLRS-A, which consists of fifty-eight Likert-type items. The estimated reliability of the instrument (Cronbach's alpha coefficient) is .87. (p. 56)

In the final section of her dissertation, Guglielmino suggests a wide variety of issues that might form the basis of further research into the SDLRS-A, and other issues of fundamental concern to those interested in the nature of self-directedness and self-direction in learning that might be facilitated by use of the SDLRS-A. (pp. 77-80) Her suggestions were preceded by a statement as to her view of the limitations of the instrument she had developed.

Specifically, she points out:

> A further limitation of the SDLRS-A is that it only measures a self-rating of traits and abilities. To maximize predictive success, the SDLRS-A should be combined with measures of achievement in a subject matter area (where necessary), motivation to perform the specific learning task, and intellectual power for the specific learning task. (p. 77)

During the twelve years since the SDLRS-A first became available, it has become the most popular instrument used to measure self-direction in learning. (Long & Agyekum, 1988, p. 255) As often happens with such instruments, it has rightly become the topic of study and scholarly debate. (Brockett, 1985; Brookfield, 1984; Caffarella & O'Donnell 1987; Guglielmino, 1989; Field, 1989; Long & Agyekum, 1983, 1984, 1988; McCune, 1989)

Field (1989) recently concluded Guglielmino's SDLRS-A "is structurally unsound and invalid." (p. 125) Indeed, his concerns led him to dismiss the instrument, and question both the ethical and intellectual fiber of others, including Brockett (1985), Caffarella and O'Donnell (1987), and Brookfield (1984) whom, he reports, "have been wary of criticizing" (Field, 1989, p. 128) (Emphasis mine) Guglielmino's instrument.

Field's (1989) indictment precipitated a rebuttal by Guglielmino (1989), Long (1989), and McCune (1989).

We seem to be caught up in a logical ping pong match in which the debate has become mired in concerns over whether the construct used in Guglielmino's (1977) original work on this topic, is an adequate representation of "self-directedness." Indeed, Field (1989) concludes,

> Lest readers interpret this conclusion as encouragement to develop alternative scales or other methodologies to replace the SDLRS-A, it should be remembered that the fundamental problem that underlies many of the flaws revealed herein is that the conceptual foundations which underpin the scale are weak. These weaknesses will need to be overcome before the issue of the measure of the construct (or constructs) can be adequately addressed. (pp. 138-139)

THE RELATIONSHIP OF CONSEQUENCES TO PREMISES

The present study has no intention of joining the ongoing, and at times vitriolic, debate over the validity and reliability of the SDLRS-A. Rather, it attempts to discern, pragmatically, whether the SDLRS-A is "valid" and "reliable" when administered to a population which fits within the limitations of the instrument as defined by Guglielmino. (1977, p. 77)

In the preface to Principia Mathematica (1910), Alfred North Whitehead and Bertrand Russell may have provided the insight needed to respond to Field's (1989) warning. They point out:

> ... the chief reason in favour of any theory on the principles of mathematics must always be inductive, i.e. it must lie in the fact that the theory in question enables us to deduce ordinary mathematics. In mathematics, the greatest degree of self-evidence is usually not to be found quite at the beginning, but at some later point; hence the early deductions, until they reach this point, give reasons rather for believing the premisses because true consequences follow from them, than for believing the consequences because they follow from the premisses." (pp.v-vi)

If this had not been understood, the top-down strategy that built the natural sciences over the past three hundred years would not have been acceptable.

For instance, understanding of the physical and chemical behavior of matter was fairly accurate even before we had knowledge of molecules. Simon (1969), notes that we have made steady progress in efforts to understand the world using,

> This skyhook-skyscraper construction of science from the roof down to the yet unconstructed foundations was possible because the behavior of the systems at each level depended on only a very approximate, simplified, abstracted characterization of the system at the next level beneath. (p. 17)

The participants in the debate over the SDLRS-A have based their positions on arguments that attempt to prove or disprove the reliability and validity of the instrument by testing consequences in light of premises which have not yet been proven to be true.

In the best scientific tradition, the unproven premise cannot be assumed to produce true consequences. Hence, the ping pong nature of the present debate.

Consider the words of William James (1907),

> Thus if no future detail of experience or conduct is to be deduced from our hypothesis, the debate between materialism and theism becomes quite idle and insignificant. Matter and God in that event mean exactly the same thing -- the power, namely, neither more nor less, that could make just this completed world -- and the wise man is he who in such a case would turn his back on such a supererogatory discussion. Accordingly, most men instinctively, and positivists and scientists deliberately, do turn their backs on philosophical disputes from which nothing in the line of definite future consequences can be seen to follow. The verbal and empty character of philosophy is surely a reproach with which we are but too familiar. If pragmatism be true, it is a perfectly sound reproach unless the theories under fire can be shown to have alternative practical outcomes, however delicate

and distant they may be. The common man and the scientist say they discover no such outcome, and if the metaphysician can discern none either, the others certainly are in the right of it, as against him. His science is then but pompous trifling; and the endowment of a professorship for such a being would be silly.

Accordingly, in every genuine metaphysical debate some practical issue, however conjectural and remote, is involved. To realize this, revert with me to our question, and place yourselves this time in the world we live in, in the world that <u>has</u> a future, that is yet uncompleted whilst we speak. (p. 99-100)

Were it not for the stature of Whitehead, Russell, and James, this observer would surely hesitate to suggest the present model in an attempt to resolve the debate over the adequacy of the SDLRS-A. What is needed is a momentary suspension of our disbelief.

SIGNIFICANCE OF THE STUDY

This study is significant in that it reports SDLRS-A scores for a population judged, over eight years earlier, to possess characteristics that are central to self-direction in learning. It is a longitudinal study. Hence, it provides insights into the validity and reliability of the SDLRS-A because we are able to view the scores achieved in light of scores one would expect to find, given the nature and history of the population.

To appreciate the point of view of the insights gained by this study, one must first recall that the SDLRS-A was designed to <u>predict</u> the performance of adult learners, by diagnosing the strength of their readiness to perform in situations where the capacity or willingness to take an active role in directing their own learning would be advantageous. (Guglielmino, 1977, p. 77)

It should come as no surprise that the debate over the SDLRS-A has focused on concerns about the validity and reliability of the instrument because such tests are typically used as a route to predictions about the future activity, or state, of people. We pre-test to determine whether candidates for a given program appear to be "ready" to benefit from a proposed intervention.   When the intervention has been completed, we use some form of ex post facto measure to assess "change" in the individual and, by inference, to assess the "effectiveness" of the intervention. Whatever we find at post-treatment, we must always be alert to the possibility that some portion of the variance may be attributable to the limitations of the pre-treatment assessment of readiness. Some, may be attributable to operator failure, or to client non-compliance. Some, may be attributable to shortcomings in the post-treatment assessment process.

In the final analysis, the researcher is left with reasonable questions as to which effect is attributable to which cause in this complex chain of events.   To date, attempts to cope with these ambiguities, as they have revealed themselves in research using the SDLRS-A, have relied upon processes that lead to predictions about future human behavior by way of analysis of results on the SDLRS-A.

This study is significant because it obviates these ambiguities by relying on processes that attempt to explain results on the SDLRS-A by way of analysis of long-term human behavior.

Operational assumption
Individuals who habitually set their own learning goals, imaginatively and aggressively pursue the resources needed to achieve their learning goals, and who are persistent in completing learning projects they set for themselves, possess traits which are essential to successful self-direction in learning.

DESIGN AND RATIONALE OF THE SELECTION PROCESS

This section goes into rather substantial detail as to the evolution of the reasoning behind the development of the selection process.   This is done because the present study asserts that the members of the population selected using this model are legitimately labelled "self-directed learners," and that they are well suited to the limitations of the instrument suggested by Guglielmino (1977). That is, they possess "achievement in a subject matter area . . . motivation to perform the specific learning task, and intellectual power for the specific learning task." (p. 77)

During the 1978-79 school year, the faculty and administrators of Johnson State College, in Vermont, established a program intended to serve up to thirty high school students who might productively participate in, and benefit from, a college-level summer program in art, creative writing, dance, music, or theatre.

Formally known as the Johnson State Early College Summer Arts Program, the mission of the "Early College" was to provide college-level instruction to high school students who were judged to be "talented" in one or more art form, to stimulate interest in eventual college study in the arts among Vermont's adolescent population, and to increase the visibility of Johnson State College as a center for the arts.

At that time, practitioners in the field of identification of the gifted and talented generally agreed that an audition or portfolio review was essential to proper identification of artistic talent. (Buttermore, 1979; Hinkley, 1980; Marland, 1971) Hence, the selection of program participants for the 1979 and 1980 Early College Programs was limited to a process of open nomination by high school arts teachers and an audition, or portfolio review, by members of the Johnson State College faculty.

During 1979 and 1980, the program proved to be an unquestioned academic success. (Confessore & Confessore, 1981, p. 261) Yet, a number of concerns about the artistic drive of some participants had begun to emerge. It appeared that talent alone was not sufficient to carry some participants through the long periods of unstructured time associated with college-level work. For some participants, the relative freedom from parental supervision, provided in college residence halls, was too great to handle. Yet, those who were most able to function creatively in an academic environment that provided little structure or direction seemed to have the most productive experiences; their freedom from parental supervision notwithstanding. Conversely, those whom the faculty judged not to be living up to their artistic potential, complained most bitterly that they could not use the long periods of free (unstructured) access to studio, theatre, and library resources productively because the faculty had failed to give specific assignments for those periods.

In point of fact, the program administrators were not surprised to learn that some students appreciate free time to pursue their interests, while others expect direction and structure for nearly every moment of a program. They were also in essential agreement with the arts faculty that the program should not deviate from traditional college standards and practices. This was especially important because it had been determined, at the outset, that the program should not be allowed to set up separate class sections for the Early College students.

On the other hand, if the program were to accomplish its mission to stimulate interest in eventual college study in the arts among Vermont's adolescents, it could ill afford to have students return to their high schools feeling they had not received sufficient instructional direction and structure during their studies.

Informed by the experiences of the first two summers, and after energetic discussions among the faculty of the Division of Arts and Humanities, and the Division of Education and Social Sciences, it was decided that participants in the 1981 Early College Program should be selected with a eye toward their readiness to work creatively and energetically with a minimum of structure and direction. At the time, the selection committee used the term "specific motivation" to describe what they believed were the necessary factors in the readiness of applicants to the program. Without these characteristics, they concluded, even very talented artists were not likely to be able to capitalize upon the full benefit of the resources made available through the program.

During the 1980-81 school year, high school arts teachers were asked to nominate students for the 1981

Johnson State Early College Summer Arts Program on the basis of the following judgements. The nominee should:

1. be recognized, by teachers and fellow students, as among the best in the school in one or more art form;
2. have a strong desire to pursue one or more art form;
3. have an established record of taking the initiative in setting his or her own learning goals;
4. exhibit imaginative and aggressive pursuit of the resources needed to achieve his or her learning goals, and;
5. be very persistent (stubborn) in completing learning goals, especially self-assigned tasks.

Once a student was nominated, guidance personnel at the student's high school were asked whether they concurred in the assessment of the student made by the arts teacher as it related to the initiative, aggressiveness, and persistence of the nominee. If the guidance officer concurred, the nominee was invited to the college campus for an interview and audition, or review of portfolio.

The selection committee at the college was instructed to review each nominee's artistic capacity as they would any other applicant for admission, as a freshman, to an arts program. Further, they were asked to recommend only those candidates who remained comfortable, and gave imaginative and thorough answers, when asked to conjecture as to their own agenda for the summer program, and to suggest how, and with what resources, they might accomplish their agenda.

At the time, the selection committee did not use the term "self-directed learner." Yet, the selection criteria and procedures appear to constitute a very useful description of persons who were ready to practice "self-direction in learning" in the art form for which they were selected into the population. Moreover, it seems reasonable to assert that the members of the population possess the specific motivation and intellectual power, in their art form, to satisfy the limitations of the instrument which Guglielmino (1977) has, from the outset, recommended.

THE POPULATION SELECTED

One hundred and fifty high school students were nominated and the process culminated in the selection of 27 participants for the 1981 Johnson State Early College Summer Arts Program. (Confessore & Confessore, 1981, p. 262) The group consisted of 14 males and 13 females who were from 17 high schools.

By all accounts, including those articulated at a mid-winter reunion, this was by far the program's most productive and talented group of Early College participants.

At the time this research was conducted eight years had passed since these 27 adolescents were identified as possessing strong specific motivation in an art form, and as possessing characteristics that led their teachers, guidance personnel, and college faculty to conclude they were likely to perform creatively and productively in learning situations which provide very little structure or direction.

It would seem to be a matter of natural, if not scholarly, curiosity to ask certain questions about this population of young adults (ages 22-26). For example, are they still inclined to set their own learning objectives, find their own learning resources, and to persist at tasks they set for themselves? Has a high proportion of them continued to pursue their art form? Do they report the program selection criteria (revealed to them for the first time in this study) fit them well as adolescents? Do they believe the criteria fit them as well, or better, at present? Do their scores on the SDLRS-A identify them as "ready for self-direction in learning?"

Twenty-five of the 1981 Early College participants were located for follow-up in 1989 (13 males and 12 females). They were asked to complete Guglielmino's Self-Directed Learning Readiness Scale. They were also asked to complete a questionnaire designed to gather information about each respondent's view of his or her learning style, the fit of the Early College Program selection criteria, work and educational history, and view of the future.

Finally, following the recommendation of Perry (1970), telephone interviews were conducted. This allowed twenty to thirty minutes to gather informal commentary about the intervening life and learning experiences of each participant.

THE DEMOGRAPHIC SURVEY INSTRUMENT

This instrument consists of three sets of Likert-type items, and twelve items which require both a yes or no response, and a brief explanation.

The first set, sixteen Likert-type items (Do you agree strongly, agree, neither, disagree, or disagree strongly that this item describes you?), is designed to determine whether the respondent views art as an important activity in his or her life, and to determine whether involvement in art has occasioned opportunities for self-direction in learning. All items are stated in the positive. For most items the highest score (five) is recorded for strong agreement. For example: "Sometimes I have had to learn a special skill (not necessarily in art) on my own, in order to accomplish a larger artistic goal." However, some are given the highest score for strong disagreement. For example: "I haven't practiced my art in a long time and I don't really miss it."

The second and third sets of Likert-type items ask the respondents to agree strongly, agree, neither, disagree, or disagree strongly with each of the following items as they apply to them at present (Now Scale) and as they believe they applied to them at the time they were selected for the Early College Program (Then Scale). This was the first time the participants were informed that these criteria were considered in the Early College selection process. The items are:

1. You have a strong desire to pursue one or more art form.
2. You have an established record of taking the initiative in setting your own learning goals.
3. You exhibit imaginative and aggressive pursuit of the resources you feel you need to achieve your learning goals.

4.   You are very persistent (stubborn) in completing tasks you set for yourself.

The "yes/no/explain" type items include:

1.   Are you presently involved in one or more of these art forms? (Art, Dance, Music, Theatre, Writing) If so, please indicate the number of hours per month.
2.   Have you completed a degree? If so, where and in which discipline?
3.   Are you presently involved in formal education? If so, give details.
4.   Have you used your art form to make an income? If so, explain.
5.   Have you had to overcome any special obstacles in life? If so, explain.
6.   Have you had to overcome any special obstacles as an artist? If so, explain.
7.   Are you working to accomplish any special goals in life right now? If so, explain.
8.   If you have any special goals right now, will you need to find special resources to accomplish them? If so, please describe them.
9.   Do you think of yourself as "self-directed?" If so, explain.
10.   Have you ever had to teach yourself something in order to accomplish a larger goal? If so, give an example.
11.   What do you think you will have accomplished or will be doing five years from now (1994)?
12.   Is there anything you would like to add to the information you have already given?

The explanations given in response to these items were inspected for indications that the respondent has historically behaved in ways that reasonably may be labelled "evidence of self-direction." For example, the following responses to item 10, above, were interpreted as indications that the respondent exhibited self-direction in that instance:

Yes.   To accomplish my duties as a governess, in Germany, I had to learn to speak enough German to get around. To take my GRE subject test in literature, I had to teach myself all about English and American poetry since I never had a poetry class and the test is predominantly poetry. (Subject #2)

Yes.   I have to study the way people do things in order to be a better actor. Once, I had to teach myself to act like an old man for a role in a play. Learning to speak with different accents requires lots of practice with a mirror and tape recorder. (Subject #3)

Yes.   I am constantly learning, on my own, things about music. I still work on theory, I am slowly teaching myself about electronics (basic stuff) and I am continually interested in how computer technology works with music, and in general. (Subject #15)

The following responses to item 10, were interpreted as not indicating self-direction in learning:

No.   (Subject #23)

Yes.   New York City, and how to survive in order to know happiness -- contentment -- even if momentary. (Subject #20)

Yes.   Work skills and phenomenal patience in those jobs to get by dollarwise. (Subject #16)

Cast in the form of a clinical report on the subjects who achieved the highest and the lowest scores on the SDLRS-A, the following statements are presented to give the reader a sense of the richness of the information gathered with this survey form:

Subject #1

This twenty-five year old female was admitted to the Early College Program at age seventeen to study dance. During the program, she decided she did not have the "body type" to be a professional dancer. That summer, she asserted dance would always remain a central part of her life.

    She scored seventy-three out of eighty points on the sixteen item Likert-type arts drive questions. The range for this portion of the survey

136

is forty-two to seventy-three, the mean is 60.48, and the standard deviation is 7.02.

She has completed a two year degree program in business management and is presently enrolled in further study in sociology/human relations.

She is employed as a fleet manager for a major car rental agency, is married, and has two children.

She reports that she "agrees strongly" that each of the selection criteria apply to her now, and that they did so when she was seventeen. Hence, her scores on those measures are twenty and twenty. The group recorded a range of ten to twenty, a mean of 17.35, and a standard deviation of 1.92 on the measure of how well they feel the selection criteria fit them today. They recorded a range of nine to twenty, a mean of 16.61, and a standard deviation of 2.32 on how well they feel the criteria fit them when they were selected for the program.

She reports that she perceives herself to be "self-directed" and, in response to item 10, she gave specific examples of having taught herself something in order to achieve a larger goal.

She presently dances with a group directed by Donna Antell. This activity requires some forty hours a month. She reports that she views her dance activity as recreation and good exercise, as well as her personal time away from the demands of work and motherhood.

She has earned an "income" from her art in that she teaches aerobic dance and children's dance classes as barter to defray the cost of her own dance lessons.

Her special goals include working toward a promotion at work, completing a degree program in human relations, seeking "some real good tap classes," and trying for a part in a local production of "Anything Goes."

She achieved a score of 289 on the SDLRS-A. This score places her in the 99+ percentile when compared to the scores of other adults for whom scores on the instrument have been reported and is the highest score achieved by the twenty-three respondents in this survey.

Subject #23

This twenty-five year old male was admitted to the Early College Program at age sixteen to study instrumental music. His responses to the survey form were generally made in the negative and without explanation.

He has completed an associate degree program and has earned certification as a court recorder, which is the source of his present employment. He reports that he is not presently involved in a formal education program, nor is he spending time with music or any of the other art forms considered in this study.

His score of fifty-four on the arts drive portion of the instrument places him within one standard deviation (7.02) of the mean (60.48) for that measure.

His assessments of the fit of the selection criteria now and when he was an adolescent score ten and nine, respectively. These scores place him at the extreme low end of the range for both scales. These scores represent -3.5 SD and -3.0 SD, respectively. As such, they constitute the strongest statement, made by any member of the population, that he does not feel the selection criteria should have been applied to him eight years ago, and that they should not be applied to him now.

In response to the item, "Do you think of yourself as "self directed? Explain.", he wrote, "No. Most things I have done and do are guided by circumstances. I have not really set any major life goals."

In response to the opportunity to give additional information (item 12), he responded, "Although I decided during the program that I didn't want to be a musician, I sometimes think about doing theatre work. Ambition is not one of my strong points, however, so that may never happen. At least that way I can tell myself I'd make a great actor/singer and never have to be disappointed!"

His score on the SDLRS-A was 198. This score is the lowest for the population studied and it places him in the twenty-second percentile of adults for whom scores have been reported.

For the sake of brevity, the information gathered with the demographic survey form are presented in tabular form in Table 8.1.

Table 8.1:   **Findings Upon Inspection of the Demographic Survey**

Attitudes	# Responding "Yes"	% of Population
Articulated Goals	22	96%
Described Resources	19	83%
Future Orientation	19	83%
Self-Directed	20	87%
Overcame Obsticle --		
in Life	13	57%
in Art	15	65%

Activities	# Responding "Yes"	% of Population
Completed Degree	18	78%
Degree in Art	9	39%
Current Education	10	43%
Current Educ in Art	5	22%
Income From Art	19	83%
Self-Taught	20	87%

Scales	Art Drive	Then	Now
Agreed Scale Applies	N/A	91%	91%
Possible Range	18-80	4-20	4-20
Actual Range	42-73	9-20	10-20
Expected Mean	48	12	12
Actual Mean	60.48	16.67	17.35
Standard Deviation	7.02	2.32	1.92

Hours of Art Per Month

Total 1750   Range 0-225   Average 76

139

Several of the group characteristics appear to support the contention that the participants are properly described in terms of the selection criteria. Moreover, these characteristics form a constellation of long-term behaviors from which one may reasonably infer self-direction.

For example, twenty-one (91%), having accumulated fourteen or more points on the Now Scale, agree the selection criteria apply to them at present. Twenty-one (91%) agree the selection criteria applied to them as adolescents. Nineteen (83%) have earned an income by the practice of their art during the past eight years. At present, their cumulative involvement in the arts produces 1,750 hours of artistic effort per month. Nine (39%) hold degrees in their art form, while five (22%) are presently pursuing undergraduate or graduate degrees in their art form. Twenty-two (96%) described specific life goals they hold and nineteen (83%) are able to articulate what resources they will need to access in order to achieve these goals.

Twenty (87%) report they view themselves as "self-directed" and they are able to explain, in terms of their long term behavior, why they hold that self estimate. Nineteen (83%) project themselves into a future (1994) condition which they believe they have, or can find, the resources to achieve.

SCORES ACHIEVED ON THE SDLRS-A

Materials which accompany the SDLRS-A report the average score for adults completing the instrument is 214 and the standard deviation is 25.59.

Table 8.2 is a replication of a portion of the information provided with the SDLRS-A.

ANALYSIS OF DATA

SDLRS-A scores for the sample responding have a mean of 244.17 and a standard deviation of 15.22. Although the N of twenty-three for this sample is small when regarded as an absolute number, it must be kept in mind that this sample represents eighty-five percent of the population selected for the 1981 Early College Program. Scores for the normative population have a mean of 214 and a standard deviation of 25.59.

Table 8.2:   How to Interpret Your SDLRS-A Score

Your score is a measure of your current level of Self-Directed Learning Readiness.

If your score is between: Then your readiness for self-directed
                                    learning is:
58-176   Low
177-201   Below Average
202-226   Average
227-251   Above Average
252-290   High

Some people have a low level of readiness because they have consistently been exposed to other-directed instruction. The most important thing to remember about your score is that it can be improved. Most persons with low or average levels of self-directed learning readiness can increase their skills with practice.

Note that the mean score for the population studied is somewhat more than one standard deviation above the mean for the normative population. Further, the standard deviation for the population studied is forty-one percent smaller (narrower) than the standard deviation for the normative population. (See Figure 8.1)

Three participants (13%) scored in the 265-290 (+2 to +3 SD)range. Two percent of the normative population scored in that range. Thirteen of the participants (56%) scored in the 240-290 (+1 to +3 SD)range. Sixteen percent of the normative population scored in that range. Twenty-one of the participants (91%) scored in the 214-290 (Above the mean) range. Fifty percent of the normative population scored in that range.

Comparison of SDLRS-A scores for the study population to their reports of the degree to which the selection criteria fit them currently (See "Now" in Table 8.1), yields a Pearson product-moment correlation coefficient of .71.

Figure 8.1:   Comparative Distribution of SDLRS-A Scores for the Normative and Early College Populations

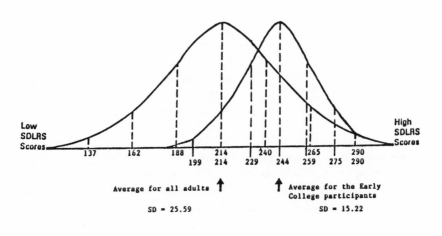

Further, the data lead to the conclusion the criteria used in the selection of the population surveyed, modified as necessary with regard to subject matter orientation, form a useful hypothetical construct to delimit the behavioral aspects of readiness for self-direction in learning.

Using the relative ranking system (See Table 8.3), the scores for nine (39%) of the participants show a "high" degree of readiness for self-direction in learning. Another eleven (48%) show an "above average" readiness. This leaves only two (9%) at the "average" level, and one (4%) "below average."

Table 8.3:   SDLRS-A Scores, Percentile, and Relative Ranks
Achieved by Participants in the 1981 Johnson State
Early College Summer Arts Program

SUBJ	SCORE	%ILE		SUBJ	SCORE	%ILE	
1	289	99		13	241	83	
2	272	98		14	239	81	
3	268	98		15	238	79	**Above**
4	261	96		16	238	79	**Average**
5	260	95	**High**	17	238	79	
6	257	94		18	237	79	
7	255	93		19	228	66	
8	253	92		20	227	66	-------
9	253	92	---------	21	223	60	**Average**
10	246	87		22	211	42	-------
11	243	85		23	198	22	**Below**
12	241	83					**Average**

CONCLUSIONS

Two aspects of the present study are directly responsive to
statements made in the materials which accompany the
SDLRS-A. (See Table 8.2) First, the scores on the SDLRS-
A, the self-estimate that the selection criteria apply today, and
the remaining demographic data provide information about
the current state of the members of the population. This is
directly responsive to Guglielmino's intention to measure the
current level of readiness. Second, the demographic data
indicate that a significant portion of the population have been
"practicing" self-direction in learning for the past eight years.
If Guglielmino's instrument works, SDLRS-A scores for this
population should, on the whole, be above average.

A population was selected using criteria designed to
ensure that participants would be inclined to work
productively and creatively in a learning environment
characterized as having very little direction or structure. The

population selected succeeded in that environment. (Confessore & Confessore, 1981)

Over an eight year period the population selected by these criteria has regularly, and in a wide variety of ways, exhibited self-direction in life and in learning.

When asked to offer a self-estimate of the appropriateness of applying the selection criteria to them, ninety-one percent said it may properly be applied to them at this time.

When asked to give specific evidence that the underlying construct of the selection criteria has been demonstrably at work in their lives, eighty-seven percent of the participants were able to do so.

Therefore, the data gathered in this survey lead to the conclusion that the selection criteria (an established record of taking the initiative in setting his or her own learning goals; exhibit imaginative and aggressive pursuit of the resources needed to achieve his or her learning goals, and; be very persistent in completing learning goals, especially self-assigned tasks) constitute appropriate descriptors for the population in the present.

If one is prepared to accept, pragmatically, that these criteria provide a useful behavioral construct for "self-direction in learning," then it seems fair to ask what can be inferred from the evidence provided by the SDLRS-A scores for the population?

Two findings should be kept in mind:

1.   Scores on the SDLRS-A achieved by the population studied are significantly higher than those for the normative population, and;

2.   With regard to factors measured by the SDLRS-A, the population studied is substantially more homogeneous than the normative population.

Hence, it seems reasonable to conclude the data gathered in this survey support the contention that the SDLRS-A is able to discern and report the high level of readiness for self-direction in learning which the population studied has exhibited as a matter of long-term behavior. Therefore, the SDLRS-A is judged to be a useful instrument when used for the purposes of identifying persons who are ready to exhibit self-direction in learning, provided, as advised by Guglielmino, (1977, p. 77), there is sufficient evidence they are specifically motivated to learn the material at hand.

Further, the data lead to the conclusion the criteria used in the selection of the population surveyed, modified as necessary with regard to subject matter orientation, form a useful hypothetical construct to delimit the behavioral aspects of readiness for self-direction in learning.

REFERENCES

Brockett, R.G. (1985). Methodological and substantive issues in the measurement of self-directed learning readiness. Adult Education Quarterly, 36, 15-24.

Brookfield, S. (1984). Self-directed learning: A critical paradigm. Adult Education Quarterly, 35, 59-71.

Brookfield, S. (1988). Conceptual, methodological and practical ambiguities in self-directed learning. In H.B. Long and Associates, Self-Directed Learning: Application & Theory, Athens, Georgia, Adult Education Department, University of Georgia, 11-38.

Buttermore, P.H. (1979). Arts in gifted education. Gifted Child Quarterly, 23, 405-414.

Caffarella, R.S. & O'Donnell, J.M. (1987). Self-directed learning: A critical paradigm revisited. Adult Education Quarterly, 37, 199-211.

Confessore, G.J & Confessore, S.J. (1981). Attitudes toward physical activity among adolescents talented in the visual and performing arts. Journal for the Education of the Gifted, 4, 261-269.

Field, L. (1989). An investigation into the structure, validity, and reliability of Guglielmino's self-directed learning readiness scale. Adult Education Quarterly, 39, 125-139.

Guglielmino, L.M. (1977). Development of the self-directed learning readiness scale. (Doctoral dissertation, University of Georgia, 1977).

Guglielmino, L.M. (1989). Reactions to Field's investigation into the SDLRS: Guglielmino responds to Field's investigation. _Adult Education Quarterly_, 39, 236-241.

Hinkley, B.J. and others. (1980) _Conn-Cept IV: Identification and programming for students with outstanding talent in the creative arts_. Hartford: Connecticut State Department of Education. ED 199 956

James, W. (1907). Some metaphysical problems pragmatically considered. _Pragmatism: A new way for some old ways of thinking_. New York: Longmans, Green & Co., 1907

Kenyon, G.S. (1968). A conceptual model for characterizing physical activity._Research Quarterly (AAHPER)_, 39, 1, pp. 96-105.

Long, H.B. (1989). Reactions to Field's investigation into the SDLRS: Some additional criticisms of Field's investigation. _Adult Education Quarterly_, 39, 241-244.

Long, H.B. & Agykum, S.K. (1988). Self-directed learning readiness: Assessment and validation. In H.B. Long & Associates._Self-Directed Learning: Application and Theory_. Athens, Georgia: Adult Education Department of the University of Georgia, 253-266.

Long, H.B. & Agyekum, S.K. (1983). Guglielmino's self-directed learning readiness scale: A validation study. _Higher Education_, 12, 77-87.

Long, H.B & Agyekum, S.K. (1984). Teacher ratings in the validation of Guglielmino's self-directed learning readiness scale. _Higher Education_, 13, 709-715.

Marland, S.P., Jr. (1971). _Education of the Gifted and Talented_. Report to the Congress of the United States by the U.S. Commissioner of Education. August 1971.

McCune, S.K. (1989). Reactions to Field's investigation into the SDLRS: A statistical critique of Field's investigation. _Adult Education Quarterly_, 39, 244-246.

Perry, W.G., Jr. (1970). _Forms of Intellectual and Ethical Development in the College Years_. New York: Holt, Rinehart & Winston. 1970.

Simon, H.A. (1969). _The Sciences of the Artificial_. Cambridge: The M.I.T. Press.

Whitehead, A.N. and Russell, B. (1910). _Principia Mathematica_. Cambridge, England: University Press.

CHAPTER NINE

THE VALIDITY GENERALIZATION OF GUGLIELMINO'S SELF-DIRECTED LEARNING READINESS SCALE

Sandra Luna McCune and
Lucy M. Guglielmino

Guglielmino's (1977/1978) Self-Directed Learning Readiness scale (SDLRS) is to date the most widely used instrument for assessing self-direction in learning (McCune, 1988). A large body of research supports the validity of the SDLRS. Significant correlations between total SDLRS score and various psychosocial/behavioral variables commonly thought to be associated with self-direction in learning have been reported. Particularly, significant correlations between total SDLRS score and degree of involvement in self-directed learning activity as measured by (a) total number of learning projects undertaken in a stated time period and (b) total number of hours of involvement in self-directed learning activity in a stated time period have been determined. These latter results lend strong support to the concurrent criterion-related validity of the SDLRS because the value of the associated criterion variable is determined by a manifestation of self-directed learning behavior. The present study is an investigation of the extent to which the concurrent criterion-related validity of such studies is generalizable to different subjects with similar characteristics.

The validity generalization model is a procedure developed by Schmidt and Hunter (1977) to establish validity of an instrument by statistically analyzing previous validity studies involving the instrument of interest. The approach does not take the observed variance in results across studies at face value. Rather, it assumes that much of the variance in

147

the outcomes of validity studies is due to statistical artifacts such as sampling error, measurement error, range restriction, and typographical and computational errors. Obviously, it is not possible to quantify all potential sources of artifactual variation; and, furthermore, when it is possible, the necessary data may not be reported in the studies. In the present study the artifactual variance will be determined from sampling error and measurement error. Correction formulae reported in Hunter, Schmidt, and Jackson (1982) allow for the determination of the extent to which the observed variance in results across studies is due to these artifacts.

The null hypothesis of interest in validity generalization is that the true variation across studies is zero. If the null hypothesis is retained, validity generalization can be assumed. To estimate the true variance across studies, the variance due to statistical artifacts is estimated and subtracted from the observed variance. If the corrected variance across studies is positive, then Hunter et al. (1982) recommend adoption of the decision rule that the null hypothesis be retained whenever 75% or more of the variance in the validity distribution is accounted for by artifactual variance.

METHOD

The steps followed in the course of this study were the following:

1.   Location and retrieval of all published and unpublished studies that investigated the correlation between SDLRS score and (a) total number of learning projects undertaken in a stated time period or (b) total number of hours of involvement in self-directed learning activity in a stated time period.

2.   Extraction of relevant data from these studies (e.g., validity coefficients, sample sizes, etc.).

3.   Estimation of the true variation across studies via the Schmidt-Hunter validity generalization procedure as follows:

(a)   Compilation of information on the distribution of the observed validity coefficients (in studies that reported, for a given sample, two or more validity coefficients, the average of the coefficients was used as the validity coefficient in computations), the distribution of the SDLRS reliabilities, and the distribution of the criterion reliabilities.

(b)   Subtraction of the sum of the variance due to sampling error and the variance due to measurement error from the observed variance.

4.   Testing of the null hypothesis using the 75% rule.

5.   Estimation of the true validity using a 95% confidence interval.

RESULTS

Five studies contributed data for this investigation of validity generalization. Table 9.2 presents data from the five studies. Table 9.2 contains summary information for the validity generalization procedure.

All studies reported Cronbach alpha coefficients of reliability for the SDLRS. While test-retest reliability would have been preferred (as suggested by Schmidt and Hunter [1977]), the Cronbach alpha reliabilities were used in the validity generalization procedure. Because such reliabilities usually overestimate the test-retest reliabilities (Schmidt & Hunter, 1977), the mean SDLRS reliability coefficient was a conservative estimate, leading to undercorrection of the mean validity estimate.

Table 9.1: **Data for Validity Generalization From Five SDLRS Studies**

Study (Year)	Sample Size	SDLRS Reliability*	Criterion Reliability	Validity Coefficient
Finestone (1984	77	.92	not given	.198
Graeve (1987	99	.87	not given	.208
Hall-Johnsen (1985)	65	.87	not given	.500
Hassan (1981/1982)	77	.87	.92	.340
Skaggs (1981)	118	.92	not given	.256

* Coefficient alpha reliability

Also contributing to undercorrection of the mean validity estimate was the lack of information regarding the criterion reliabilities. This information was reported in only one study. The reported value was a split-half reliability of .92 which would likely be an overestimate of the true reliability, leading to further undercorrection of the mean validity estimate.

Table 9.2 shows that 93.7% of the total variance can be attributed to statistical artifacts indicating that the null hypothesis of no true variation be retained. Thus, validity generalization for the SDLRS is justified.

Table 9.2:   **Summary Information From Validity Generalization**

Weighted mean validity coefficient estimate	.286
Corrected mean validity coefficient estimate	.316
Mean SDLRS reliability	.89
Mean criterion reliability	.92
Variance due to SDLRS reliability differences	.000168
Variance due to criterion reliability differences	.000000*
Variance due to sampling error	.009669
Total observed variance	.010335
True variance estimate	.000796
True standard deviation estimate	.028210
Percent of variance due to artifactual variance	93.7%

*Only one study reported criterion reliability information; therefore, the sample variance was zero.

Therefore, the variability in the reported SDLRS validity coefficients can be attributed to statistical artifacts in the data. This result suggests that conducting a new SDLRS concurrent criterion-related validity study is unnecessary and that the concurrent critierion-related validity of the SDLRS indicated in the sample of studies is generalizable to different subjects with similar characteristics. The 95% confidence interval for this study was .261 to .371.

Table 9.3 provides a summary of validity coefficients for the five studies reviewed.

Validity

Table 9.3: **Summary of Validity Coefficients**

Study (Year)	Sample Size	Criterion	Criterion Instrument	Validity Coefficient
Finestone (1984)	77	Total number of learning projects undertaken in past year	Tough's Interview Schedule	.094
	77	Total number of hours of involvement in SDL activity in past year	Tough's Interview Schedule	.301**
Graeve (1987)	99	Total number of hours of involvement in SDL activity in past 6 months	(Modified) Tough's Interview Schedule	.208*
Hussan (1981/82)	77	Total number of learning projects undertaken in past year	Tough's Interview Schedule	.340**
Skaggs (1981)	118	Total number of hours of involvement in SDL activity in past year	Self-Directed Learning Activity	.256**
Hall-Johnsen (1985)	65	Total number of learning projects undertaken in past year	(Modified) Tough's Interview Schedule	.500**

*	Significant at the .05 level
**	Significant at the .01 level

DISCUSSION

Guilford (1954) stated that "The key to a successful validation study is a good criterion measure or combination of measures" (p. 402). The wide acceptance of the learning projects research of Tough (1971) and his followers attests that the criterion measures used in the studies analyzed in the present investigation are acknowledged criterion measures of self-direction in learning. Using Cohen's (1988) guidelines for assessing correlation coefficients, the 95% confidence limits for the true mean validity coefficient range from low (.261) to moderate (.371); however, owing to the probable overestimates of the SDLRS reliabilities and criterion reliabilities, the determined limits are likely underestimates of the true limits for the validity coefficient. Therefore, one might assume that the true SDLRS validity coefficient is even higher than estimated in the present study.

Because correlations in behavioral research tend to be low Nunnally (1978) asserted that the average is probably below .40), the mean SDLRS validity coefficient of .316 found in the present study indicates a moderate but <u>definite</u> relationship between total SDLRS score and degree of involvement in self-directed learning activity. The results of this analysis lend strong support to the continued use of the SDLRS as a valid predictor of involvement in self-directed learning activity.

REFERENCES

Cohen, J. (1988). <u>Statistical power analysis for the behavioral sciences</u>. Hillsdale, NJ: Lawrence Erlbaum.

Finestone, P. (1984). A construct validation of the self-directed learning readiness scale with labour education participants (Doctoral dissertation, University of Toronto, 1984). <u>Dissertation Abstracts International, 46</u>, 05A.

Graeve, E. (1987). Patterns of self-directed professional learning of registered nurses (Doctoral dissertation, University of Minnesota, 1987). Dissertation Abstracts International, 48, 04A.

Guglielmino, L. (1978). Development of the self-directed learning readiness scale (Doctoral Dissertation, University of Georgia, 1977). Dissertation Abstracts International, 38, 6467A.

Guilford, J. (1954). Psychometric methods. New York: McGraw-Hill.

Hall-Johnsen, K. (1985). The relationship between readiness for and involvement in self-directed learning (Doctoral dissertation, Iowa State University, 1985). Dissertation Abstracts International, 46, 07A.

Hassan, A. (1982). An investigation of the learning projects among adults of high and low readiness for self-direction in learning (Doctoral dissertation, Iowa State university, 1981). Dissertation Abstracts International, 42, 3838A-3839A.

Hunter, J., Schmidt, F., & Jackson, G. (1982). Meta-analysis: Cumulating research findings across studies. Beverly Hills: Sage.

McCune, S. (1988). A meta-analytic study of adult self-direction in learning: A review of the research from 1977 to 1987 (Doctoral dissertation, Texas A&M, 1988). Dissertation Abstracts International, 49, 11A.

Nunnally, J. (1978). Psychometric theory. New York: McGraw Hill.

Schmidt, F., & Hunter, J. (1977). Development of general solution to the problem of validity generalization. Journal of Applied Psychology, 62, 529-540.

Skaggs, B. (1981). The relationship between involvement of professional nurses in self-directed learning activities, loci of control, and readiness for self-directed learning measures (Doctoral dissertation, University of Texas at Austin, 1981). Dissertation Abstracts International, 42, 1906A.

Tough, A. (1971). The adult's learning projects: A fresh approach to theory and practice in adult learning. Toronto: Ontario Institute for Studies in Education.

CHAPTER TEN

SPARK GAP TO SPACE:
A STUDY IN SELF-DIRECTED LEARNING*

Terrence R. Redding

Every man who rises above the common level has received two educations: the first from his teachers; the second, more personal and important, from himself. ---Edward Gibbon, 1923 (Houle, 1988)

PURPOSE

The attributes of the self-directed learner require further research and refinement. Identifying the characteristics of the self-directed learner and gathering information on whether these attributes are natural or nurtured will permit educators to determine whether the learning environment can be managed in order to permit the individual's self-directedness to emerge. Identifying a group of self-directed learners that encompasses a wide range in age, education, life experiences, vocations, and other social characteristics is essential to studying the attributes of self-directed learning.

It is not unique to have a desire to learn and acquire skills that the more common person only dreams of having. Within every society there is a collection of individuals that demonstrate the ability, desire, and drive to independently acquire knowledge and develop their individual skills in a highly notable way. These individuals may be thought of as the innovators or experimenters. Houle has said, "The desire to learn, like every other human characteristic, is not shared

* This research was supported by the Oklahoma Research Center for Continuing Professional and Higher Education, University of Oklahoma, Norman, Oklahoma.

equally by everyone (1988, 3)." Recognizing that individual ability is a variable in terms of knowledge acquisition, it is of interest to identify and define those characteristics that increase the likelihood to successfully learn independently. In particular this research is designed to study the attributes of the self-directed learner.

This research project began as an effort to further investigate self-directed learners, identify their attributes, and qualify them. The study was designed as a pilot study to collect data on a unique group of self-directed learners, amateur radio operators, thus the results reflect aspects associated with this population.

The study is based on a sample of convenience of 43. As a result some of the subgroups within this sample have small Ns. A follow-on study will attempt to gather a sample of approximately 300 in order to permit the segmenting of the sample into subgroups with sufficiently large Ns to be statistically useful.

LITERATURE REVIEW AND CULTURAL FRAMEWORK

A key component of this pilot study was the use of the Self-Directed Learning Readiness Scale (SDLRS). The SDLRS was developed under the assumption that self-direction in learning exists along a continuum, and that it is present in each person to some degree (Guglielmino, 1977). As of this writing it is still considered to be the best that we have in this area of study and most widely used (Long & Agyekum, 1988; Guglielmino, 1989). The SDLRS has been challenged in the area of validity and reliability, but continues to be the most widely used and accepted means of identifying and measuring an individuals readiness for self-directed learning (Field, 1989). It is a Likert scale instrument containing 58 items. Ary (1985) refers to the Likert scale as one of the most widely and successfully used instruments to measure attitudes.

In part the concern over the SDLRS and the notion of self-directedness in learning is a concern that the instrument, and most studies of self-directed learning, have been conducted using primarily adult, middle-class samples. Caffarella and O'Donnel (1988), called for additional verification studies using subjects from different economic, ethnic, and cultural backgrounds. Brookfield focuses the concern on whether age is a factor with his declaration, "We really need to caution loudly and longly, against the phrase `all adults are self-directed learners' being uttered as an adult educators' truism" (1988, 24). To address this issue requires a population with a less restricted range in the age of its respondents. To answer these concerns requires that data be collected on a group of self-directed learners that represents a wide range in socioeconomic, education, ethnic, and age. That is not to say that one could find a group of self-directed learners that had members from every segment of the population. Rather any group selected should provide an open opportunity for participation to the widest possible number of individuals in order to represent a group that is heterogeneous.

Amateur radio operators fit the recommendation. Access to the amateur radio hobby is available to literally every segment of the population. The only prerequisite is the ability to receive mail via the U.S. Postal Service. Age, educational level, economic level nor even physical ability are considered. That they are self-directed learners is demonstrated by the manner in which they enter their hobby. Because amateurs are not permitted to earn money from their amateur activities (FCC, 1961) the motivation to participate comes from within the individual; the hobby, therefore, contains members with varied backgrounds.

Amateur radio operators, as they exist today, are an out-growth of a colorful and interesting history. Initially, in the middle to late 19th century their forerunners consisted of a wide variety of individuals ranging from home laboratory experimenters to physicists trying to understand the complexities of the newest discoveries. They comprised a loose network of tinkerers and scientists, who accomplished break-through discoveries beginning with Volta (1823) and his development of wet-cell batteries that were to provide much of the power for other experimenting with electricity, to Deforest (1922) and his development of the vacuum tube, which made modern radio communications possible. In between were such notables as Samuel F. B. Morse with the invention of Morse Code (1867), which was first used extensively by telegraph operators, and Marconi with his initial experiments with radio waves and wireless telegraphy (Janke and Fay, 1989).

The origination of the term "ham" has often been attributed to professional telegraphers in reference to their disdain for the amateurs that used Morse Code for other than commercial communication purposes. Their complaint was that the "hams" sent Morse Code as if it were being sent with a slab of meat (ham) rather than professionally with the care of a "real" telegrapher.

Historically, it has been the amateur radio operator's ability to provide communications in response to public need, rather than their contribution in the technical area, that has resulted in the hobby being federally established and protected. Initially hams provided communications in support of the U.S.A. involvement in WW I. Amateur radio operators were the only available large pool of trained radio communicators. Their contribution to the war effort, and the federal government's recognition that they were a self-taught, highly capable group, led to their treatment as a national resource. This resulted in frequency allocations within the short wave bands, federal regulation through licensing, and ultimately to the development of an incentive licensing program that encourages amateurs to continue to study and develop their individual technical and operating skills.

Their ability to keep pace with increasing technology, and their exploration and ultimate successful use of the short wave bands, permitted them to again support military operations during WW II. Constantly updating their knowledge and skill, they continue to demonstrate a unique ability to establish and maintain communications from disaster sites (earthquakes, hurricanes, forest fires, floods, tornados) when commercial means fail or are inadequate.

Amateur radio operators (hams) are individuals from every walk of life (ARRL, 1990). Some are highly educated while others have not completed a formal education. However, they all share a common bond. Normally through independent self study, each individual has learned a unique but common language, a language that has been described by some as archaic and of little real value. The language is a code developed by one of the founders of their group. Each has acquired communicative skills of a highly technical nature that, before they could be exercised, required formal certification within federal guidelines similar to those imposed on aviation. And yet, all of their individual and collective efforts are precluded from providing a livelihood or even partial income directly from activities in the Amateur Radio Service. As a result the motivation that drives their individual learning efforts cannot be associated with traditional motives such as earning a living or providing for ones social responsibilities.

Part 97 of the Federal Communication Commission's regulation (1961) dictates the conditions under which the Amateur Radio Service is operated. It stipulates that amateur radio operators will be self-taught and engage in activities that cause improvement in their ability to conduct radio communications from a procedural and technical point of view. To encourage hams to continue to improve their operating skills and knowledge-base the Federal Communications Commission has imposed a program of incentive licensing. Incentive licensing includes five levels of competency, with each succeeding level authorizing additional modes of communication, frequencies of operation (referred to as privileges by the hams), and recognition. As a federally regulated activity with over 400,000 participants in the United States of America and nearly 1.5 million world-wide, the Amateur Radio Service is an example of a unique body of dedicated self-directed learners (Call Book, 1989).

But more importantly for the purposes of this study, they fit the unique descriptors used to describe self-directed learners. They are goal oriented, activity-oriented and learning-oriented (Houle, 1988, 15). The nature of their hobby imposes structure but the individual must bring to the learning activity the natural inclination to acquire knowledge. They are what Long described as plugged in learners (Long, 1987). Also of importance is the wide variety of people attracted to this hobby. Astronauts (Owen Garrett), senators (Barry Goldwater), kings (Jordan's King Hussein), and private individuals are among the ranks of amateur radio operators world wide.

Taken as a group these individuals are highly similar with respect to the rigorous training and knowledge acquisition processes they have followed. Their willingness to acquire knowledge, committing hundreds possibly even thousands of hours, sets them apart from the general population. Continually improving their skills through additional knowledge acquisition and study is also provided for in the federal regulations that govern their activities. They are perceived by those around them to be technically oriented.

The following description of the process that allows one to become an amateur radio operator indicates the level of self-direction required. While it is not necessary that one enter at the bottom, the licensing structure in the USA is such that it is easier. There are five classes of license: Novice, Technician, General, Advance, and Extra. Each succeeding license class requires additional knowledge, and is structured in such a way that demonstrated proficiency in a given area is not repeated during subsequent testing for the higher classes of license. A way of viewing the licensing structure and comparing difficulty is depicted in Table 10.1.

The Novice class is the entry level license. Electronic theory and communication principles are at the introductory level. A Morse Code proficiency of 5 wpm permits the Novice to copy individual elements of the letters, numbers, and punctuations for follow-up deciphering. The Technician class requires a better understanding of electronic theory, radio wave propagation theory and operating procedures. Note that it does not require additional code proficiency. Code proficiency is not re-tested.

Table 10.1:   **Class of Amateur Radio License and Difficulty**

Class	No. of Questions	Code Speed	Remarks
Novice	25	5 wpm	Basic theory and regulations
Tech	20	5 wpm	Additional theory and regulations
General	20	13 wpm	Detailed theory and regulations
Advance	45	13 wpm	Advanced theory
Extra	50	20 wpm	Additional theory and regulations

The General class license is a relatively minor step over the Technician class in terms of additional knowledge required.   However, it is considered a major step in upgrading because of the additional code skill requirement. At 13 wpm, the operator can no longer hear or count the individual elements of the characters being sent.   One must hear the "rhythm" of the letters and be able to write them down automatically.   Passing the 13 wpm code proficiency test allows the ham to move from entry level status to full amateur in terms of the range of privileges and activities in which he or she can be involved.   It is at this license level that the ham is first permitted to participate in the licensing of other hams.   General class licensees are permitted to conduct Novice class testing.

The Advance class license provides increased status and is associated with a significant increase in the amateur's knowledge of electronic theory, radio design, antenna theory, radio wave propagation theory, and the wide variety of communications skills associated with being an active radio amateur.   The Advance class license is the first level at which a ham can participate in the formal licensing of other amateurs through the federally regulated Volunteer Examination Program. They are permitted to participate in the examination of Novice and Technician class applicants. It is also at this license level that a ham is considered knowledgeable enough to teach Novice and Technician licensing classes.

The highest class license is that of Extra class. The major difficulty in achieving Extra is the code proficiency requirement. At 20 wpm, the operator must be able to recognize complete words and phrases. It takes literally hundreds or even thousands of hours of practice for an amateur to reach this level of proficiency. If the amateur's favorite mode of operation is constant wave (CW), which uses exclusively Morse Code, then he or she may appear to build proficiency without apparent effort. However, most find achieving the Extra class license extremely difficult because of the code requirement. The written portion of the exam covers a wide range of not often used methods of communicating including slow and fast scan television, facsimile, all digital modes, and communications with space platforms, which itself includes unique antenna theory and the physical properties of the Doppler effect. Additionally, the written exam places emphasis on rules and regulations because it is the Extra class licensee that has the bulk of the responsibility for the Volunteer Licensing Program. The Extra class amateur is authorized to conduct testing for all classes of amateur radio licenses to include Extra.

Methodology
In order to further establish that amateur radio operators constitute a group of self-directed learners a sample of opportunity was collected and administered the SDLRS. Those selected to participate included some gathered through on the air (communications via amateur radio) contacts. The investigator invited members of the Lawton Fort Sill Amateur Radio club, including participants in that Fall's 1989 licensing class and prior class members (from the licensing class in the prior year) to complete surveys. The class members were

surveyed immediately following their successful completion of the entry level novice exams which allowed a tentative comparison between their scores and those of the previous class. This procedure was designed to provide an indication of the immediate effect successful completion of the course had on the indicated level of self-directedness. The class instructor was evaluated at the same time to indicate if his score was effected by his environment (role as an instructor). During a volunteer examination session, the volunteer examiners were also surveyed to evaluate whether this group of Extra Class hams' scores differ from the majority of hams at the same level of licensing. These small samples (snapshots of like groups) provided an opportunity to consider the impact of "state" versus "trait" as they pertain to SDLRS scores.

Additionally, birth year, gender, education level, date each class of amateur license was achieved, study habits, reason for becoming a ham, level of family support for the hobby, location of amateur station, other hobbies, and occupational information was collected. This additional information was required to enable the investigator to formulate a more complete picture of the amateur self-directed learning situation. It further permitted the exploratory correlation of a variety of factors to determine if they provided a comprehensive qualitative description of the self-directed learner.

FINDINGS

The pilot study used the SDLRS with each of the 43 respondents in an effort to quantify their inclination or attitude toward self-direction in learning. The mean of their scores was 235.86 with a SD of 24.93. Guglielmino reports, in the instructions for interpreting SDLRS scores, that the average for adults is 214 and SD 25.59. This produces an effect size of .85 which supports the notion that amateur radio operators as a group are more self-directed than average adults.

The SDLRS is helpful as a tool to differentiate between different segments of the sample. Additional elements of information gathered was primarily to gain a more objective view of the sample and population being evaluated. Certain elements are clearly objective (age, education, license class, other members of the family licensed), however, other elements of information collected were not so objective. These subjective elements included study habits, self direction, why did you become a ham, family support and occupation. Some of the subjective elements provided the greatest insight as to why or how one became a ham, and how that success at becoming a ham related to the notion of being self-directed.

Descriptive data gathered from the sample are displayed in Table 10.2 and Table 10.3.

Table 10.2:   **Descriptive Demographics of Amateurs**

Variable	Mean	Std.	Min.	Max.
Age (yrs)	44.3	15.1	14	80
Educ (yrs)	14.4	2.5	9	19
Fam Members Licensed	2	1	1	5

Table 10.3:   **Descriptive Statistics of the Amateur Sample**

Variable	Frequency	Percent
Gender		
Male	40	93.0%
Female	3	7.0%
License Class		
Novice	2	4.7%
Technician	20	46.5%
General	2	4.7%
Advance	5	11.6%
Extra	14	32.6%
Study Habits		
No response	5	11.6%
Individual	36	83.7%
Group	2	4.7%
Self-Direction		
No response	6	14%
Self	36	83.7%
Other	1	2.3%
Ethnic Group		
White	42	97.7%
Pacific Isl	1	2.3%
Black	0	
Am Indian	0	
Asian	0	
Hispanic	0	
Other (Pacific Islander)	1	
Why Ham?		
Other	6	14%
Interest	29	67.4%
Love to Learn	8	18.6%

(Continued on next page)

Table 10.3 (Cont'd.):   Descriptive Statistics of the Amateur Sample

Variable	Frequency	Percent
Level of Family Support		
Not supportive	1	2.3%
Somewhat	10	23.3%
Supportive	15	34.9%
Very	17	39.5%
Station Location		
No Answer	5	11.6%
Separate	2	2.3%
Garage	2	2.3%
Spare Room	28	65.1%
Family Area	6	14%
Other Hobbies		
None 15	34.1%	
One	13	30.2%
Two	9	20.9%
Three	3	7%
Four	2	4.7%
Greater	1	2.3%
Occupation		
Non-profess	10	23.3%
Semi-profess	22	51.2%
Professional	10	23.3%
Researcher	1	2.3%
Surveyed Group		
Vol Examiner	4	9.3%
Instructor	1	2.3%
On-the-air	9	20.9%
Class 14	32.6%	
Club 10	23.3%	
Pri-class	5	11.6%

DISCUSSION

One element of the survey addressed "why" the individual became a ham. In order to differentiate between those that did it for some one else (other), those that simply indicated a keen interest in learning, and those that expressed an emotion (love) in regards to why they chose to become a ham, a self-evaluation item was completed. But the aggregate answer appears to be that they exert the effort primarily for self gratification, because of an interest in some aspect of communicating via radio, and to place themselves in a position to provide service to their fellow man. Typical of the responses were that they did it for someone else (i.e., to communicate with a spouse or parent), did it because of a high level of interest developed at an early age in ham radio, or just for the love of learning.

It was noted during the analysis of the responses that many of the amateurs cited a particular situation, early in their life (between ages 8 and 12), that created a high level of interest in ham radio. This leads one to surmise that a maturation linkage may exist between becoming self-directed in learning and becoming excited about learning during a particular stage of human development.

Two of the respondents were less than 18 years of age (14 and 16). Their data were retained because it appeared not to adversely effect the validity of the study and provided an opportunity to evaluate their data in light of the larger sample (follow-on study). The oldest respondent was 80 years old and the overwhelming majority of participants in the survey were white adult males.

Pearson correlation coefficients were run for SDLRS, age, educational level, license class, number of family members licensed, level of family support, and other hobbies.

The correlation between age and SDLRS score was r.07, which indicates that, given the wide range of ages present in the sample, the SDLRS score is affected very little by the age of the respondent. The correlation between age and license class is r.50 which means that as age increases one would expect license class to increase. Simply stated, the older you are the more time or opportunity you have had to up-grade to the higher class licenses. In the same way the correlation between level of education and license class, r.38, partially reflects the function of age, in that the older you are, the more time you have had to increase your level of education.

More difficult to understand is the correlation r-.41 between number of family members licensed and SDLRS. This indicates that as the number of family members licensed as amateur radio operators increase their SDLRS scores decrease. A causal relationship is not implied. Rather, the datum seems to support the notion that the family unit and the support that it provides to the members of the unit permit some members of the family to successfully license as amateur radio operators who might not otherwise be successful on their own. This premise is further supported by the positive correlation between family support and the number of family members licensed, r.32.

One other correlation of some interest should be mentioned. The correlation between the number of other hobbies and level of license class is r-.33. This may indicate that the more "other" hobbies one has the less likely it is that he or she will upgrade to the higher classes of license. This is probably not surprising. It suggests that as the number of hobbies increases the ham has less time to devote to amateur radio and the process of upgrading to higher class licenses. There was also a small correlation (r.26) between SDLRS and the number of other hobbies. This implies that, in some slight degree, those who have more hobbies score higher on the SDLRS.

One might assume that, from the discussion on licensing structure, there would be a clear correlation between each higher license class and SDLRS scores. That is not the case as the following table will show.

While it is obvious that class of license and educational level will correlate, because both reflect the function of age, just comparing license class and SDLRS can be misleading.

Table 10.4: **License Class vs SDLRS**

Class	N	SDLRS	Mean Age	Mean Educ Level
Novice	2	238.50	15.00	10.00
Tech	20	237.35	39.65	14.00
Gen	2	251.00	47.00	15.00
Advan	10	231.00	51.00	14.60
Extra	14	232.93	52.00	15.50

A quick glance at the figures might lead to falsely concluding that the General class hams are in someway more self-directed in their learning. However, that is more likely to be as a result of the small N of this subgroup. Still, if one concludes that the level of effort required to progress to the higher levels of license are not attractive to truly self-directed learners, and that social pressures or group dynamics are involved in motivating the ham that continues to work toward what could be described as diminishing rewards, maybe the choice not to progress is in fact the more self-directed choice. It is difficult to say. The small N associated with Novice and General make any conclusions drawn from their samples questionable.

Included as an element of the study were questions concerning the location of the amateur station in the home. The notion was that respondents might not accurately report the level of family support, but that the same information could be derived by simply asking where the amateur station was located. This is not to say that the respondents were not being truthful, rather that the possibility exists that they may feel they are receiving more family support than actually exists. The following table displays the mean SDLRS scores for each response group.

Again, the sample sizes for most response groups were too small to allow any conclusions to be drawn.It would appear logical that, if the family is supportive or very supportive then the station location would be closer to the center of the family, i.e. in the house and possibly in the primary family living area.

Table 10.5:   Amateur Station Location and SDLRS

Location	N	SDLRS	Minv	Maxv
NA	5	238.20	216.00	268.00
Separate	2	249.50	237.00	262.00
Garage	2	254.50	251.00	258.00
Fam Area	6	229.17	185.00	265.00
Spare Rm	28	234.57	170.00	280.00

Further study may demonstrate an association between number of family members licensed, level of family support, and station location. Further it is hypothesized that those factors will be negatively correlated with the SDLRS score. It is reasonable to conjecture that when a family provides strong active support for all members to become hams, some individuals within the family successfully achieve licensing that might otherwise not have become hams. These individuals should score lower on the SDLRS and therefore lower the group scores. It is also interesting to note that when the station location is other than in the house, the SDLRS score is higher. This may indicate an aspect of autonomy or independence that positively correlates with an SDLRS score.

Other subgroups within the amateur sample were broken out and looked at for exploratory purposes to include survey groupings by who was sampled and occupation. Maybe not so surprising was the discovery that, while there is no significant correlation between age or educational level and SDLRS score, the same can not be said for sub-sample "survey group" and sub-sample "occupation". As data were collected the respondents were classified. Those listed as Volunteer Examiners (Volexam) were sampled during a Volunteer Licensing session. The Instructor (Instruc) was sampled immediately following a ham class session. The group identified as "On air" were all individuals that were met while operating in the amateur radio bands and who agreed to participate in the survey. The group labeled Class were surveyed immediately following their successful completion of a complete licensing course (all were newly licensed Novices, all but two upgraded to Technician). Those identified as Club were sampled at an amateur radio club meeting and those listed as Prior Class (PriClass) are members of the club which had completed a ham licensing class the previous year. The survey groups were broken out as follows.

Table 10.6:   **Sample Subgroup**

Group	N	SDLRS	Minv	Maxv
Volexam	4	228.25	185.00	265.00
Instruc	1	251.00	251.00	251.00
On air	9	238.56	195.00	280.00
Class	14	240.79	201.00	268.00
Club	10	234.20	198.00	255.00
PriClass	5	223.60	170.00	271.00

The volunteer examiners were all Extra class hams. As a class of license their SDLRS is 232.93, but when grouped as just those conducting licensing examinations their score is 228.25. The main study should contain a large enough N to permit further evaluation to determine if the difference between Extra Class (232.39) and volunteer examiner (228.25) is significant. However, the difference between their scores points to the possibility that individual scores reflect the perceived role of the respondent at the time the sample is collected.

Looking more closely at the data associated with the "Class" and "PriClass" additional inference may be drawn. The implication is that as a student, individuals have a positive, empowered attitude that causes their SDLRS scores to be somehow higher. However, when the role is that of an examiner, more structured and confined by guidelines, somehow the individual is less empowered and the SDLRS scores reflects this change in role. Assuming that what is being observed is a change in attitude, then the findings are in keeping with Ary's comments concerning the reliability of using a Likert scale to measure attitude (1985). It further supports the notion that controlling the learning environment can enable self-directed learning.

Somewhat surprising was to the discovery that the group identified as a Prior Class also had a lower score. The implication might be that somehow being licensed for less than a year (which the Prior Class was) and away from the influence of the instructors (no longer being empowered by the role of student), and now at the bottom of a new and somewhat strange hierarchy (new member of an amateur radio club), has contributed to their scores as a group to fall. It is difficult to say why there is a difference. Again a larger sample will have to be available to determine if it is significant. It is possible that there is simply a difference in the two samples. The Prior Class and the Class were both recruited exactly the same way. However, imbedded in the Class are two different groups of new amateurs that by and large are more professional and affluent. As a result, their scores may not be comparable to that of the Prior Class. This is but another indication of the need for a follow-up study.

While it might be argued that the instructor with an SDLRS score of 251 is feeling more empowered because of the role that he played in the licensing process, a different view is possible. With an N of 1 it is impossible to draw any meaningful conclusions. If an in sufficient number of instructors participate in a follow-on larger study this question may have to be addressed qualitatively using ethnographic or phenomenological procedures.

There is an inherent difficulty in determining status in terms of who is and is not a professional. Rather than asking the respondent to self select the category in which they believed themselves to fit, they were asked to identify their current, and previous occupations. Their status was than determined based on their highest occupational category during all occupations. This solved the problem of retired respondents simply indicating that they were retired and therefore not being properly categorized. It further allowed one individual involved in laser research and the development of computer-directed video systems to be placed as a researcher even though he described himself as a semi-professional.

The following table shows a clear trend toward higher scores as the level of occupation, as a function of mental complexity, increases. There are two possible explanations for this trend. First, that occupations, by the status and the sense of well-being that they bring, can influence individuals' attitude about themselves and cause a heightened view, causing the SDLRS score to be higher. The other possibility is that the SDLRS score represents a stable construct, and that it can be used to predict the possible ultimate potential success of an individual. In either case it indicates fertile ground for further study. The figures are below.

Table 10.7:   **Occupational Subgroup and SDLRS**

Occupation	N	SDLRS	Minv	Maxv
Non-prof	10	228.80	170.00	262.00
Semi-prof	22	234.68	195.00	280.00
Professional	10	241.40	185.00	271.00
Researcher	1	277.00	277.00	277.00

CONCLUSIONS/RECOMMENDATIONS FOR FUTURE RESEARCH

This was a pilot study designed to apply Guglielmino's Self-Directed Learning Readiness Scale to further define the uniqueness of amateur radio operators and establish them as a group of self-directed learners.

Further study is now required to quantify the attributes of the amateur radio operator. This call for additional study is timely in that the U.S.A. amateur population is rapidly aging, but still contains many active hams that first licensed immediately following WW I at the inception of federal regulation. The follow-on study is designed to include qualitative aspects of this self-directed population and to increase the richness of the data by adding historiographic procedures. The historical method is critically important as a research tool because of its emphasis on the individual and his or her point of view and concepts of the phenomena being studied. The historical methods will be used to capitalize on the existing population (still living) pioneer amateur radio operators.

By further studying amateur radio operators it is hoped that additional attributes of self-directed learners can be identified and qualified. Questions of whether a typical type of family, or similar experiences is shared by self-directed learners must be asked. The SDLRS provided a clear indication as to the self-directedness of the amateur radio population. Questions concerning the point at which an individual becomes excited about learning and his maturation level also need to be explored.

The indication that SDL is effected by attitude or life roles is of interest and will provide fertile ground for further analysis and study. The amateur radio population as a segmented and highly stratified population is suited to this area of study.

Family support for learning endeavors and the effect it has on outcomes coupled with the self-directed nature of the individuals involved also need to be studied further. The negative correlation between SDLRS and a family member's ability to be successful in an educational effort is a clear indication that something is going on.

REFERENCES

Amateur Radio Handbook (1990). Published annually by the American Radio Relay League, Newington, CT.

Amateur Radio's Newest Frontiers (1985). Video tape produced and distributed by the American Radio Relay League, Newington, CT.

Ary, Donald, Jacobs, Lucy C., Razavieh, Asghar (1985). Introduction to research in education. New York, NY: CBS College Publishing, p. 95, 195.

Caffarella, Rosemary S., and O'Donnell, Judith M. (1988). Research in self-directed learning: Past, present, and future trends. In Huey B. Long and Associates, Self-directed learning: Applications and theory. Athens, GA: Adult Education Dept. of the University of Georgia, 39-61.

Call Book North America (1989). Published annually by the American Radio Relay League, Newington, CT.

Federal Communication Commission, Part 97 (1961). Amateur Radio Service. Pueblo, CO: Federal Publishing Office.

Field, L. (1989). An Investigation into the structure, validity, and reliability of Guglielmino's self-directed learning readiness scale. Adult Education Quarterly, 39, 125-139.

Houle, Cyril O. (1961). The inquiring mind. 2nd ed. Norman, OK: Oklahoma Research Center for Continuing Professional and Higher Education.

Guglielmino, Lucy M. (1977). Development of the self-directed learning readiness scale. Unpublished doctoral dissertation, University of Georgia, Athens.

Guglielmino, Lucy M. (1989). Guglielmino responds to Field's investigation. Adult Education Quarterly, 39(4), 236-241.

Jahneke, Debra A. and Fay, Katherine A. (1989). From spark to space. Newington, CT: The American Radio Relay League.

Long, Huey B. (1987). New perspectives on the education of adults in the United States. New York, NY: Nichols Publishing Co., 182.

Long, Huey B., and Agyekum, Stephen K. (1988). Self-directed learning readiness: Assessment and validation. In H. B. Long (Ed.), Self-directed learning: Application and theory. Athens, GA: Adult Education Department of the University of Georgia, 253-266.

Spark Gap

PART THREE

PART THREE

CHAPTER ELEVEN

REFLECTION ON A PERSONAL SELF-DIRECTED, INDEPENDENT LEARNING ACTIVITY

Sara M. Steele

This is an autobiographical study. It provides one view of self-directed learning from a learner rather than a teacher or agency perspective.

I have only a passing awareness of the literature on self-directed learning. As a professional evaluator I have a general interest in learning. I usually look at learning from a specific program, but often have come across clues which have reminded me that a single program is only a small part of the information a program participant draws upon. I wanted to attend the 1990 Self-Directed Learning Conference to explore the idea of self-directed learning in more detail. When the call for proposals for this conference came, I decided to reflectively analyze my learning in a non-vocational area to see if the process or findings would be useful in helping us better understand self-directedness.

You are aware, as I am, that it is unwise to generalize from one case because people differ greatly. I may differ from others in 1) my age 2) my personal resources for learning, 3) my past experience in controlling my own learning and 4) my concept of learning being a mental process through which something is done with information. However, we can find hypotheses to be further examined from looking at specific case studies.

This revised paper is divided into three sections. The first section summarizes the reflective experience. The second includes some issues and modeling in relation to my experiences. The third section presents some implications for adult educators and agencies related to completely self-controlled learning on the part of adults.

Reflection on Self-Controlled Learning in Non-Vocational Areas

This section becomes shorter each time I revise this paper.

Areas of Learning
I started my reflective analysis by looking at my most recent personal learning project - family history. In attempting to find where my ancestors came from, I've covered the following content areas.

Primary areas: My ancestoral lines including those of spouses, how to use a variety of genealogical research tools, better understanding of myself, differences between genealogy and family history.

Secondary areas: Geography of the New England states and British Isles, U. S. history from 1620 to 1860, British history pre-1800, migration patterns in the United States, history of Eastern Dane County, relationship of past, present and future.

Peripheral areas: Local history of thirty New England communities, DAR and other organizations, LDS genealogical resources.

Because I have never taken a course in genealogy or family history, I felt that this was truly self-directed and independent learning. After I was into the analysis, I found parallels with experiences in another area--quilts and quilt making which I had pursued for several years.

Reflective Methodology
When I presented the paper, people asked about the methodology used. Someone asked if I kept a journal. I did not. I used retroactive reflection as opposed to reflection-in-action. (Mezirow, 1990) I did not search through the many "artifacts" in my genealogy rooms--five or six discs of

correspondence and stacks of papers. It seems strange to say that things just came to me, but that's what happened. It was not reflection as a structured consciously organized research activity, but reflection as an everyday thoughtful activity (the kind of reflection which occurs when we interview someone about past experiences).

I had previously reviewed the activities used in exploring family history by doing a rough guide to sources for some friends who were starting genealogy; and by preparing some very rough notes for a chapter on methodology to eventually be added to the family history.

In starting the reflection for this paper, I stood in the doorway of my workroom and simply looked at objects for a few minutes and then rather aimlessly scanned a few things. I also went back to two or three of the family ancestral lines where I started and thought about what had occurred. Then I did active things like dishes, washing, aerobics, occasionally thinking about the paper and developing ideas. When I came to write, I simply sat down at the word processor and the key lists flowed from my fingers. The "sets" of items simply appeared. I printed them, thought about them (possibly evaluated, perhaps critically analyzed them), and made additions or changes. I used them to examine my experiences in learning about quilts and quilting to see the extent they applied in both projects and again did some revisions.

What I Learned About Self-Controlled Learning

The elements common to both learning through exploring family history and learning through quilting grouped into three categories: affective elements, direct resources, and facilitating resources. I found the affective factors surprisingly important.

Affective Factors. I am basically lazy and will not invest time in things that I don't enjoy. Therefore, for me to have carried out focused learning activities in the areas of family history and quilts, I had to receive value beyond the information I received.

Reflection

       In retrospect, affective factors were extremely important in keeping me going. (Both projects were quite intensive. I pieced more than 100 quilt tops before my quilting fever ceased. I'm currently about 80% complete on all of my mother's family lines back to the mid 1600s). Affective factors included:

o   **Interest.** Something aroused my interest in the general area and provided a starting question. Satisfying the first question opened up new areas of exploration.

o   **Awareness.** I was aware that there were easily accessible free resources in terms of both genealogy and quilting that I could secure and use on my own. In neither case was I aware how many resources there were. I started with quilts just before publishers began to produce full color quilt books and hobby magazines came into vogue.

o   **Satisfaction.** I had to get <u>value received as I went along</u>. Both learning projects produced tangible results at each step. Quilt blocks grew under my hands. Branches of the family tree emerged.

o   **Creativity/Self Actualization/Activeness.** On further analysis, this factor may break into several subfactors. Neither of the two learning projects were passive. I was not absorbing knowledge held and organized by someone else, but was finding my own information. Activeness may not be an affective factor, but it wasn't just being active; there was a creative activeness involved in both learning projects which gave me the feeling of accomplishment and self-actualization. The quilt making offered simple creativity in terms of choosing color and pattern and making adaptations. The family history project provided the creative challenge of searching out the parents of someone who lived at the time of the Revolutionary War.

o   **Curiosity.** I've heard experts say that curiosity is a strong factor in motivation to learn. As I reflected, I realized that I am especially attracted to "unfolding" learning and unfolding in areas where I am curious. I am not curious about every subject. In fact, I am wondering if I can find a new area which will give me satisfaction when I wear these two out.

o   **Encouragement.** Although the close involvement of others is not necessary to me, it helped that my mother, sister, and two aunts had at least a casual interest quilts. Linking with at least one other person who is searching the same ancestral, and that the information is useful to more than myself, has given me added impetus in the family history project.

Before revising this paper, I scanned the two publications from previous Self-Directed Learning Conferences. McCune and Garcia's reference (1989) to Jahoda's (1958) characteristics of psychological health in relation to self-directed learning seemed relevant to the importance of certain affective elements. Among the conceptualizations of psychological health that seem to apply in my analysis are: attitudes toward my self (and my ability); growth, development, and self-actualization, inner-directedness, successful mastery of the environment.

Learning Resources. The major learning resources used were common to the two projects.

o   **Informal networks.** My first step in the family history activity was to get in touch with relatives who were interested in genealogy. Then I found colleagues who were into this area. Lately, I've been networking with other descendants from the same early ancestor. In quilt making, I turned to the expert quilters who were doing quilting for me. I also networked with people who had interests in similar kinds of quilts.

Networks are very important in independent learning activities. You replace some of the contributions of a teacher by interacting with a variety of people who you can help you and who you can help in return. My networking was casual and mostly via mail. However, some networks develop into self-help groups that meet regularily. Hammerman (1990) has examined the commonalities between self-directed learning and self-help groups. As a socially independent person, it surprised me to discover through reflection how much I had networked in relation to these two activities.

o   **Newsletters.** In both instances I used newsletters and periodicals extensively for short pieces of information. The newsletters and periodicals were well organized, and easily accessible through indexes. I subscribed to quilter's newsletters. I found I could access many of the various genealogical newsletters at the Wisconsin Historical Library.

o   **Books.** Books were a main resource in both projects although I seldom read a book from cover to cover. I looked at the pictures in the quilt books. I skimmed through the family and local history books searching for my particular ancestors.

o   **Consultants.** In both projects I used a variety of people as consultants. Specialized librarians were especially helpful. In the family history project I located and paid searchers at various locations. In the quilting project I sought out local quilters.

o   **Exhibits and Conferences.** I learned a great deal about quilts from going to various quilt shows. I went to the national genealogist association meeting one year and studied the exhibits. What I found there was more of a verification of already found sources and procedures rather than much new material.

Perhaps the most significant reflection on learning resources came as I revised the paper and realized the number and flow of sources I used in the two projects. I tapped resources more than 1,000 times in the course of each project. Some resources I went back to several times--certain local history books and certain books on quilting--some I used only once or twice. But perhaps the most insightful finding for me was that from a learner's standpoint a particular resource is only one of several. From an agency or educator's standpoint their particular resource is all they are interested in.

Facilitating Resources. Another conclusion I reached out of reflecting upon my two major learning projects is the importance of facilitating resources to the success of self directed, independent projects.

o   **Electronic Technology.** Microfilm, microfiche and computers all have been useful in accessing stored material in the family history project. I would certainly add my computer and the library's fast copy machines as resources for the family history project. There is ABSOLUTELY NO WAY I would have copied all the material and written all of the letters and summaries that I have written if I had had to do them by hand.

o   **Travel.** Opportunities to travel have also helped. I usually was able to include a trip to a quilt store, or to a library which had a good genealogy or local history collection when I went to a professional conference.

o   **Space.** Some self-directed, independent learning projects may not require space, but I'm a bit of a pack rat. In both projects the paper trail grew and grew and grew. I needed both working space and storage space.

o   **Time.** I spent many hours on each of the projects, but I could adjust the number of minutes or hours spent at any one time. I could spend twenty minutes writing one letter, or a whole day reviewing a file and putting pieces together in the family history project. The quilting project worked in especially well in airports, doctors' offices, hospitals, etc.

o   **Confidence and Courage.** Even though I was used to libraries, I was a bit uneasy the first time I took a subway across Washington to the Library of Congress and figured out the routine of using that library. Quilting required a different kind of courage on my part. I enjoyed quilting because I could work creatively with color and design but I was not a careful seamstress and I had to be courageous enough to be true to my own interests and not get crowded into a perfection of stitchery which I did not enjoy.

Reflection

Again in a second reflection in revising the paper, the availability of facilitating resources makes considerable difference in the efficiency and ease of pursuing a learning project.

Other Insights

This reflective study "unfolded" much like the two learning projects I was examining. It surprised me to identify so many elements common to the two major learning projects. Here are a few of the other insights I identified from the experience.

1. In many areas, both in terms of one's occupational and leisure life, the resources for self-structured and self-controlled learning are available to people with adequate time, money, and/or energy. They do not have to be dependent on teachers. The invention of the printing press reduced dependence; the electronic age makes accessing information much easier and is loosening dependence upon a teacher still farther.

2. Considering the wealth of special publications and auxiliary materials available related to both of these projects, it is apparent that the hobby and leisure area attracts a multitude of learners. Some learn from a teacher, many learn on their own. Some of the experts and lay consultants have formal preparation in education, but many do not.

3. Many of the people who provide the resources most likely to be used in self learning projects are people who are not intentionally teaching. However, because their services or materials are very useful to the independent learner they are essential to independent learning.

5. Associations and societies make a major contribution to providing resources and opening networks to independent learners in relation to hobbies and non-vocational learning activities.

6.   Dependence on a teacher is lessened when there is adequate access to other sources of information and consultations with knowledgeable others.

7.   Able learners may chafe at being controlled by a teacher. A teacher should be able to recognize that fact and not be hurt by it. (I wonder how many others feel they don't want to be yoked to one teacher's view of content and one teacher's control of learning situations).

8.   Discovery learning can lead to self-actualization and great satisfaction for some people.

9.   Active seeking out of information may be less efficient than passively receiving it, but it is more stimulating.

10.   One can't be self directed or independent unless one has a starting point and some source of direction. Some people need a teacher at least for the start of a major learning project. However, rather than using a class as a take-off point, some become so teacher dependent that their activity stops when the class stops.

11.   I tend to think of learning as a cognitive process and it was surprising to see the major role of affective elements in these two projects. It is possible that some people have access to the resources they need to learn, but if one or more of the affective elements is weak or missing less, learning will occur.

12.   Drawing insights from one's own experiences can be valuable if one does not try to over generalize from them.

Issues, Modeling and Further Insights

As a professor, I found myself identifying and dealing with some related issues as I developed this paper. One of those issues is one which is frequently dealt with - what is self-directed learning? Another involves what the extent to which learning is dependent upon planning, and the third involves acceptable sources of knowledge for learning.

Elements of Control Involved in Self Directed Learning

When I started writing this paper I was confused about the relationship of self-directed learning and independent learning. Some years ago Allan Tough's work in relation to independent learning projects interested me greatly. I thought I knew what self-directed meant. I became confused when I saw people including learning contracts in graduate programs in self-direction literature. Another confounding factor is the way some people entangle distance learning and independent learning. At the 1989 Commission of Professors meeting, one of the business meetings developed into a discussion of whether the self-directed learning and the distance education interest groups should merge. Some feel that learning is independent when there is no direct face-to-face contact with a teacher. In distance education, the student is independent of the regimentation of a class meeting at a specific time and at a specific place, but is not necessarily independent of the direction and control of a teacher.

I decided that both terms were open to several conceptions and I needed to identify what was happening in my own context. I took time out and tried to define the kind of self-directedness I was discussing. Rather than dealing either with directedness or with the independence, I was dealing with several dimensions which define the degree of control held by the learner versus that held by someone else. Each of those factors can be viewed as a continuum. It is easiest to see two major dimensions.

1) <u>control of the content</u>. - To what extent does a learner define the content to be covered and/or how it will be covered?

2) <u>control of learning activities</u>. - To what extent does the learner control when, how, where, the learning will occur?

The two continuums form the matrix shown in Figure 11.1. Cells A and I are opposites and are most easily identified.

Cell A - Learner Control of Both Content and Activities.
My paper deals with learning where I was completely in control using other resources but giving them no real control over what content I explored and retained or how I accessed that content. This is the only cell where the learner is completely independent of control or guidance by others.

Cell I - Teacher Control of Both Content and Activities.
When the teacher controls both the content and activities, there is little opportunity for self direction. Society expects most University courses to be teacher controlled both in terms of content and major learning activities.

Figure 11.1:   Degree of Control of Content and Learning Activities

| | Control of the Learning Activities: | | |
	By Learner	Jointly/Negotiated	By Teacher
Control of Content:			
By Learner	A	B	C
Jointly/Negotiated	D	E	F
Teacher Controlled	G	H	I

Cells C and G involve situations where the learner controls one part and the teacher controls the other.

Cell C - Learner Controls the Content; Teacher Controls the Learning Activities.
In some instances, independent study as a part of a resident credit program is an illustration of this cell. The student identifies the content, but the Professor determines how the learning activity will be structured.

<u>**Cell G - Teacher Controls the Content; Learner Controls the Activities**</u>. Problem focused teaching may fall into this category. The teacher controls the general area of learning through the kind of problem which is posed, but the learner or learners are free to develop their own approach to the problem. Some computer programs and workbooks might fall into this category when the content is defined, but the learner has several choices as to how he or she will interact with that content. At least in theory, much of the adult education offered by agencies or private consultants involves joint control.

<u>**Cell B, D, E - Joint or Negotiated Control of At Least One of the Dimensions**</u>. Learning contracts and mentoring usually fall into Cells B, D, or E depending upon who does the initiating and who has most control. They are usually planned and controlled either jointly or through negotiation.

After working with this matrix, I became more accepting of the wide range of learning activities that people fold into self-directed learning. It is possible for some degree of self-direction to occur when there is an ongoing relationship with a teacher. Thus, as I revised my paper, I began to talk more of the independent self-directed learner--or the person who was in total control and in no way dependent upon a teacher for either content or learning activities.

I notice in previous papers at these conferences that various authors have recognized that control is a decisive element in self-directed learning. Long (1989), for example, identified the importance of the psychological factor of control and distinquished between Autonomous Learning, Pedagogical Self-Directed Learning, and Traditional Institutional Settings as a continuum of the probability with which self directedness occurs. It is clear that my focus has been on autonomous learning. Garrison (1989) separated the terms self-directedness and control and points out that self-directed learning as a fully self-instructional process has been questioned. Such a statement makes me more comfortable with sorting out the difference between self-direction which can occur in varying degrees within teacher directed learning activities, and autonomy from a teacher which occurs when a learner does not follow content and structuring of learning activities established by another person.

Autonomous (from a teacher but not from resources) learning is the basic thrust of "street learning" and most of the rest of the learning which we engage in. However, the information age and technological revolution is making it much easier for people to learn successfully autonomously in scholarly pursuits or in areas which have usually been the domaine of the school and the educator.

Life after retirement gives more people the time to engage in such learning. Therefore, as someone said a few years ago, the self-directed, independent learning arena (autonomous learning) shows great potential for development. Educators need to find a place for themselves in organizing and presenting materials via print and media which will stimulate and facilitate the learning of people that the educator will never see or never know used the materials.

Planning as Involved in Learning Activities
As I narrowed my attention to Cell A and began to reflect upon the nature of that particular cell I saw two dimensions which further helped to clarify the nature of autonomous self-directed learning. One of the two is the extent to which preplanning is involved. Although I have used the term "learning project" in the first pages of this paper, I was using the words as a convenient label rather than in the academic sense.

Three categories of degree of planning emerged as I reflected.

o   **Preplanned.** At a minimum the learner has thought out a rough plan of what they want to find out, by when, and how they will go about it.

o   **Unfolding.** The learner starts with a question, problem, interest, or goal but no boundaries as to how much time will be invested or the specific direction the learning will take. The activity develops as it goes along. Planning is done a step at a time and may not be done rationally or consciously.

o   **Serendipitous.** Learning occurs in relation to another activity and is a byproduct of that other activity. For example, we learn from talk shows when we use them as company while we are driving.

I saw the last two patterns in my major approaches to non-vocational learning. The learning from my family history activities was about 75 % unfolding and 25 % serendipitous. It definitely was not preplanned. I did not set out to learn any of the things that I did learn. Each problem I encountered involved learning more about family history resources and about local history in different areas of the New England states. The learning simply kept unfolding as I went along.

The serendipitous learning came about because I could not escape history. In order to find ancestors, I often had to explore the history of the town where they had settled. I hadn't realized there were so many organizations in addition to DAR that related to the colonial era, nor that there there as many genealogical and family history associations and libraries as there are.

Quilts and quilt making, which had held me enthralled for fifteen years previously, also was an unfolding learning project. I didn't plan what I would study about quilts. One thing led to another. Again, serendipitous areas emerged that I would not have considered putting effort into learning but I eventually valued--color, textiles, history, origination of various designs, the Amish, Hawaiian missionaries, etc.

As I reflected, I realized that I not only was comfortable with a learning project which "unfolded", I definitely preferred it. It is very hard now to subject myself to a preplanned study of something, even though I know most of the steps and processes. For me, preplanning takes away the fun of discovery, stymies self actualization, and lessens my sense of accomplishment. Taking part in a teacher structured activity is like making a quilt out of a precut kit.

All the decisions about color and design have been made and you just have to find the pieces and put them together.

Some of those who view learning from the standpoint of educational institutions, would say that unfolding learning activities and learning which is serendipitous don't quality as self-directed learning. Some focus on deliberate learning and exclude any learning where there wasn't an original intent to deliberately increase knowledge. If we exclude unfolding and serendipitous, we ignore the bulk of everyday learning and especially the learning activities of relaxed, creative people. We may need to be open to new paradigms. Jarvis (1990) appears to be advocating a broader definition of what adult educators accept as learning activities.

I briefly thought about three of my other non-vocational interests: collecting murder mysteries, aerobics, and travel. (There is a tremendous amount of serendipitous learning from novels which have special ambiance.) It is interesting to compare the five learning situations, and to realize that I learned from all three categories. I enjoyed the unfolding projects as major projects, but accepted preplanned when it was needed and valued preplanned activities where they took less energy. However, the projects where I invested heavily in my creative energy gave me more satisfaction than did the serendipitous or passive learning situations.

When adult educators first opened education to considering self-directedness, they also opened doors to a broader consideration of learning. It is likely that adult educators could increase their contribution if they thought about how they could facilitate learning when the learner is not engaging in a pre-planned activity. Often this facilitation comes through products the educator has produced and filed in a library. Or it comes from an informal question in a social situation.

Source of What is Learned
Another way of subdividing and better understanding autonomous learning is by examining sources of knowledge

about what is being learned. As I reflected upon my experiences, I found four major sources of content.

<u>Own experiences</u>. We can learn a lot from our experience. Considerable learning comes from the learner using his or her own experiences as the source of content as I am doing in this paper. Some researchers may negate experiential learning as appropriate self-directed learning. However, transformational education credits experience as being a source of content. Fortunately, Schon, Mezirow and others are helping us return to and build upon the work of Dewey and Lindeman in accepting experience as a source of knowledge. (Gerstner, 1990)

<u>Information from others which is not intended to educate</u>. In each of my leisure learning activities, I have drawn information from others either directly or from print materials which were not designed to educate anyone. Local histories and genealogies are designed to capture and record information. Quilt books are designed to provide enjoyment or make patterns available. All of the materials were designed to share information, but very few of them were organized to "teach" the user. Information drawn directly from people often came through an answer to a question or listening to other people's experiences.

<u>Information from teachers</u>. Sometimes we draw information from teachers without giving them any opportunity to structure or control our learning. Reading an expert's book is probably the best example. The teacher may have prepared it as a text, but I scan and take only those parts that I want to take. The first quilting newsletter I subscribed to was started by a Home Economics teacher and I could recognize her teaching techniques without being controlled by them. Orientation videos to the National Archives and to the Salt Lake Family History Library also would fall into this category. They were clearly designed to educate and were well structured but they were short enough that I did not feel the teacher was in control.

<u>Instruction.</u> When the autonomous learner wants something and cannot get it otherwise, or is in a hurry, he or she will attempt to use formal instruction as a means of learning. I went to an expert quilter to learn the hand movements in quilting. I wanted to be instructed, but I did not want to take a class. I went to orientation programs explaining the use of

genealogy or history. An autonomous learner does not completely boycott instruction. Such a learner goes into an instructional setting and keeps control of his or her own learning. Usually the amount of time one submits to a specific instructional situation is small compared to the total investment in various learning resources.

SUMMARY

Autonomous learning, where the learner does not permit a teacher either to structure content or learning activities, can be categorized and examined in terms of the extent of pre-planning and the source of content. Again we can try a matrix.

Figure 11.2:   Differences Within Autonomous Learning

	Source of Content:		
	Experience Non Experts	Experts	Instruction
Extent of pre-planning:			
Preplanned			
Unfolding			
Serendipitous			

Much of preplanned autonomous activity relates to the use of experts or instruction. One has defined what one wants to know sufficiently to have decided the best way is to use someone who knows. Also, although unfolding and serendipitous are most associated with experience and non-experts, there is serendipitous learning from both experts and instruction if the expert/teacher is able to relax and not instruct.

Reflection

As I reflect upon the ideas in this section - autonomy, non-preplanned learning, multiple sources of knowledge - I am recognizing a paradigm shift away from thinking of education as the province of the professional with interest in learners a key to being more effective in teaching, to a view that adults are active learners, sometimes calling upon teachers and other authorities. In part the shift in the professional field is coming from within the field with the growing recognition of self-direction and transformational education. In part it is occurring because of advances in technology which increases opportunities for autonomy, and population factors which change who is reached through traditional instructional modes.

Implications
There are many points that could be discussed. But the one that interests me most is the nature and role of people who facilitate the learning of those autonomous adults who want to control and structure their own learning.

First some conjectures about the past and future of autonomous learning.

o   Autonomous learners have always been with us. The extent of survival or success of the lay person regardless of formal education often rests with the quality and amount of autonomous learning. In addition, experts in most fields often become experts because they do a great deal of autonomous learning.

o   Autonomous learning is often associated with those areas of learning which involve local knowledge or can be easily acquired through books. Instruction has usually been associated with disciplines.

o   Autonomous learning for some people or in some content areas has come about because of lack of access to instruction. Lack of access may be due to instruction not being available or not available at a time or cost that fits the individual. "I couldn't afford to go to college, so I had to pick it up on my own."

Therefore, for some people and content areas autonomous learning is a forced choice.

o   In other areas it is an alternative selected by the individual. It is the alternative I selected for non-vocational education. It's possible that autonomy often is more likely to be used in areas where we feel completely free of other's expectations or sanctions.

o   However, as educational technology develops more products at lower prices, it will become possible to access most disciplines in considerable depth autonomously. Today, the kind of video overviews provided at most cultural and historical locations such as Amana or the Truman Library help the adult learn more about history than a teacher ever can in an instructional setting. Tomorrow, a person will be able to rent or borrow the video from the Truman library and interact with it via computer.

o   In the future it is very likely that people in the communications field and those with specialized interests will have more influence on the learning of middle America than will adult education professionals.

o   Thus, more people will be free to "shake off" teachers in more areas if they want to. However, all of us will prefer dependent, teacher-directed learning situations at times such as:

---   when we don't want the responsibility of making choices or finding resources.

---   when we want to gulp something down in a hurry. Self direction and independent learning can take a lot of time.

---   when we feel unable to evaluate the soundness of the information available through other sources.

---   when there is someone whose ideas we really respect and we want to place ourselves at his or her feet and absorb what that person professes.

o　　With the increase in autonomy the role of professionals related to helping adults learn will change. It will be important that we:

　　a.　　Help adults recognize their choices and their ability to learn autonomously. In part that means helping them redefine their concept of learning. Learning can be done without a teacher.

　　b.　　Develop informative materials that can be accessed and used effectively and appropriately by autonomous learners.

　　c.　　Give more attention to those who facilitate autonomous learners in their search for understanding.

o　　There is a major difference between instructing people and facilitating learning. Educating assumes the teacher is educating people in regard to something. Facilitating learning means that someone is stimulating or assisting a learner. It is possible to facilitate learning while one is teaching, but the two activities are not synonymous.

　　True "facilitators" of autonomous learners are not trying to "profess" or "instruct." The facilitator does not make decisions about what the learner should learn, but is free to listen to where the learner wants to go and help him or her get there. We have courses preparing "teachers" of adults and program "coordinators," but do we have courses for facilitators? Librarians, the clergy, journalists, consultants, nurses, and policemen, grandparents, talk show stars, and others find themselves in the role of facilitating learning. Many of the techniques used by the facilitator are the exact opposite of those of an instructor. For example, the facilitator asks and answers questions but does not discourse or direct.

o   Even though the activities of facilitators of self directed, independent learning increase greatly, instructors of adults will not erode away like unuseful appendix. There will continue to be people who prefer passive learning (putting all of the responsibility on the teacher) all of the time.

Autonomous learning (uncontrolled by teachers) is an important area within self-directed learning which needs considerable more attention both in terms of research and in terms of philosophical examination. In addition to more attention to the nature of autonomy, consideration is needed in terms of adult educators' responsibilities for helping autonomous leaners and to the extent to which professionals who facilitate autonomous learning are adult educators.

REFERENCES

Garrison, D. R. (1989). Facilitating self-directed learning; not a contradiction in terms. In H. Long and Associates. Self-directed learning: Emerging theory and practice. Norman, Oklahoma: Oklahoma Research Center for Continuing Professional and Higher Education, University of Oklahoma, 53-62.

Gerstner, L. (1990). On the theme and variations of self-directed learning. In H. Long and Associates, Advances in research and practice in self-directed learning. Norman, Oklahoma: Oklahoma Research Center for Continuing Professional and Higher Education. University of Oklahoma, 67-92.

Hammerman, M. L. (1990). Commonalities of self-directed learning and learning in self-help groups. In 31st Annual Adult Education Research Conference proceedings. University of Georgia.

Jarvis, P. (1990). Self-directed learning and the theory of adult education. In H. Long and Associates, Advances in research and practice in self-directed learning. Norman, Oklahoma: Oklahoma Research Center for Continuing Professional and Higher Education, University of Oklahoma, 47-66.

Reflection

Long, H. B. (1989). Self-directed learning: Emerging theory and practice. In H. Long and Associates, Self-directed learning: Emerging theory and practice. Norman, Oklahoma: Oklahoma Research Center for Continuing Professional and Higher Education. University of Oklahoma, 1-12.

Mezirow, J. (1990). A Transformational theory of adult education. In 31st Annual Adult Education Research Conference proceedings. University of Georgia.

McCune, S. K. and Gonzalo, G. Jr. (1989). A meta-analytic study of the relationship between self-direction in learning and psychological well-being: a review of the research from 1977 to 1987. In H. Long and Associates. Self-directed learning: Emerging theory and practice. Norman, Oklahoma: Oklahoma Research Center for Continuing Professional and Higher Education. University of Oklahoma, 87-98.

CHAPTER TWELVE

THE STAGED SELF-DIRECTED LEARNING MODEL

Gerald Grow

Current education does not necessarily produce self-directed adult learners. "The structure of higher education ...does little to foster self-directed adult learning," Hiemstra (1985) wrote. "Further, much in that very structure effectively hampers such learning efforts." A similar conviction was the starting point of Carl Rogers' Freedom to Learn in the '80s, a book that described educational experiments which had, as one of their primary goals, "to learn how to learn" (1983, p. 18). Dependency and passivity on the part of students may be built into what McLaren (1989) and others have called "the hidden curriculum," such that "the present educational system is geared to creating dependent rather than independent learners" (Cross, 1984, p. 249). Several esteemed approaches to teaching have recently been critiqued as hampering, rather than furthering self-direction. Brookfield, for example, notes how teacher-generated learning objectives foster dependency (1986, p. 211ff). Other frequently-valued methods, such as intensive tutoring with immediate feedback, may have the unintentional side effect of leaving students more dependent upon external reinforcement as a reward for learning (Deci & Ryan, 1981). Indeed, public schooling tends to replace the child's natural desire for learning with a dependency on being told what, when, and how to learn -- a dependency complicated by the student's rebellion and resentment against being over-controlled.

By the time they reach college, many students have developed complicated dependencies upon teachers and the educational system. Some seem locked in rituals of passive aggression -- demanding to be told what to do, then resenting having to do it. From them, a teacher may receive "outright defiance, veiled opposition, or studied indifference" (Brookfield, 1986, p. 11). Others have gotten too good at school: They follow directions well, do exactly what they are told and succeed beautifully in the artificial environment of schooling. Yet, as Sternberg (1986) emphasizes, students in this group may not do well in a more open-ended environment -- such as graduate school or a profession -- where one must often act without direction or supervision.

The educationally disadvantaged present a special challenge in the development of self-direction in learning and in life. Educational programs that neglect to develop self-direction may build upon the strengths of well-prepared students from professional parents and penalize students from educationally disadvantaged and/or working class backgrounds, where authoritarian forms of discipline may have interfered with the development of self-direction. The high dropout rate among Blacks and American Indians could be related to the failure of educational programs to identify and train such students in the attitudes, motivations and cognitive strategies that lead to self-direction. British sociologist Basil Bernstein has argued that children of the professional class grow up learning the importance of "individual initiative, long-term planning, and interpersonal cooperation." Consequently, they are able to function well in schools and jobs that require self-direction. But, due to the structure of family life, children of working-class families may be at a disadvantage in schools that give students freedom without training them in how to use that freedom productively (Tuman, 1988). College-level programs may attempt to avoid such problems by admitting as majors only students who already possess the basic skills of self-direction. Programs actively recruiting minority students, however, may find themselves suddenly needing to teach such skills in order to retain and graduate minority recruits. The "haves" -- those who arrive at college already possessing the basics of self-direction -- may succeed, while the "have nots" -- those whose family background and earlier education did not equip them with self-direction -- may drop out. Without teaching the higher-order skills that culminate in such life-skills as self-direction, higher education may perpetuate the successes and failures of earlier schooling, rather than teaching students what they need to learn.

Adult educators commonly maintain that the purpose of adult education is to produce self-directed, lifelong learners. Adults are assumed to have an inherent ability for developing self-directed learning, and self-directed learning is often treated as something that comes easily and naturally to them. But if the educational system is producing dependent, even resentful, learners, will these suddenly learn to be self-directed in the non-directive, humanistic settings so often promoted by adult educators?

The top priority of education should be to produce self-directed, lifelong learners. The ability to continue learning may be the most important single skill a human being can possess in the twenty-first century. All levels of education should contribute to this one overriding goal, for the simple reason that the world is changing too fast for any one educational program to equip its graduates with all they need to know. This paper presents a model -- the Staged Self-Directed Learning (SSDL) Model -- that suggests how self-directed learning may be encouraged at all levels of education. The model is expressed in terms of "teachers" and "students," and was devised with educational institutions in mind. It may be extended, however, to less formal learning situations.

Self-directed learning has many complexities that we will not consider here. Those interested can consult Brookfield (1984; 1985), Oddi (1987), and Candy (1987).

THE MODEL

The SSDL model takes as its starting point key ideas from the Situational Leadership Model of Paul Hersey and Kenneth Blanchard. One of the leading concepts of modern management theory, Situational Leadership is described in full in The Management of Organizational Behavior. In many ways even more useful is the non-technical account of it in their book applying the model to parenting, The Family Game: A Situational Approach to Effective Parenting.

In the SSDL model, good teachers are like good parents: They prepare students to carry on without them. As children mature, the parent's role changes; as learners mature, the teacher's role changes in a similar way. Figure 12.1 introduces the four stages of the SSDL model, which are discussed in more detail below.

I was inspired to develop the SSDL model after I moved to a historically Black university and began having difficulty with non-directive, humanistic teaching techniques that had worked elsewhere. After developing the main elements of the model on my own in order to solve a specific teaching problem, I reviewed the literature on self-directed learning as preparation for extending the model. At that time I discovered that some of the key ideas of the model are accepted among adult educators but there is no program for teaching self-directed learning at other levels. I also discovered that a few writers had developed several of the same ideas in similar models, but limited to adult education-- such as Pratt's, "Andragogy as a Relational Concept" (1988).

The Staged Self Direction Model proposes that students move through stages on the path toward self-directed learning. Good teaching reaches them where they are, and it enables them to move further toward self-direction. For each of the 4 stages, this section sketches the characteristics of learners at each stage, suggests what a good teacher for that stage might do, and gives sample instructional activities and educational models for each stage.

The concepts in this paper may generalize to other situations, but they were developed in a college classroom and have teachers in mind. In this paper "self-directed learners" are those who, within a teacher-controlled setting, take greater charge of their own motivation, goal-setting, learning, and evaluation.

Figure 11.1 introduces the four stages of the SSDL model, which are modeled after the four stages of employee readiness and manager style described in Situational Leadership.

Figure 12.1:   The SSDL Model, Overview.

Stage	Student	Teacher	Examples
Stage 1	Dependent	Authority coach	Coaching with immediate feedback. Drill. Informational lecture. Overcoming deficiencies and resistance.
Stage 2	Interested	Motivator, guide	Inspiring lecture plus guided discussion Goal-setting and learning strategies.
Stage 3	Involved	Facilitator	Discussion facilitated by teacher who participates as equal. Seminar. Group projects.
Stage 4	Self-directed	Consultant, delegator	Internship, dissertation, individual work or self-directed study-group

Stage 1: Learners of Low Self-Direction:
"Coaching"Learners.
Dependent learners require explicit directions on what to do, how to do it, and when. Learning for them is teacher-centered. They may simply lack the knowledge and confidence to be more self-directing, they may have chosen Stage 1 learning for reasons of personal style, or they may have chosen a subject that is traditionally taught in this mode. Being a Stage 1 learner is situational; a person who is a

dependent learner in the classroom may be much more self-directed in projects that have no instructor.

Teaching Stage 1 Learners. There are at least two ways to approach the teaching of dependent learners-through coaching and through insight. The coaching approach probably works better for children and youth; the insight method requires the learner to have some life-experience and reflection.

To use the coaching method, first establish your credibility and expertise. Stage 1 learners respond best to a clearly-organized, rigorous approach to the subject. Prescribe clear-cut objectives and straightforward techniques for achieving them. Provide discipline and direction. Keep such students busy learning specific, identifiable skills. Create and reward success.

When dealing with Stage 1 students, avoid giving choices. Keep your communication clear and keep your focus on the subject -- not on the learners. Grading must be objective and cleanly related to the learning tasks. Feedback should be immediate, frequent, task-oriented, and impartial.

Teacher expertise and effectiveness are the key in dealing with the dependent learner. This is a potentially friendly but distinctly "all-business" approach to teaching and learning. Many learners at this stage depend on teachers to make decisions they themselves will later learn to make. Be prepared to make those decisions.

In the insight method, teachers involve Stage 1 learners in the design and content of the learning. Students gain insight into what they need to learn. Adult educators customarily begin this way. Another learner-involvement approach derives from the work of Paulo Freire (Freire, 1968; Christians, 1988; Shor, 1987; Shor & Freire, 1987). Called "critical pedagogy," this approach encourages the teacher to lead students to take responsibility for their own learning, especially by confronting the ways they have internalized societal oppression.

Examples of Stage 1 Teaching. Formal lectures emphasizing subject matter. Structured drills. Highly specific assignments and graded exercises. Intensive individual tutoring. Examples of the insight method: developing critical awareness of one's life situation; needs analysis; goal-setting.

Models: Coaches in sports, drama, music. Vocabulary and spelling drill. A karate instructor. Drill sergeants. A high school band conductor at the phase of getting the mechanics of the music right.

Alcoholic Anonymous, Toughlove, Vision Quest, and similar therapies insist that learners acknowledge dependency as the first step of regaining self-control.

A successful Stage 1 teacher can be seen in the film, Stand and Deliver. That teacher drives, goads, pushes, and cajoles a group of disenchanted underachievers until they learn calculus almost to spite him. Then he lifts their self-esteem with the realization that they did it, and they can do it again. He prepares them (as a good Stage 1 teacher must do) for higher levels of achievement and self-direction.

Stage 2: Learners of Moderate Self-Direction:
"Motivating"Learners.
Stage 2 learners are interested or interestable. They respond to motivation and are willing do assignments. They are confident but may be largely ignorant of the subject of instruction. These are what most teachers know as "good students."

Teaching Stage 2 Learners: "Motivating." Stage 2 teaching is what is widely known as "good teaching." The Stage 2 teacher sweeps learners along with enthusiasm and motivation. Such a teacher will persuade, explain, and sell -- using a directive but highly supportive approach that reinforces learner willingness and enthusiasm. To teach at this stage, give clear explanations of why the skills are important and how the assignments help attain them. Show concrete results in what you teach. Motivated and encouraged, S2 students will learn more on their own.

It is important at this stage to begin training students in such basic skills as goal setting, so they will later be able to learn without such high-powered teaching. Use praise, but with an eye to phasing out praise (extrinsic motivation) and phasing in encouragement (which builds intrinsic motivation). Build confidence while building skills.

Communication is two-way. The teacher explains and justifies each assignment and persuades students of its value. Students communicate their responses and interests. A good Stage 2 teacher ties the subject to the learners' interests.

Examples of Stage 2 Teaching. The lecturer as inspiring performer. Industry training programs. Teacher-led discussion. Demonstration by an expert, followed by guided practice. Structured projects with predictable outcomes, close supervision, and ample encouraging feedback. Highly interactive computerized drill and learning games.

Models. Great lecturers. Evangelists. Charismatic TV teachers, such as Carl Sagan and James Burke (of the series, Connections). Directive therapy with willing clients. Aerobic dance classes combine Stage 1 directiveness with Stage 2 motivation. Many inspiring school teachers are Stage 2 teachers. The teacher's own enthusiasm motivates students until they have overcome difficulties and learned enough to become more self-motivated.

The Robin Williams character in Dead Poets Society is an example of the Stage 2 teacher as lecturer-performer. He challenges a jaded but accessible group of boys to become excited about poetry. His methods are theatrical; he is a master performer when he lectures. He also requires them to become involved, to stand before the class and recite their own work, to take risks. Interestingly, in response to his encouragement, they move to a version of Stage 3: they form their own poetry group.

Stage 3: Learners of Intermediate Self-Direction:
"Facilitating" Learners.
In this stage, learners have skill and knowledge, and they see themselves as participants in their own education. They are ready to explore a subject with a good guide. They will even

explore some of it on their own. But they may need to develop a deeper self-concept, more confidence, more sense of direction, and a greater ability to work with (and learn from) others. Stage 3 learners will benefit from learning more about how they learn, such as making conscious use of learning strategies (Derry, 1988/9).

As part of the process of weaning from other-direction, students in Stage 3 may develop critical thinking, individual initiative, and a sense of themselves as co-creators of the culture that shapes them.

Stage 3 learners may not be experienced or motivated enough to continue on their own. They need to be involved with teachers and other learners and to be respected for who they are and what they can do. Stage 3 learners work well with the teacher and with each other in the design and implementation of learning projects.

Stage 3 can be an exciting phase, and many students don't want to leave it.

Teaching Stage 3 Learners: "Facilitating." The teacher comes closest at this stage to being a participant in the learning experience. Teacher and students share in decision-making, with students taking an increasing role. The instructor concentrates on facilitation and communication and supports students in using the skills they have.

As students mature toward greater self-direction, the Stage 3 teacher will help them structure the transition toward independence. The "facilitator" might begin by negotiating interim goals and interim evaluations, then give learners more rope. Standards at this level are not the teacher's; they are negotiated with the student and often related to some external standard -- such as professional accreditation requirements. Stage 3 learners can be assigned to work in groups on open-ended but carefully-designed projects. Written criteria, learning contracts, and evaluation checklists help learners monitor their own progress. As they become more competent at setting goal and pace, learners can take on greater freedom and more difficult assignments. The facilitator's goal is to empower learners.

Examples of Stage 3. Seminar with instructor as participant. Student group projects approved and facilitated by the instructor. Group projects progressing from structured assignments with criteria checklists, to open-ended, student-developed group projects performed without close supervision.

Models for Stage 3. Humanistic education. Humanistic group therapies. Critical pedagogy as described in Shor (1987). Developmental approaches to elementary education, such as the British Infant School. Training literature for adult professionals. Non-directive teachers who develop students' own motivation rather than provide that motivation.

Carl Rogers (as seen on film) is a good example of a Stage 3 teacher: listening, drawing out, facilitating, encouraging, validating feelings, honoring risks, supporting those who venture beyond what is safe and known for them, cultivating personal awareness and interpersonal respect.

Stage 4: Learners of High Self-Direction: "Delegating"Learners.
Self-directed learners set their own goals and standards -- with or without help from experts. They use experts, institutions, and other resources to pursue hese goals. They are essentially inner-directed. Being independent does not mean being a loner; many independent learners are highly social and belong to clubs or other informal learning groups.

Learners at this stage are confident, both able and willing to take responsibility for their learning, direction, and productivity. They exercise skills in time management, project management, goal-setting, self-evaluation, peer critique, information gathering, and use of educational resources. The most mature Stage 4 learners can learn from any kind of teacher, but most Stage 4 learners thrive in an atmosphere of autonomy.

Teaching Stage 4 Learners: "Delegating." In Stage 4, the progression is complete from the subject-matter focus of the earliest stages to the learner-focus of Stage 4. The Stage 4 teacher's role is not to teach subject matter but to cultivate the student's ability to succeed, in a specific project, as a self-directed learner. The ultimate subject of Stage 4 is the learner's own personal empowerment. The teacher may: Consult with learners to develop written criteria, an evaluation checklist, a timetable, and a management chart for each project they develop. Hold regular meetings so students can chart and discuss everyone's progress and discuss problems. Encourage students to cooperate and consult with each other, but not to abandon responsibility. Focus on the process of being productive, as well as the product. Work on more advanced projects with clear meaning outside the classroom. Emphasize long-term progress in career or life, through stages such as: intern, apprentice, journeyman, master, mentor. Bring in speakers who represent each stage in such a journey. Suggest biographies of role models. Require self-evaluation.

There is clearly more than one way to be a good Stage 4 teacher. The Situational Leadership model -- which assumes an organizational setting in which the manager is trying to produce self-managing subordinates -- advocates a lessening of interaction between teacher and student. Due to the psychological maturity of Stage 4 students, the instructor gradually reduces both two-way communication and external reinforcement. As enjoyable as it is to interact with such advanced learners, a good Stage 4 teacher will fade back, so that the learner's own efforts become the unequivocal focus. The relationship between teacher and student is collegial and distinctly not intense; relationship is high between students and world, students and task, and perhaps among students. The teacher actively monitors progress to ensure success, but steps in only to assist students in acquiring the skills to be self-directing and self-monitoring. The teacher weans the student of being taught.

There are other S4 roles besides delegating. Another S4 teacher might inspire and mentor. Another might challenge or provoke the learner, then step back. Another might become the externalized professional conscience of the learner, directing and evaluating the learner in almost oppressive detail -- but ensuring that the learner internalizes those functions thoroughly. (S4 learners sometimes need the enlightened reapplication of S1 methods.) Another might plant concepts, questions, or paradoxes in the learner's mind which require a lifetime to work through. Such seeds usually require well-tended gardens.

Fully self-directed learning is not possible in an institutional setting, and the SSDL model does not require it. Rather, self-directed, lifelong adult learning is offered here as the single most important outcome of a formal education.

Examples of Stage 4. Internship, term projects, independent study, senior project, dissertation. Student-directed discussion with teacher involved mainly as asked to join. Student newspaper or magazine with faculty sponsor. Creative writing. (Many other examples occur outside educational institutions, such as discussion groups, hobby clubs, geneaolgy groups, family therapy, union training programs, weight loss, and home repair.)

Models. Non-directive therapies and meditation. Consultants. Writing coach for professional reporters. Inservice teacher training. Mentoring.

In Stage 4, the learner may not need a teacher at all. A Stage 4 teacher might set a challenge, then leave the learner largely alone to carry it out, intervening only when asked to help -- and then not help meet the challenge, but help empower the learner to meet the challenge. Castaneda's Don Juan, Gandhi, and Joseph Campbell are possible models. Judging from the Tao Te Ching, Lao Tzu must have been one of the ultimate Stage 4 teachers.

Many graduate professors are Stage 4 teachers. They supervise the learner in a project or thesis, stay far enough away for the student to progress alone, but remain available for consultations. They monitor to assure that students make progress, rise to the occasion, and use what they know. They are always ready to step in to offer a change in direction, to suggest a skill, to help evaluate, to serve as a sounding board, to empower. But the ultimate task of a Stage 4 teacher is to become unnecessary.

APPLICATIONS OF THE MODEL

<u>Mismatch between Teaching Styles and Learning Stages</u>
Problems arise when the teaching style is not matched to the learner's degree of self-direction. Out of the grid of 16 possible pairings between teaching styles and learning stages, six pairings are mismatches, and two of those are severe.

Figure 11.2:   Match and Mismatch between Learner Stages and Teacher Styles.

S4: **Self-Directed** **Learner**	**Severe Mismatch** Students resent authoritarian teacher	Mismatch	Near Match	Match
S3: **Involved** **Learner**	Mismatch	Near Match	Match	Near Match
S2: **Interested** **Learner**	Near Match	Match	Near Match	Mismatch
S1: **Dependent** **Learner**	Match	Near Match	Mismatch	**Severe Mismatch** Students resent freedom they are not ready for.
	T1: **Authority,** **Expert**	**T2:** **Salesman,** **Motivator**	**T3:** **Team Leader**	**T4:** **Delegator**

211

The S4/T1 Mismatch. When Stage 4 self-directed students are paired with a Stage 1 authoritarian teacher (referred to here as T1), problems may arise. Some S4 learners develop the ability to function well and retain overall control of their learning, even under directive teachers (Long, 1989). Other S4 learners will resent the authoritarian teacher and rebel against the barrage of low-level demands.

This mismatch is one of the fundamental difficulties with the public school system. Students who are capable of more individual involvement in learning are often relegated to passive roles in authoritarian classrooms. This mismatch may also occur when adults take college classes from teachers accustomed to teaching students in late adocescence.

The S1/T4 mismatch. A different problem occurs when dependent learners are paired with a Stage 3 or Stage 4 teacher who delegates responsibility that the learner is not equipped to handle. With such students, humanistic methods may fail. Many will not be able to make use of the "freedom to learn," because they lack the skills to do so. In this mismatch, students may resent the teacher for forcing upon them a freedom they are not ready for. Wanting close supervision, immediate feedback, frequent interaction, constant motivation, and the reassuring presence of an authority-figure telling them what to do, such students are unlikely to respond well to the delegating style of a nice humanistic facilitator, hands-off delegator, or critical theorist who demands that they confront their own learning roles.

Several telling examples of this kind of mismatch can be found in the case studies of humanistic teaching in Carl Rogers' Freedom to Learn in the '80s. One student, whose ability to respond with self-direction was less than that demanded by the course, wrote:

> I am the product of a system built around assignments, deadlines, and conventional examinations. Therefore, with this course graded by the flexible method and four other courses graded by the more conventional methods I tend to give less attention to this

212

course than it merits due to lack of well-defined requirements. (Rogers, p. 91)

In another section, Rogers acknowledges "the shock and resentment that sometimes occur when students are faced with the necessity of making responsible choices" (p. 93). Other teachers in the book blame such students for not taking responsibility for their own learning, concluding that in dependent learners "old conditioning feels safe and operates well" (p. 66). The teachers quoted in this book want students to be more self-directing, but they have no pedagogical method for helping students move from dependency to self-direction. That is what the Staged Self-Directed Learning Model fosters.

Working in learning groups set up and subtly managed by an expert facilitator also does not, of itself, necessarily promote self-direction. A letter reported in Freedom to Learn in the '80s provides an example:

> I think a lot about my experiences [in the class], especially the cooperative group of friends (teachers and students) and the stimulating environment and intellectual excitement which I have rarely experienced anywhere else... The places I've lived and studied have not been nearly so supportive or rather have not encouraged the kind of growth I experienced in our class. (Rogers, 1983 p. 78)

The tragedy is that this student did not leave college able to create learning environments she could thrive in. She left dependent upon a high-level of facilitation which she was not able to find elsewhere, lacking the empowerment Spencer described:

> Self-directed learners do not necessarily need to have an atmosphere created for them in order to explore their own capacities. A positive view of self gives the self-directed learner a portable supportive atmosphere, an aura, that provides... a sense of personal power. (Nancy Spencer, "The Development of

213

the Self-Directed Learner as the Aim of Education" quoted in Della-Dora & Blanchard [1979], p. 8).

Discussion of Mismatches. The S1-T4 mismatch (or the milder mismatch of S2-T4) points to a fundamental problem with the extreme "free school" approach to education (practiced by Neill [1960] and attempted by many). This approach trusts that, left alone, children will learn on their own. The literature on self-directed learning, however, suggests that "learning on your own" requires a complex collection of self-skills and learning skills which not all learners spontaneously acquire. Unless self-direction is explicitly encouraged, "free" schools and "open" programs may work only for those whose family background has already prepared them for self-direction (Tuman, 1988).

Teachers using critical pedagogy have also reported difficulties when the method does not match the learning stage of the student. Even though critical pedagogy is specifically designed to address the learning problems of students in their real situations (including the classroom), some students do not respond. "Most of my mainstream college students...are waiting for the teacher to speak and do all the work and leave them alone to copy down what should be memorized," Ira Shor reported. "They generally begin passively alienated, and many stay that way until the end" (Shor & Freire, 1987, p. 129). For all its virtues, critical pedagogy alone is not sufficient to move students from dependent to independent learning. The SSDL model suggests that problems may arise when the teacher's S3 approach conflicts with S1 students.

Though adult educators recognize that adult learners are not necessarily self-directed learners, it is widely assumed that adults will become self-directed after a few sessions explaining the concept (See, for example, Rutland and Guglielmino's excellent program for enhancing self-direction in adult learners.) This is not necessarily true. Adult learners can be at any of the four learning stages (Pratt, 1988, voiced a similar conclusion). Teachers of adults often describe using what the SSDL model would call a Stage 3 method -- a facilitative approach emphasizing group work (epitomized by the generous, gentle approach in Knowles, 1975). Teachers of adults, however, may need to approach certain learners in a directive, even authoritarian style, then gradually equip those learners with the skills, self-concept, and motivation necessary to pursue learning in a more self-directed manner.

Freire, advocate of a classroom in which student and teacher receive equal respect, paradoxically acknowledges the need to be directive:

> On the one hand, I cannot manipulate. On the other hand, I cannot leave the students by themselves. The opposite of these two possibilities is being radically democratic. That means accepting the directive nature of education. There is a directiveness in education which never allows it to be neutral... My role is not to be silent (Shor & Freire, 1987, p. 157).

Every stage requires balancing the teacher's power with the student's emerging self-direction. If I emphasize the need for directiveness, it is because, coming from a humanistic background, I had to learn to use directive methods wholeheartedly, without apology or shame, as part of the long-term cultivation of self-direction in certain dependent learners.

Good Teaching

The SSDL model shows why "good teaching" is widely misunderstood. Most people seem to think that good teaching is a single thing, and award the teacher who maintains discipline, or the one who inspires students, or the one who encourages students to develop on their own, or the one who engages the most advanced students with deep, open-ended problems.

What is "good teaching" for one student in one stage of development may not be "good teaching" for another student in another stage of development. And stages of development bear no relation to age. There are college juniors who learn at a lower level of self-direction than some first-graders.

Active and Reactive Roles
Models always present a simplified view of real conditions
and their value lies in taking you to the point where you no
longer need the model. The SSDL model will certainly not
cover all learning situations, and other approaches to teaching
may work far better in some circumstances.

Extending models is risky; most models are metaphors
that work at only one or two levels of connection to the real
subject. Take them further and the model begins to distort
the teaching; what results is ideology, not education. The
SSDL model, however, can be productively extended by
adding another variable: "active" and "reactive" responses by
students and teachers. Figure 12.3 outlines some active and
reactive responses teachers and students can make at each
stage. Active responses promote the long-term development
of self-direction. Reactive responses promote dependency.

Reactive teachers and reactive students lock each other
into a symbiotic dependency. Authoritarian teachers can lock
with dependent, passive-aggressive students. Teachers who
love to perform as if on a stage can lock with students who
become an excited, appreciative, but still dependent audience.
Teachers who love to treat students as equals and facilitate
them in humanistic encounters can lock with students who
grow to depend upon the ideal family created by such safe
groups. Stage 4 teachers who prematurely demand that others
learn on their own can lock into conflict with students who
need specific skills to empower their ability to be more self-
directed, or they can lock into symbiosis with students
looking for an educational guru.

Reactive learners at Stage 1 are (in my experience) the
most difficult students to teach. They are the ones who
habitually come to class late, turn in assignments late and
unfinished, permit small obstacles to stop their progress, miss
class often, refuse to do assigned work and then expect an
inordinate amount of personal tutoring.

Figure 12.3: Active and Reactive Roles.

Stage	Reactive		Active	
	Teacher	Student	Teacher	Student
1. Dependent	I'm the authority. I'm in control.	I don't want to be here and I can defeat your efforts to control me.	I'm here to show you how to get started.	I'm ready to learn and I need your help.
2. Interestable	This ought to wake them up.	Impress me.	How can I connect the subject to their interests?	This class inspires me to learn on my own.
3. Involvable	We will learn this together as equals.	I already know how to do that. This is dumb.	How can I empower them to teach one another?	How can we work this out as a group?
4. Self-directed	You should be able to learn this without me.	(a) Let me alone; I'll do it my own way! (b) This teacher is failing to teach us.	How can I help you become a fully self-directed learner?	It's good to know you're there for when I need you.

These are the students who will work harder to get out of doing something than they would have to work to do it. They fail to hear correctly. They sit together in the back of the room and daydream or write letters during class. They hide behind a naivete that masks a calculated effort to escape responsibility.

It would be convenient to discover that such dependency has a specific cause in class, parenting, historical background, self-esteem, or community culture. But I have encountered (what I interpret as) such dependency among women, poor Whites, Afro-Americans, American Indians, hippies, two-year-olds, paranoid bureaucrats, and heroin addicts, and I have not found a simple way to explain its origins.

Reactive roles resemble the active, constructive roles taken by teachers and students developing self-directed learning -- but there are fundamental differences. Good learners progressively take greater responsibility for their learning. Good teachers empower learners to move to higher stages of self-direction.

The False Stage 4 Learner
A certain kind of student gives the appearance of being a Stage 4 self-directed learner but turns out to be a highly dependent student in a state of defiance. The one who shouts loudest, "NO! I'll do it MY way!" is unlikely to be self-directed and more likely to be acting out half of an internalized tyrant-rebel fight. The "false independent" student may resist mastering the necessary details of the subject and try to "wing it" at an abstract level. Such students may apply for early admission to graduate seminars, for example, before they have the background knowledge or learning strategies to handle Stage 3 and Stage 4 learning situations. False independents need to have their knowledge and skills brought up to the level of their self-motivation. They may well need to learn how to learn productively from others. They may benefit from a strong-willed facilitator who challenges them to become not only self-directed but also effective.

<u>Dependent Learners as a Product of the Educational System</u>
So far I have spoken of a theoretical progression through four stages, from dependent to independent learning. In educational institutions, the student often arrives ready to function at Stage 2 or higher. Stage 1, especially the reactive form of Stage 1, is probably not a natural condition. Most preschool children seem naturally to be Stage 2 learners, with burgeoning abilities in Stages 3 and 4. They are available, interested, excitable, and have a spontaneous creative energy that they are willing to direct into satisfying projects under the guidance of a capable teacher.

Dependent learning is probably a product of culture, upbringing, and -- most of all -- the public education system. Students do not naturally arrive at high school or college heavily dependent upon teachers. They become that way as a result of years of dependency training.

The creation of dependency through parenting is a standard theme in psychological literature. Don Dinkmeyer and Lewis Losoncy describe such dependency in a way valuable to educators. They distinguish two forms of feedback -- praise, which fosters external control, conformity, perfectionism, and dependency; and encouragement, which fosters internal control, the courage to be imperfect, and self-direction. (Their examples have been expanded into Figure 12.4). The shift from praise to encouragement suggests the kind of modulation in motivational strategy teachers must use as students progress to greater levels of self-direction. (Excellent, detailed methods for motivating learners can be found in Keller [1987] and Wlodkowski [1987]). As used by Dinkmeyer and Losoncy, "praise" characterizes many of the activities of Stage 1 teachers working with dependent students. In Stage 1, the focus is on external control, clear directions, external evaluation, and the teacher's expert judgment. Students conform to an external set of requirements. Such teaching produces dependent students, and a vicious cycle begins. Dependent, uninterested, unmotivated, and perhaps rebellious students further reinforce the Stage 1 teacher's tendency to authoritarian methods.

Figure 12.4: **Praise vs. Encouragement: The Nature of Motivation Changes as Learners Become More Self-Directed.**

Praise	Encouragement
Focus on external control.	Focus on internal control.
Focus on following directions.	Focus on development of life skills.
Focus on external evaluation.	Focus on internal evaluation.
Rewarded only for well-done, completed tasks.	Encouraged for improvement and good effort in the right direction.
Focus on self-criticism and personal gain.	Focus on assets, contribution, appreciation.
Student learns to conform or rebel.	Student learns personal responsibility.
Need to be perfect and live up to another's expectations.	Courage to be imperfect; willingness to try.
Self-worth based on another's judgment.	Self worth based on own values and evaluation.
Setting of unrealistic standards, tending toward perfectionism and paralysis	Standards anchored in specific competencies and achievements.
Teaches dependency and self-manipulation by introjected standards.	Promotes independence and self-direction.
	Easily internalized by self-monitoring methods such as journals, checklists, project- and time-management charts.

Based on Don Dinkmeyer and Lewis E. Losoncy, *The Encouragement Book.* Prentice-Hall, 1980.

What we see is the mutual dependence of tyrant and victim, locked in an unsatisfying but totally absorbing dance of mutual frustration.

We need a better understanding of the conditions that create dependency and we will have to face the possibility that certain forms of help only make the problem worse.

Applying the Model in Curriculum, Course, and Class

Returning to Figure 12.2, we can see that there are six areas of significant mismatch. Blocking out the mismatches produces a simple diagram of the "learning field" in which teacher style and learner stage are matched (Figure 12.5). The learning field is a powerful way of mapping several educational activities.

Figure 12.6, for example, applies the learning field to curriculum planning. In this figure, teaching methods are changed to match the increasing self-direction students gain as they progress from introductory college courses, through intermediate to advanced and graduate work. The learning field can also be used as a planning tool for coordinating faculty efforts so that students do, in fact, progress toward greater self-direction as they move to upper-level college courses.

The learning field can also be used to plan a single course, so that students move from dependent to more self-directed learning over a semester. Paul Hersey, co-author of the Situational Leadership Model, described an experimental course in which students were moved through more dependent roles into self-directed roles (Hersey & Blanchard, 1988, p. 192). The course began with lectures (Stage 1), moved to directed discussions (Stage 2), then to less-structured discussions (Stage 3), and finally to student-directed discussions (Stage 4). Figure 12.7 maps this progression onto the learning field. During the semester, the teacher in Figure 12.7 gradually changes role from expert, to guide, to facilitating participant, to consultant for student-directed activities.

Figure 12.5:   The "Learning Field" Created by Matches Between Student Stages and Teacher Styles.

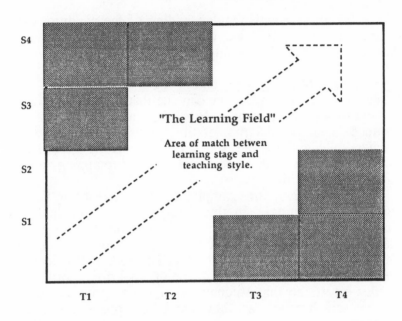

Figure 12.6:   Applying the Staged Self-Direction Model to Curriculum Design.

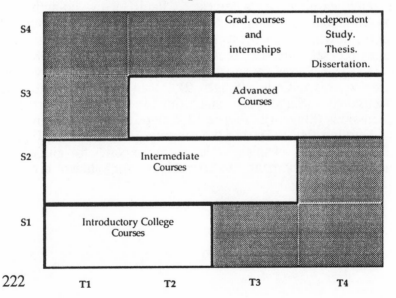

Figure 12.7: Applying the Staged Self-Direction Model to a Course.

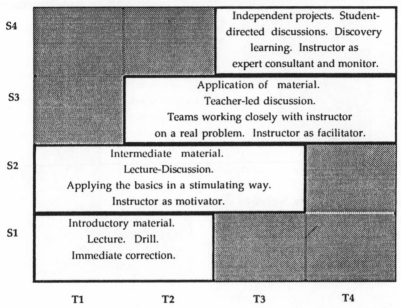

S4			Independent projects. Student-directed discussions. Discovery learning. Instructor as expert consultant and monitor.	
S3		Application of material. Teacher-led discussion. Teams working closely with instructor on a real problem. Instructor as facilitator.		
S2	Intermediate material. Lecture-Discussion. Applying the basics in a stimulating way. Instructor as motivator.			
S1	Introductory material. Lecture. Drill. Immediate correction.			
	T1	**T2**	**T3**	**T4**

Figure 12.8 diagrams how the learning field can be used to map out a single class meeting so that students move from dependency, through intermediate stages, to more self-directed learning. The teacher can demonstrate a skill, guide students through a discussion on it, guide them through an application of it, then have them work in groups to create new situations in which to practice the skill on each other. On a small scale, this progression takes students through the stages of increased self-direction.

Learners come in all stages of self-direction. A student may be more self-directing in some subjects or circumstances than in others. This model does not prescribe that teachers must start at Stage 1 and progress through the other three. You start at whatever stage learners are in and advance (or even backtrack) to stay matched to them.

223

Figure 12.8: **Applying the Staged-Self-Direction Model to a Single Class Meeting.**

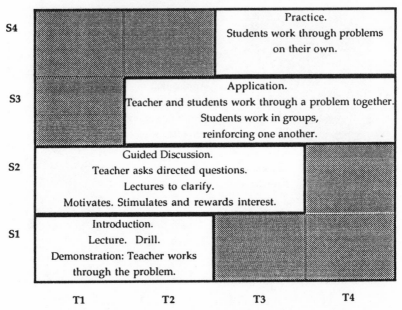

Many teachers already use parts or even all of this progression in designing units of instruction, courses, and pro-grams. hope the SSDL model will provide a framework for helping teachers do so more systematically and more effectively, in a curriculum and an entire educational system someday dedicated to producing self-directed, lifelong adult learners.

REFERENCES

Brookfield, Stephen. (1984). "Self-directed adult learning: A critical paradigm," Adult Education Quarterly, 35 (2), 59-71.

Brookfield, S. (1985). Self-Directed Learning: From Theory to Practice. (New Directions for Continuing Education, Number 25.) San Francisco: Jossey-Bass.

Brookfield, S. (1986). Understanding and Facilitating Adult Learning. San Francisco: Jossey-Bass.

Brookfield, Stephen (1987). Developing Critical Thinkers: Challenging Adults to Explore Alternative Ways of Thinking and Acting. San Francisco: Jossey-Bass.

Caffarella, R. S., & O'Donnell, J. M. (1987). Self-directed adult learning: A critical paradigm revisited," Adult Education Quarterly, 37 (4), 199-211.

Candy, P.C. (1987). Reframing research into `self-direction' in adult education: A constructivist perspective. Doctoral dissertation, University of British Columbia. Ottowa: National Library of Canada, canadian Theses (Microfiche: 0-315-40011-0.).

Cross, K. P. (1984) Adults as learners: Increasing participation and facilitating learning. San Francisco, Jossey-Bass.

Deci, E.L., and Ryan, R. M. (1981). Curiosity and self-directed learning: The role of motivation in education. Urbana, IL: ERIC Clearinghouse on Elementary and Early Childhood Education. (ERIC Document Reproduction Service No. ED 206 377).

Della-Dora, D., & Blanchard, L.J. (Eds.). (1979). Moving toward self-directed learning. Alexandria, VA: Association for Supervision and Curriculum Development.

Dinkmeyer, Don & Losoncy, Lewis (1980). The encouragement book. Englewood Cliffs, NJ: Prentice-Hall.

Freire, Paulo. (1968). Pedagogy of the oppressed (trans. M. B. Ramos). New York: Seabury Press.

Guglielmino, L.M. (1977). Development of the Self-Directed Learning Readiness Scale, Unpublished doctoral dissertation, Department of Adult Education, University of Georgia, 1977.

Hersey, Paul, & Blanchard, Kenneth. (1988). Management of organizational behavior: Utilizing human resources (5th ed.). Englewood Cliffs, NJ: Prentice-Hall.

Hersey, Paul, & Blanchard, Kenneth. (1978). The family game: A situational approach to parenting. Reading, Mass.: Addison-Wesley.

Hiemstra, Roger (Ed.). (1985). Self-directed adult learning: Some implications for facilitators. (ERIC Document Reproduction Service No. ED 262 260.)

Keller, John. (1987) Development and use of the ARCS model of motivational design, Journal of Instructional Development, 1987, Vol. 10, No. 3, p. 2 - 10.

Knowles, M.S. (1975). Self-directed learning: A guide for learners and teachers. New York: Association Press.

Knowles, M.S. (1980). The modern practice of adult dducation: From pedagogy to andragogy (2nd ed.). Chicago: Follett.

Knowles, M.S., & Associates (1984). Andragogy in action. San Francisco: Jossey-Bass.

Long, Huey B. (1989). Self-directed learning: Emerging theory and practice, in Huey B. Long & Associates (Eds.), Self-directed learning: Emerging theory and practice. Norman: University of Oklahoma Research Center for Continuing Professional and Higher Education.

McLaren, Peter. (1989). Life in schools: An introduction to critical pedagogy in the foundtions of education. New York: Longman.

Neill, A.S. (1960). Summerhill: A radical approach to child rearing. New York: Hart.

Oddi, L. F. (1986). Development and validation of an instrument to identify self-directed continuing learners, Adult Education Quarterly, 36(2), 97-107.

Oddi, L. F. (1987). Perspectives on self-directed learning, Adult Education Quarterly, 38(1), 21-31.

Pratt, D.D. (1988). Andragogy as a relational construct, Adult Education Quarterly, 38(3), 160-181.

Rogers, C. (1983). Freedom to Learn for the '80s (2nd edition). Columbus, Ohio: Merrill.

Rutland, A.M., & Guglielmino, L.M. (1987). Increasing readiness for self-directed learning: A facilitator's manual for ten self-directed learning group modules for adults. Boca Raton: Florida Atlantic University, Adult Education Office.

Shor, Ira (1987). Freire for the classroom: A sourcebook forlLiberatory teaching. Portsmouth, NH: Boynton/Cook Publishers.

Shor, Ira, & Freire, Paulo (1987). A pedagogy for liberation. Portsmouth, NH: Boynton/Cook Publishers.

Sternberg, R.J. (1986). Identifying the gifted through IQ: Why a little bit of knowledge is a dangerous thing. Roeper Review, 8(3), 143-147.

Tuman, Myron C. (1988). Class, codes, and composition: Basil Bernstein and the critique of pedagogy. College Composition and Communication, Vol. 39, No.1 (pp. 42-51).

Wildemeersch, Danny, & Leirman, Walter (1988). The facilitation of the life-world transformation, Adult Education Quarterly, 39 (1), 19-30.

Wlodkowski, Raymond J. (1987). Enhancing adult motivation to learn. San Francisco: Jossey-Bass.

CHAPTER THIRTEEN

FACILITATING THE SELF-DIRECTED LEARNING OF PROFESSIONALS: AN EXPLORATION

Lilian H. Hill

It has been my observation in the past several years of participating in and facilitating learning experiences which are intended to be self-directed in nature, that there is a transition to be made from teacher-directed learner to self-directed learner and that this transition can involve varying degrees of uncertainty and doubt about ones' capability as a learner. Negotiated successfully, the transition may lead to increased excitement and confidence. Taylor (1987) describes the reactions of graduate students who chose to participate in a course in which "people were expected to take primary responsibility for their own learning" as including "shock, confusion and ambivalence" (p. 180). This occurred despite having chosen to participate in the course because of its reputation including the fact that it was self-directed in nature.

This difficult transition is not surprising when one considers that many participants have extensive experience in teacher-directed classes in which the when, what and how of learning is pre-determined and is not particularly amenable to individual needs. In particular, those students who have achieved in degree programs may have become adept at meeting the expectations of others including instructors, faculties and graduate committees. Posing the classic question, "What would you like to learn?" may not immediately produce desired results, and initially produce only confusion, irritation and inaction.

Adult educators who are interested in facilitating self-directed learning within their classes need to be aware of the difficulties inherent in the transition towards self-directedness in learning for many people, and to develop the skill of facilitating this transition. As one person in a recent course said to me, "I can be as self-directed as you want, just tell me what to do!" This man had no problems with responsibility or hard work, he just had difficulty with discovering what he might want for himself.

The following pages describe an experiment on the part of myself and my colleague, Dr. H.K. (Morris) Baskett, in which we attempted to facilitate the transition towards self-directedness for seven professional women. In another chapter, Baskett discusses the learning processes; this paper will focus on facilitation.

DEVELOPMENT OF THE PROJECT

The project arose out of a series of conversations between myself and Morris in which we discussed ideas and issues related to autonomous learning and professional growth.

A subsequent literature search revealed that while there was considerable material on self-directed learning, much less existed which linked self-directed learning, professional learning, and planning and design. Therefore, we proceeded to create our own design. The core of this design was a workshop where in we used such instruments as Kolb's Learning Style Inventory (1976), Guglielmino's Self-Directed Learning Readiness Scale (1977), Hogan and Champagnes's Personal Style Inventory (1987), and a list of tools and exercises that appeared to be relevant to facilitating the autonomous learning of professionals.

In planning the workshop, the following objectives were established. They were to:

1)   provide tools and the impetus for the participants to be more self-directed in their

learning 1) about their professions and 2) about their lives

2)   help participants to understand their own learning and to identify their personal theories, ie. their "theory in use" vs, their "espoused theories" (Facilitators planning notes).

Six elements were identified as being critical to the achievement of the above objectives. They were as follows:

Energy.   Marge Denis (1985) comments on the energy generated by people learning together. Although in this case she is referring to learning partnerships, we felt that this would be the case in a group such as the one were planning to convene. We did not in fact comment on this, nor did any of the participants, but upon reviewing the tapes of the proceedings a lot of energy is observable.

Inside-out approach.   It was assumed that "professionals learn from practice all the time, but that (the learning) needs codifying, organizing" and that there was a "problem with legitimation without a theorist to hang it on. Because many professionals work in isolation group discussion is vital." (Facilitators planning notes).   Hunt (1987) and Belenky et al (1986) comment on the difficulty of working with one's own ideas without the validation of an "expert". It was our intention to move the focus to the professionals learning obtained through practice. The validation would come from the articulation and the comments of the group.

Self-esteem.   We knew that some work would be necessary that would allow people to maintain their self-esteem in the face of activities that required reflecting upon themselves as learners. Ultimately, we hoped that people's self-esteem would not only be maintained , but enhanced, but we realized that in what Taylor (1987, p. 183) has termed the **disorientation** phase of a **learning process sequence** people may suffer a crisis of confidence when certainty about what they know is temporarily elusive. Griffen (1977) comments that:

> Because we are socialized to perform well in educational settings, and to expect to be judged, and are taught to be competitive, learning situations remain threatening places. (p. 11)

It was not the investigators' intent to judge, nevertheless one must be prepared for apprehension on the part of participants in almost any class or group one convenes.

Trust. It was anticipated that the workshop, as planned, would require a high degree of trust on the part of all participants, including the staff. Since we discussed instrumental strategies for improving learning capacities, rather than the involvement of participants in self-reflective activities and discussion, self-disclosure would necessarily ensue. This could only occur if people felt safe to do so. In part, this was engendered by self-disclosure on the part of the facilitator and participant observer. As well, when self-disclosure on the part of the participants did occur there was no attempt on the part of the staff to judge this disclosure, and in fact it was met with a lot of acceptance and encouragement.

Fluid agenda. The investigators intent was that the agenda would be fluid and not restricted by timing and content. It was very difficult to resist the urge to plan in a programmatic way, and in fact at one point the facilitator began to plan in this way and needed to be reminded that we were attempting to change our approach as one of our other goals was to explore how the university might provide a different, non-programmatic service. The temptation to map out every minute and hour gives the facilitator a sense of control, but by giving up some of the control that might be achieved in this way, some very real gains can be made by allowing conversations to develop as they will thereby moving the incidental to the centre of our attention.

Inter-weaving of roles. It was expected that while each member of the staff would have a role such as facilitator, participant-observer and research assistant, Baskett and Hill would be able to share responsibility by monitoring each other and stepping in when necessary. This was done on occasion very simply by asking each other questions such as "Do we need to spend more time on that?" or "Is it time to move on yet?" It was hopefully anticipated also, that the participants would be enabled to contribute to the proceedings as well.

Reflection. It was assumed that some time would have to be set aside for reflecting upon the exercises and experiences that participants would partake in. This would be necessary both for them to integrate new information and for them to provide feedback about how useful these exercises actually might be. Quoting Griffen again:

> I emphasize the taking time to notice, to reflect, and to formulate the principle, because if these steps aren't done ... the learning benefit can slip by us, and dissolve into the ether. (Griffen, 1977, p. 6)

While it is true that the need for some reflection time was anticipated, the planners were unable to predict the amount of time this would require and the importance of it.

STRUCTURE OF THE EXPERIENCE

The format consisted of a workshop lab spread over a five week period. The first session was an intensive one and one-half days, followed by three follow-up meetings of four hours duration. In total, 24 hours of formal sessions were held.

The writer facilitated the meetings and Baskett took the role of participant observer. Urmil Chugh acted as research assistant. These roles were clear to all participants

In the initial session introductions were made and an exercise was presented which enables people to express fears and hopes about the ensuing processes. Much discussion was engendered by this exercise. We then attempted to express our intentions and orientations, including our commitment to involving the group in jointly carrying out the program.

A resource menu, from which participants could select activities they wished to pursue much as one would select from a restaurant menu, was presented. Members also were invited to make their own contributions to the list. The resource menu included:

- Kolb's Learning Style Inventory (L.S.I.)
- Personal Style Inventory (P.S.I.)
- Guglielmino's Self-Directed Learning Style Readiness Scale (S.D.L.R.S.)
- Image Learning by Judy Miller and Lilian Hill
- Intuitive Learning by Margaret Denis
- Strategies of Action
- Stress, Self-Concept and Learning
- Farquharson's (1983) Ten Competencies for Learning
- Values Clarification Cards by Allen Tough

Two participants volunteered to present materials with which they were familiar and these were added. One participant had expertise in the area of stress management and volunteered to try to link stress, self-concept and learning. Another had developed a personal development system based on a synthesis of her readings and study. She presented a portion of it about graphic visualization.

After negotiations with the group a tentative schedule of activities was developed, with the expectation that deviations could occur whenever the group wished. Virtually all items on the menu were eventually covered in varying degrees of thoroughness.

In all but the first meeting, the first hour to one-half hour was spent in discussion of what had gone on in the previous sessions, or of what had been happening in the minds and lives of the participants in between sessions. The intent of this discussion time was to allow group members to integrate their various experiences in and out of the group as it related to their learning as professionals and as individuals.

PARTICIPANTS

Invitations were sent to 60 professionals in human resource development and adult education. Seven registered, and an additional four expressed interest but were unable to participate.

Of these seven, two were staff development officers in hospitals, one was a college continuing education department manager, one a senior instructor at a vocational college and chair of the staff development committee, two were private consultants and one a government consultant. All were female. Median age was 43, with an age range of 35 to 52. One participant held a Ph.D., three held masters degrees and three held bachelor degrees. Two of the three bachelor degree holders were enroled in adult education graduate masters programs.

In describing themselves as learners, all descriptors were positive or neutral, ("excited", "auditory learner", "learn by doing".) Self-descriptions of learning weaknesses included "poor self-concept", "low motivation unless topic is perceived as useful", "emotions get in the way", "resent authority". Time, and workload were most often described as external barriers to learning.

JOURNALS

As an aid to reflection and for the purposes of data collection the participants were asked to keep a journal. They were instructed to describe their insights, learnings and problems as they related to their learning. This is similar to Simons (1978,) who suggests that the individual who has chosen to:

> set down in writing the melange of events, feelings, inspirations, ideas which make up his or her life , [is

engaged] for some purpose variously described as
understanding, growing, reflecting, praying, finding
direction, knowing oneself or sharing one's story. (p. 2)

Permission was given for the investigators to read the
journals. The investigators were aware that the request to read
the journals might influence or restrict what participants
would choose to include; however, it was felt that the
journals might provide valuable insight into what was
happening for people in the project. The analysis of the
information as discussed by Baskett can be found in chapter
fourteen.

Several people found keeping a journal to be a useful
aid for learning and wrote in their journals extensively. Some
stated that they probably would not keep a journal without the
incentive of a course. Others did not seem to find a journal a
useful concept; these people kept a journal but theirs were not
as lengthy as others. Simons (1978) states that "not all people
adapt to or enjoy journal writing" and that "the expenditure of
time seems to be for some a deciding factor." (p. 19)

INSTRUMENTATION

Four instruments were used during the workshop: a learning
preference questionnaire designed by the research assistant,
the Learning Style Inventory (Kolb, 1976), the Self-Directed
Learning Readiness Scale (Guglielmino, 1977) and a
Personality Style Inventory (Hogan and Champagne, 1987)
The intention of using the instruments was partially for the
purpose of data collection, but more importantly from the
point of view of facilitation the instruments were interesting
because they provided participants with feedback about
themselves and others in the class. This provided a basis for
discussion, as well.

Even though no attempt is made to draw conclusions
from the data collected, it is interesting to note in passing that
upon completing Kolb's LSI three people were divergers, and
two each were accomodators and assimilators. Therefore, the

humanities and the orientation towards the concrete was well represented. In regards to Guglielmino's SDLRS, all participants scored in the above average category according to reported norms. We felt that the group was self-selecting and tended to come from the upper range of autonomous learners and this was confirmed; the median score was aggregately at the 85th percentile. As well, of the seven, two had first degrees in Nursing, two in English, two in Arts and one in Sociology. So again, humanities and the concrete were dominant. It is possible that the experience in the Enhancing Project could have been very different if a different group had assembled.

CLIMATE

Great effort was put into climate setting in order to build the atmosphere of trust and safety that we felt was important. This included having coffee available and providing a meal on the first all-day session. Flowers were placed in the room, candies were available and music was playing when people entered the room. Several quotes were written out on flip-chart paper and posted on the walls and books related to self-directed learning were placed around the room. By the time we had completed the first exercise which involved writing out collective hopes and fears for the ensuing sessions on flip-chart paper and these were also posted on the walls, the room was pleasantly crowded.

Different rooms on the University of Calgary campus had to be used so there was some variation in the actual physical space. The room we used for our first session was the smallest and was used more often as a department library than a classroom. The greatest amount of sharing also appeared to occur on that day.

Every effort was also made to create a safe atmosphere by being non-judgemental and sharing about ourselves. The intent was to build a space where people felt free to be self-reflective and to share about themselves as people. The learners in this group were involved in examining themselves as learners, but it must be pointed out that learning involves relationships. Having people to share with, to understand and to compare similarities and differences with in an accepting way is essential to the learning process. Marilyn Taylor (1981) in describing eight learners in a somewhat similar situation writes:

> While common patterns in the experiences of these learners include essential periods of solitude, these data suggest that this process literally would not occur without relationships of a particular quality including specific communication events between the learner and those whom (s)he perceives to be associated with the theme or issue around which this process is occurring. Assumptions that we can learn independently of other people appear to be not only ill-founded as far as coming to a new understanding is concerned, but they may also lead to initiatives that inhibit the process. (p. 2)

One reason why people need others in a learning situation is that one's own thoughts can seem be obscure even to oneself. One thought that I expressed as the facilitator was that "I often don't know what I'm thinking until I hear myself say it". This seems to have struck a chord for many participants. Someone else described it as needing an In/Out Loop. I was surprised to find a quote from Marshall McLuhan that is almost identical: "I don't know what I think until I've said it." (quoted in Simons, 1978, p. 41) Unless one is an avid journal writer many thoughts would go unexpressed and hence unknown. While it is true that many people cultivate support groups of friends and family, it is not often that one convenes a group to examine learning, even as an adult educators.

FACILITATING ISSUES

There were several issues to be dealt with during the facilitation of such a learning experience.

Retaining responsibility vs. flowing with the group. First of all, because the group became self-regulating very quickly and needed little facilitation to become involved in meaningful discussion the facilitator had to maintain a split consciousness, becoming at times almost a group member, yet at the same time retaining responsibility for both timing and structure. This was something that had to be remembered at all times preventing one from fully flowing with the group because one was always monitoring the atmosphere in the room. Was it time to move on? Was the exercise or discussion currently involved in still useful? This is true in most situations when one is responsible for facilitation; in this case it was even more so because of the fluid agenda employed.

Modelling. The learners in the Enhancing group were involved in self-awareness activities, and a lot of energy was directed toward rediscovering themselves as learners and revaluing of their learning. It is the type of learning that Mezirow (1985. p 18) would term "self-reflective learning, in which we come to understand ourselves." This requires a certain sensitivity on the part of the facilitator, and I would suspect that these sensitivities would be developed by having had similar experiences. Much as counsellors learn to deal with their own issues during their training so that they are able to deal with their clients without inserting their own issues into the dialogue, emotional house-keeping if you will, facilitators of self-awareness must have discovered their own learning style, capabilities, and needs. This does not mean that one would then hold oneself up as an example, but rather that one would have come to terms with one's own strengths and weaknesses, and be able to act as a fellow traveller on the path. My observation has been that many people have doubts about their capabilities as learners, but that we learn to keep them to ourselves due to the competitive nature of schools and schooling. In this situation it became legitimate to talk about these doubts and a lot of excitement was generated because of this.

Reflection time. A related issue was the amount of time devoted to reflection. This was what we came to term far-ranging discussion that encompassed many ideas that participants had, and after the first session it encompassed events that had occurred in the past week and people's reflections and learning from that, their thoughts on the previous session and the kind of exciting talk that occurs when people are able to bounce their ideas off each other. This reflection would often take from an hour to an hour and a half at the beginning of each session. In fact this amount of time was needed on the very first day after participating in introductions and an exercise that is designed to elicit participant's hopes and fears for the ensuing session. So much excitement was generated and there were so many ideas to discuss that it was important to discuss them immediately. This became the pattern for the rest of the lab-workshop. The struggle that I had at the time was with how much time to allow, although I quickly began to realize that the reflection time was probably one of the most valuable activity that occurred. Having a fluid agenda without the emphasis on completing a curriculum meant that we could allow for as much time as seemed necessary for reflection and issues that would normally not be discussed because they were "off-topic", "there isn't enough time", "others wouldn't be interested", "it's too personal"; in short because of the impersonal norms of the classroom and the lack of time. Schon (1987) and Brookfield (1986) are among those who have argued for the power of reflection in adult learning.

Credibility. It was interesting that credibility was an issue for many of the participants. This included the credibility not only of the staff, but also of the other participants. Having others who are perceived as credible within the group allows learners to identify with them and readily learn from them.

For some, but not all, of the participants there seems to have been doubts about themselves as learners, that the way they learned was not as effective, as "correct" or "right", as others. Many people, including the facilitator, felt themselves to suffer from what Brookfield has termed the **Imposter Syndrome**, in which outwardly successful people feel less capable and credible than other learners in the class. Realizing that others in the group shared this feeling helped to alleviate it.

WOMEN

It is interesting to speculate about the fact that the Enhancing group was made up entirely of women with the exception of Baskett. However, this was not intentional. The group felt they had a lot of freedom with each other. A lot of fun and laughter characterized the sessions. The taped proceedings even generated grins and laughter when reviewed by the author. One of the participants very early established that the group felt safe. There was sharing of personal stories that occurred quickly in a way that does not often occur in mixed groups, but often does in women's groups. People felt free to make comments about learning that resulted from their roles in life other than that of worker or student; for example what one learns from parenting was seen as legitimate information.

There was also a greater ease with admitting doubts and insecurities than one would expect to find in a mixed group with a competitive atmosphere often associated with the classroom. There is real strength that women have in being able to admit to weakness.

> In no society does the person - male or female - emerge full-grown. A necessary part of all experience is a recognition of one's weaknesses and limitations. That most valuable of human qualities - the ability to grow psychologically - is necessarily an ongoing process, involving repeated feelings of vulnerability all through life. (Miller, 1986, p. 31)

At the Symposium in Oklahoma where some of this information was originally presented the comment was made that these women appeared to be unsure of themselves and to need a lot of reassurance. This occurred during a discussion of learning processes which included validation, credibility and revaluing (as presented in chapter fourteen by Baskett). In actual fact, the group assembled for the Enhancing Project was made up of accomplished and confident women. These are professional women with good educations; yet it is significant that they had doubts about their learning abilities and potential. According to Miller (1986), it is precisely because women are willing to admit to doubts that they are able to move forward, I would suspect that this ability is something that one should see more of in all classroom and learning situations. The authors of **Women's Ways of Knowing** (Belenky, et al. 1986) describe what they term the connected classroom in which "no one apologizes for uncertainty. It is assumed that evolving thought will be tentative." (Belenky et al. 1986, p. 221) Butterwick et al. (1990) also emphasize the importance of a tentative voice. Perhaps one of the things functioning in this group is that for a short time the participants were able to let go of the need to appear knowledgeable and confident.

The women in the Enhancing group were also very supportive of one another. They listened to each other and did not appear to be busy formulating what they would say next as someone else spoke, a common fault in conversation in which competition dominates. This was commented on by the participants themselves: "I'm slower than I used to be because I'm listening. Can't learn unless you're listening." (from taped proceedings) Included with this listening was a withholding of judgement:

> (I) notice that in [listening] professionals who have developed a level of comfort, confidence and security. That is demonstrated through their quietness and composure because they're withholding judgement and they are reflecting in action and they don't have an overriding need to ask questions immediately. (From taped proceedings)

CONCLUSION

The above is not intended to be proscriptive; it is most especially not meant to be a "how-to" article, although I admit to searching for such guidance when planning the project. The major aspiration underlying this chapter is to convey the concerns the investigators were struggling with while planning and conducting the project itself.

The "Enhancing Project" was a privileged experience in which the participants taught me much. We had a very exciting and positive time together, but it must be pointed out that the Enhancing project was not the only factor that contributed. Several people in the group said that this was only one part of a greater search that they were involved in.

Perhaps none of what is stated here is new. However, just as the participants spoke of "really knowing", I have come to understand many issues in greater depth and complexity.

REFERENCES

Argyris, C., Putnam, R., & Smith, D.M., (1985). Action science. San Francisco: Jossey-Bass.

Belenky, M., Clinchy, B., Goldberger, N., & Tarule, J. (1985). Women's ways of knowing: The development of self, voice and mind. New York: Basic Books, Inc.

Boud, D.J. & Griffen, V. (Eds.) (1987). Appreciating adults learning: From the learners' perspective. London: Kogan Page.

Brookfield, S.D. (1984). Self-directed adult learning: A critical paradigm. Adult Education Quarterly, 35,(2), 59-71.

Brookfield, S. (Ed.) (1985). Self-directed learning: From theory to practice. San Francisco: Jossey-Bass.

Brookfield, S. (1986). Understanding and facilitating adult learning. San Francisco: Jossey-Bass.

Exploration

Butterwick, S., Collard, S., Gray, J., & Kastner, A. (1990). Research and soul search: Feminism and adult education. In Proceedings of the Ninth Annual Conference of Canadian Association for the Study of Adult Education. Victoria. B.C. June 1-3.

Garrison, D.R. (1989) Facilitating self-directed learning: Not a contradiction in terms. In H.B. Long (Ed.), Self-directed learning: Emerging theory and practice. Norman, OK: Oklahoma Research Center for Continuing Professional and Higher Education, University of Oklahoma.

Griffen, V. (1977). Self-directed learners and learning. Unpublished paper presented at the Wisconsin Adult Educator Lyceum, Pewaukee, WI, July 15-16.

Grow, G. (1990). Staged self-directed learning. Unpublished paper presented at the 4th Annual Symposium on Adult Self-directed Learning, Norman, OK.

Guglielmino, L.M. (1977). Development of the self-directed learning readiness scale (Doctoral Dissertation, University of Georgia, 1977). Dissertation Abstracts International, 38, 6467A. (University Microfilms No. 78-06004)

Hogan, C.R. & Champagne, D.W. (1987). Personal style inventory. Bryn Mawr, PA: CH Publications.

Hunt, D.E. (1987). Beginning with ourselves: In practice, theory and human affairs. Cambridge, MA: Brookline Books.

Keirsey, D. & Bates, M. (1984). Please understand me: character and temperament types. DelMar, CA: Prometheus Nemesis Books, Co.

Kolb, D.A. (1976). Learning style inventory technical manual. Boston: McBer.

Long, H.B. (1990). Changing concepts of self-direction in learning. In H.B. Long (Ed.), Advances in research and practice in self-directed learning. Norman, OK: Oklahoma Research Center for Continuing Professional and Higher Education, University of Oklahoma.

Mezirow, J. (1985). A critical theory of self-directed learning. In S. Brookfield (Ed.), New directions for continuing education: Vol 25. Self-directed learning: From theory to practice (pp. 17-30). San Francisco: Jossey-Bass.

Miller, J. B. (1976). Toward a new psychology of women. Boston: Beacon Press.

Robinson, J., Saberton, S., & Griffen, V. (1985). An Interview with Marge Denis.

In J. Robinson, S. Saberton & V. Griffen (Eds.) <u>Learning partnerships: Interdependent learning in adult education.</u> Toronto: Ontario Institute for Studies in Education.

Schon, D.A. (1983). <u>The reflective practitioner: How professionals think in action.</u> New York: Basic Books, Inc.

Simons, G.F. (1978) <u>Keeping your personal journal.</u> New York: Paulist Press.

Taylor, M. (1981). The social communication dimension of the learning processes where learning constitutes perspective change. Prepublication draft for Salter, L. (Ed.) <u>Communication studies in Canada.</u> Toronto: Butterworth Publishing.

Taylor, M. (1987). Self-directed learning: more than meets the observer's eye. In Boud, D. & Griffen, V. (Eds.), <u>Appreciating adults' learning: From the learner's perspective.</u> London: Kogan Page.

Exploration

CHAPTER FOURTEEN

PROCESSES INVOLVED WITH DEVELOPING AUTONOMOUS LEARNING COMPETENCIES

"Morris" H.K. Baskett

Seven professional adult educators and staff development officers participated in a twenty-four hour experimental workshop/demonstration project designed to assist them in enhancing their autonomous learning skills. The workshop, held at the University of Calgary, was entitled Enhancing Professionals' Self-Directed Learning Competencies.

The participants were all female, with a median age of 43, and a range of 35 to 52. All held a bachelors degree, three held masters degrees, and one a PhD. The participants were self-selecting from an invitational list of 60 professionals in the human resource development and adult education field. These 60 were identified by the author to be in positions to influence the learning of other professionals.

The workshop primarily used the mode of inquiry, "...the process of creating some new synthesis, idea, technique, policy, or strategy of action." (Houle, 1980, p.31.) It took place over a period of three months and involved five separate sessions. The data-collection began with the commencement of the program and was finished a year later.

Research focused on three components of the project; facilitation, impact evaluation, and processes. A companion article in this volume (Hill) reports on the facilitation aspects. Impact data are reported by Baskett and Hill (1990). This article reviews findings about the processes involved in the development of autonomous learning competencies.

REASON FOR THE STUDY

We know very little about how professionals learn and change (Fox, Mazmanian and Putnam, 1989). We know even less about means and processes by which professionals can improve their skills to learn and change autonomously. Yet, given the rapidity with which new understandings and knowledge occur in any profession and given that very few professionals have available in packaged and organized form the specific knowledge, skills and understandings they require at any one time, it seemed reasonable that an examination of means by which professionals can increase their ability to learn how to learn and change would be most fruitful.

The focus on the learner, rather than on the instructor or instructional process is a relatively new departure in adult education literature, and has considerable promise in helping us to understand adult learning. Continuing professional education systems of the future, according to Cervero, Azzaretto & Tallman (1990) "...will emphasize what the learner does in determining what is learned, rather than what the instructor does." (p.8). As Smith (1983) has stated:

> The idea of organized help for taking control of one's learning has been accepted as desirable, but until now rationales and procedures for doing it have been scarce. (p.2).

DIMENSIONS OF ENHANCING SELF-DIRECTED LEARNING AND CHANGE

There appear to be a variety of ways in which one can examine professional learning and change, and as yet, these approaches do not seem to have been well articulated and integrated in the literature. Some authors have focused primarily on the improvement of delivery systems to ensure maximal learning (Cervero, Azzaretto and Associates, 1990; Cervero, 1988). The perspective here is institutional;

agencies such as continuing professional education programs in universities, in-service education and training units in business, service and industry, and professional bodies can improve the effectiveness of their employees/members by certain kinds of institutional interventions.

Some work has focused on the quantification of self-directed learning. Models or instruments which are said to reflect or examine self-directed learning tend to be developed deductively from previous models or theories (Jarvis, 1990; Bonham, 1989) or from experts (Guglielmino, 1977). Very little work, as Candy (1990) and Peters (1990) indicate, has examined learning as experienced by the learners themselves, although several recent works, including studies by Danis and Tremblay (1988), Spear (1988), Fox, Mazmanian and Putnam (1989) and Peters (1990) are beginning to add considerable richness and depth to our understanding of self-directed learning and self-directed learners.

Another direction of inquiry and of intervention is on those skills and competencies which professionals need in order to learn how to learn. Farquharson (1983), for example, identifies seven major competency domains in which beginning professionals should be equipped to prepare them to learn in a self-directing manner. Improved reading and study skills, time-management, and use of approaches such as "Super-Learning" are variations on this theme. This approach may be characterized as a deficit model: given additional skills, one should be able to learn more effectively. Many dimensions of what Mezirow (1981) has called "Instrumental Learning" are apparent in this approach. They seem to derive from behavioral or functionalist perspectives.

Another direction of study and practice has been insight development in which learners are helped to understand their own particular learning tendencies, styles, strengths, weaknesses, and self-imposed barriers. This perspective implies that the problem is not one of skill deficit, but of lack of knowledge of self, one's learning styles and preferences, and the conscious and unconscious processes by which learning occurs, or does not occur. This point-of-view derives primarily from the humanist perspective:

> Through the processes of self-discovery, self-expression, and self-mastery the adult learner will come to gain self-knowledge which permits that person to determine and guide his life course. (Gerstner, 1990,p.71)

Belenky et al. (1986) and Hunt (1987) represent this perspective. Women, or professionals, are thought of as being socialized into a dependency role whereby they are unable to see themselves as agents of their own learning and constructors of their own meanings. The implicit understanding of this perspective is that learners, through a process of insight, can bring about change in the way they learn and be empowered to take charge of their own learning. This perspective may involve some features of what Mezirow (1981) has termed "transformative" learning.

RESEARCH DESIGN AND METHODOLOGY

Candy (1990) and Spear (1988) have argued for assuming an interpretist perspective toward research of autonomous learning and autonomous learners. Peters (1990) has criticized textbook models of learning processes for poorly representing self-directed learning experiences.

An initial search revealed that while there was considerable literature on the provision of continuing professional education, some on professional learning, and a growing literature on self-directed learning, very little could be found which linked self-directed learning, professional learning, and program planning and design on learning-how-to learn. Given that these were relatively uncharted waters, the study was cast in the "Context of Discovery" (Kaplan, 1964), in which the dimensions of the phenomenon under study are unclear, and the researcher's role is to develop an initial map of the territory.

Because no previous works were found which clearly identified the factors involved in learning processes in workshops such as the one undertaken, qualitative data-collection methods were primarily employed, although three instruments, the SDLR Scale (Guglielmino, 1977), the Kolb Learning Style Inventory (Kolb, 1976) and the Personal Style Inventory (Hogan and Champagne, 1987) were used both for data-collection and for programme design purposes. Data-collection methods included participant-observation, audio taping of the sessions, audio taped interviews, and participant's learning journals.

What constitutes "learning processes" is problematic, inasmuch as there were few precedents to this project. Rather than define these "a priori", an emergent strategy was adopted, using Glaser and Strauss'(1967) methods of constant comparison and theoretical saturation. During the participant-observation phase, ongoing field notes were kept which tentatively noted the dynamics and processes which appeared to be occurring. These were used as "foreshadowing" concepts in analyzing the audio tapes of the workshops, the participant's journals, and the transcriptions of the follow-up interviews which were held six months after the end of the workshop.

To check validity, it was initially planned that the data would be analyzed independently by the three individuals involved (the research assistant, the facilitator, and the author). However, due to a variety of circumstances, the penultimate analysis was carried out by the author, and Lilian Hill examined the completed analysis against the transcripts to check for alternative interpretations. As another check for validity, four of the seven participants met with Hill and the author to review the conceptualization of the process. These had been sent to them in advance in the form of an initial draft of a paper. Based upon input from this group, adjustments and changes were made to the analysis and ultimate reporting. The minor revisions were reported to the Fourth International Symposium on Adult Self-Directed Learning (Baskett and Hill, 1990).

Participants were asked to maintain a journal for the duration of the workshop, and to include in the journal their insights, understandings and problems as these related to their learning and to their staff's learning. At the end of the workshop, they were asked to review these journals, and to make observations about their learning processes in the right hand column, which they had been asked to leave blank.

The journal entries formed the basis of the follow-up interviews, which were conducted six months after the end of the workshop. The investigators shared in the task of interviewing, each conducting three interviews separately, and one jointly. They read each of their interviewee's journals in advance and noted instances where participants seemed to have insight, commit themselves to future action, or indicate unresolved problems or difficulties. During the interview, they were given their journals, and asked to read the noted passages. They were then asked "What was happening then?", meaning what was going on in terms of their emotions, thinking, and the context at the time of the entry. In most cases, participants were able to recall the incident or the moment easily, and to describe the circumstances more fully. Then, they were asked if any change had occurred as it related to the statement, and, if a change was indicated, to then describe the nature of the change, and the conditions which brought it about. To some degree, this approach reflects what Peters (1989) has described as the Action-Reason-Thematic method. In this case, the journals acted as the initial and first interviews (actually, self-interviews), and the follow-up interviews six months afterwards provided the one additional iteration.

Analysis of the journal entries and the follow-up interviews observed the normal procedures of coding, memoing and propositions used for analyzing qualitative data (Miles and Huberman, 1984). Categories and themes were tentatively identified during site observations, analysis of the tapes of the meetings, and reading of the journals. By going back and forth between successive conceptualizations and these data, concepts and themes were confirmed or revised. Finally, sections of the field notes and transcripts were assigned categories and then re-arranged manually under these categories, seeking examples which would confirm, refute or extend the conceptualizations.

By using the journals as a base, we were able to gain a before-after description around significant learning issues, as well as the dynamics and processes involved. Through employing this technique, we were able to counteract some of the effects of imperfect recall, a common criticism of the Learning Projects interviewing approach. Several participants provided evidence that they could clearly recall six months later the issues about which they had written.

The use of the journals as base-line also affected the nature of the data obtained. By tracing individual changes, the assumption was made that self-directed learning processes would be unique, idiosyncratic, and personal phenomena, a point made by other researchers (Spear,1988; Candy,1990). In taking this direction we were able to trace individual change, to extrapolate more universal processes and as well, to gain some impressions about these processes over time.

PROCESSES

The lack of pre-existing models or frameworks dictated that the investigation would be inductive in nature. The main research question addressed in this part of the data-collection was, "What are the experiences of the learners as they go through this learning journey?" The focus was on understanding the life-world of the learner, rather than attempting to confirm an already-formed hypotheses of learning processes and dynamics. It was reasoned that by better understanding the life-experiences of the learner, we would be able to construct a typology which could then be put forward for examination by other investigators as well as ourselves, while at the same time, moving toward a set of substantive propositions about learning under these conditions.

In what follows, the processes which emerged out of the analysis of the data are identified, together with examples of excerpts which were seen as confirming and explaining each process. References to other pertinent research are also made. Following the presentation of the processes, the manner in which they were seen to interact with each other is elaborated through a composite representation of this group of learners.

Not all of the processes which might be involved have been identified, and some may remain unrecognized and unnamed. Some may be epiphenomenal. Most overlap and intertwine with each other. The purpose here is to portray as faithfully as possible within the limits of print those processes either perceived directly by the participants or those which appeared to the investigators to be operating.

<u>Verbalizing</u>
This process involved putting meaningful labels on experiences. Sometimes, this occurred when listening to someone else:

> When she said that, it...catalyzed me. Before, I hadn't articulated what was happening to me.

Sometimes it involved hearing oneself talk out loud:

> The way that I described it to you helped me to crystallize it even further.

The presence of others who can be an appreciative, attentive and non-judgemental audience seemed to be a critical component of verbalizing. By having to describe ideas and feelings to another individual, learners were forced to put these as yet inarticulate ideas and feelings into words, and in so doing, these ideas took on a life and reality of their own.

In the case of some of the participants, talking out loud, as a means of labelling experiences, had been previously seen as negative, or "talking too much". Through their experiences in the project, they came to see this as a natural and acceptable way of learning for some individuals:

> I feel so confirmed that I learn through talking...that it's not a waste of my time.

Objectifying

A process of observing and objectifying the self seemed evident. It was as if the participants had moved beyond or out of themselves, and looked back on themselves with a "third eye". This process seemed to be a kind of monitoring activity involving growing self-awareness:

> As I was working on it, I was also cognizant of, like, another (self) was observing how I was going.

While there are many elements of affect in this process, the act itself seemed to be primarily that of conscious reflection which involved the ability to "get out of oneself." The results of this ability seemed to be new, or newly articulated, understandings and insight into just what kind of learners they were:

> I'm learning...how relationships and discussions with people is my strongest and most valuable form of learning.

> As I learn more about Kolb, ...the feeling (end of the continuum) is so strong in me, and I'm so low on... the abstract.

These insights into themselves as learners were constantly changing as they interacted with each other, the learning activities in the workshop, their daily experiences, and others outside of the group. Understanding of self was a fluid, and sometimes personally frightening activity in which they could articulate over time more and more clearly the kind of image they held of themselves as learners.

> I started to analyze my own thinking. I wasn't afraid of analyzing it any more.

Connecting

Another process to which participants referred was connecting, in which learners linked one idea with another, to create a new (at least, to them) idea or concept.

> With me, it's connecting. I'm always thinking and connecting
> it's really exciting when you start connecting.

During the site observations, participants could be noticed looking off into space, or seemingly to not pay attention to the proceedings. Clues that they were creating connections came as they emotionally re-entered the groups with remarks such as "You know, I've been thinking about that remark you made a while ago".

Sometimes, this linking was deliberate, as the comments of this participant, who was one of two assimilators in the group, and high on the thinking end of the Personal Style Inventory indicate:

> I try out new ideas. If they work, I incorporate them. If not, I
> toss them out and go on to the next one.

Linking of ideas was not random. The elements which were being linked had to be have meaning to the member in order for it to gain their attention in the first place, a point which Danis and Tremblay (1988) make.

The process of journal writing served to make connections for several of the participants. One interviewee wrote in her journal

> Here I am writing in a journal.. I feel like I'm circling my target-
> getting closer, but taking long sweeps around.

Asked about the meaning of this entry six months later, she explained:

> ...I don't look at things logically. That's why writing (in the
> journal) is good... eventually I pick up all the pieces.

Sometimes, connecting of disparate ideas occurred a considerable time after the initial understandings were established. This individual had completed her masters degree recently, and had time to reflect:

> It is like sifting through all (previous ideas and learning).... Some
> things are starting to make sense because I was now outside of the
> structure. I could sit and listen and absorb and make some kind
> of connection and say, "Oh! That's what that was all about!"
> Which is why I said I must not be particularly bright, and why is
> it hitting me now? I guess it must just be a mental state of
> readiness.

Harri-Augstein and Thomas (1976) have also noticed
this rather circular way in which learning occurs in everyday
life.

> The learner is purposive and yet it is in the nature of learning that
> you often cannot know what exactly you are going to learn until
> you have learned it. This means that the purpose can only be
> specified completely when it has been achieved ... Effective
> learning almost always consists of ... cycles in which purposes
> become progressively more clearly articulated, and the outcomes
> become more precise and determined and well mapped onto
> purpose. (Cited by Candy, 1990, p.28)

Spear (1988) makes a similar observation:

> Learning sequences progress, not necessarily in linear fashion,
> but rather as the circumstances created during one episode
> become the circumstances for the next necessary and logical step
> in the process. (p.202)

Danis and Tremblay's (1988) in-depth study of ten
autodidacts also corroborates these findings:

> Self-taught adults proceed in a heuristic manner, within a learning
> approach which they organize around intentions, redefine and
> specify without following any predetermined patterns. (p.178)

Conceptualizing
Connecting seemed related to another process which I have
labelled conceptualizing. Conceptualizing involved more

than simply linking ideas, it involved organizing these ideas into a higher level of understanding together with placing a meaningful label on them or "naming" them. There was only one clear statement relating conceptualizing, but, there were no data to refute, consequently it is included here.

When asked if a theme of "putting things into packages" which was evident in her journal entries, was typical of her, one of the participants answered:

> Very much so. Naming-giving it a label. For example, multi-cultural training and development. That is a new label. Naming to crystallize, by putting disparate elements into a new whole. The new framework may not be all that new, but it allows (one) to look at things differently.

Constructing

As part of the conceptualizing process, some referred to a process of constructing their own knowledge. It should be noted that the entire group was familiar with the book, Women's Ways of Knowing. (Belenky, et al., 1986). The essence here seemed to that of deliberateness, in which they not only know that they constructed new (for them) ideas, but that this was part of their learning processes. In the following comments, one can also sense that this act is empowering for the learner-a phenomenon referred to by Belenky et al. (1986).

> Now I know. Now, it's starting to make sense... Getting to that point where you can create your own design, create your own knowledge, do your own connecting of ideas.

> I know that I do it quite naturally. My husband can attest to this (constructing new concepts out of disparate ideas.)

Testing

Related to the processes of conceptualizing and constructing is that of testing or bouncing ideas off of other individuals or situations. Only one individual actually referred to this process directly. In this case, she was designing a particular approach to a workshop, and this was uppermost in her mind when she had a chance encounter with a work colleague:

> As I'm having a conversation with this guy, I'm, relating everything that is said to my workshop and to the organization.

The process of testing seems to involve confirming an idea or conceptualization. Almost unconsciously, one seeks clues as to whether the conceptualization or idea stands up against some other reality, such as the experiences, in this case, of her colleagues:

> ...hearing other people talk about it, I was able to scrutinize my own learning.

The presence of others provided opportunities for members to check their ideas, actions, anticipated moves, or their self perceptions, against some alternative model. Several mentioned this as helpful:

> I was giving more credibility to these people and their reflections on their learning. I was consciously listening... because it was subjective and very real that I seemed to absorb a lot from that exchange...

> Then, listening to what other people did... it was like I needed some models for what to do and where to go.

Not only were other people used as means of testing oneself and ones' ideas, but books, articles, previous experiences also seemed to act in a similar manner.

Ideas or issues were also being constantly revisited by the learners, and this could be seen throughout their learning journals. Each had a set of recurring agendas or themes upon which they were working, for example, deciding whether to change jobs, learning to involve students more in decision-making about program design, or learning to think abstractly. Some of these agendas arose from growing insights as to the kinds of learners and individuals they were, sometimes facilitated by the workshop process. Some of these agendas were broad, such as learning to let go of a sense of total responsibility for what their learners or trainees learned. Others were quite specific, for example, deciding how to use the Kolb Learning Styles Inventory in a workshop the following day.

<u>Clarifying</u>
Participants were not always fully conscious of their agendas. In fact, the processes of reflection and journal-writing during the workshop helped to raise these agendas to a conscious level. Moreover, as these agendas rose and fell in priority for attention by the learner, and as they were able to bring new light onto them, changes seemed to occur in their appreciation and understanding. Several participants referred to this deepening and sharpening:

> ...theory is becoming real to me. It was a more concrete experience of process. Like, I was feeling the process.

> I used LSI in teaching (before). But, only (now) did I really understand the significance.

When asked to elaborate six months later, the person who made the last comment replied,

> It's when I'd experienced it in this class... that put the extra dimension in it that gave the understanding... It was the dimension of feeling. I had the information. But I didn't have the understanding that comes from adding that affective part of it.

The pattern of re-visiting issues time and time again was noted often in the experiences of the participants. Confirmation of this as a more universal pattern comes from Harri-Augstein and Thomas (1976) previously quoted, Spear (1988), and Danis and Tremblay.(1988)

Idling
The learning and insights which the participants gained did not occur in a logical, linear fashion. Like a lot of our reflection, insights sometimes occur when we aren't consciously thinking about an issue. Several referred to this activity, which is labelled here as idling.

Idling involves periods of seemingly doing nothing or doing something else. One participant described her habit of automatically going to the kitchen at times when she was concentrating on an idea. She said that she was

> ...letting the brain do its work. Very often I would... stare into the refrigerator.

Another learner described her need for idling:

> I get to a certain point in my reading and I stop. I feel overwhelmed. I know that's the time. I stop, then I do something else so my brain can work on its own.

Sometimes a connotation of overload was detected, whereby all "circuits were busy", and some time for reflection was required:

> I had a need to escape to get some work done and to sort out my thoughts.

Insights into issues or agendas were sometimes only gained after extended times of idling, as this participant recognized:

> And the importance of confusion... there is a stage in the learning process where everything is confused, and sometimes you have to wait and let things sift through and fall together, and have patience that it will happen.

This idling process was in evidence during group meetings. Members could be observed gazing off into space during presentations or discussion. The evidence that something was happening to them internally occurred when they joined the conversation a bit later with such remarks as "When you mentioned unlearning a while ago, I got to thinking....", or "You know, I just realized....".

The comments made above suggest points where the mind is not focused or engaged on the specific task or issue or agenda. There is a powerful unconscious dimension involved in which people simply abandon themselves to the brain, and a time dimension which is almost floating. Driving for example, was mentioned by several as a time for this reflection. In another study, Baskett and Garrison (1989) found that adult education researchers reported this sort of seemingly disengaged reflection occurring during jogging, cutting the lawn and other "mindless" activities.

Learning about oneself as a learner is an emotionally challenging experience to many. The organizers of the workshop were cognizant of the affective dimensions of learning, and consequently built into their design opportunities for sharing and reflection and creating a climate of acceptance and trust. Most participants commented upon this climate as being one of the most helpful aspects of the experience.

Four processes which emerged from data analysis and which seemed to contain a higher degree of affect than the previous processes were freeing up, affirming self, validating, and re-valuing.

Freeing Up
One of the characteristics of adulthood is the myriad of competing demands, obligations and emotions with which one contends in everyday life. Some of these are truly of traumatic proportions: for example dealing with children's crises, or dealing with bereavement of those close to us. All of these are background presences in any learning situation. One of the most noticeable activities of the learners, as indicated in the journals and in the interviews, was finding time and emotional space to gain maximally from the learning experience, given these other demands. In various ways,

each individual in the learning group struggled to find enough time and energy to devote to the task at hand.

> ...I realized in (the workshop) that I needed dead air. I needed time to get my own thoughts together.

Freeing up also involved giving oneself permission to not have to learn it all at one time:

> ....there is a stage in the learning process where everything is confused, and sometimes you have to wait and let things sift through and fall together... and have the patience that it will happen.

Life stages and events intermingled with the participants' learning and influenced the amount of energy and time they had free to devote to learning and reflection. Referring to her recent divorce, one participant described the sense of release she experienced. However, while the divorce gave her a sense of freedom, she was still completing a graduate degree:

> ....but I was still locked into the tightness and structure of being in the program. When that was over, that was a separation too. The calmness and peace that I felt after I left my marriage... wasn't complete because I was still caught up in the chaos of course-taking. When that was over, it was the last structured thing, and then I was free.

Freeing up was not only an activity in response to external forces. Emotions, attitudes and assumptions were also blocks to their learning, and many references to this struggle could be found throughout the journals, meetings, and interviews. This comment is typical:

> I started to analyze my own thinking. I wasn't afraid of analyzing it any more. I didn't feel like I should be embarrassed anymore about how I thought...

Processes

Self- Affirmation.
Associated with emotional freeing was a companion process
of validating oneself as a learner. A considerable amount of
our data gave evidence of the manner in which group
members had come to positively value aspects of their
learning:

> I now think that I'm a good learner. Before I always felt I was a
> mediocre learner who just lacked a lot of discipline.

> I wasn't less than-inferior. I was different. We all were
> learning.

It was apparent that members held a variety of views
of themselves as learners, and their sense of agency as
learners. Although all scored well above the median of the
SDLR Scale, there were quite different perceptions about the
degree to which they were the active ingredient in the
learning process. Some seemed very assured in their ability
to create (for them) new perspectives, interpretations and
concepts. Others seemed to require external legitimation of
thoughts and ideas in order to accept them as "real"
knowledge:

> I still need to read it in a book and then I feel like... my idea is
> OK... because somebody else said it.

> Women's Ways of Knowing was another milestone. It gave me
> permission to be the kind of learner I am.

Several authors refer to this sense of agency or lack of
it. Belenky, et al. (1986), refer to the way in which many
women assume that only expert knowledge is legitimate
knowledge, and see themselves as only recipients of this
knowledge whereas others see themselves as active agents in
constructing their own knowledge and ideas, and feel
empowered to do this. Candy (1990) refers to "personal
learning myths" which are "...convictions held by a learner
about himself or herself based on past experience." (p.34). It

was quite apparent that each held myths of themselves as learners, and these varied by the individual. It was also apparent that a major struggle for several of the participants was to change their self-image from that of a mere receiver of knowledge to having a greater sense of agency in creating their own understandings and personal knowledge.

As mentioned by Lilian Hill elsewhere in this volume, the fact that the group was composed of women may very much affect the data. If it had been an all men's group, agency in learning might not have been an issue at all.

Re-Valuing
Confirmation of self as learners was an objective of the workshop facilitators, and it is apparent from the data that this objective was achieved (Baskett and Hill, 1990). In some cases, this validation process involved re-valuing of old behaviors or attitudes, often seeing these in a different, more positive light. The behavior or attitude itself hadn't changed:

> In the past... I gave myself a lot of negative feedback about the way I approached learning. Now I accept it and try to make the best of it.

Some of the accounts of change in self-perception, and the affirmation of themselves as learners suggest almost transformative qualities (Mezirow, 1981). Just what was involved may only be guessed, but the re-labelling of aspects of themselves from a less to a more positive light was evident. Permission to change their self-perceptions, the absence of any insistence that there were only certain correct ways of learning, the opportunity to think about themselves in a personally non-threatening environment, as well as having available examples or models of alternate ways of seeing themselves and their learning, were some of the components which supported this re-valuing of learning approaches and of themselves as learners.

THE ROLE OF EXPERIENCE

These processes did not occur solely because of the Enhancing project, nor did they occur in isolation. Participants brought with them their outside experiences and carried their experiences in the Enhancing group to other aspects of their life. Each sphere was used as a test for developing and broadening their insights and understandings, as these excerpts imply:

> What I was trying to do was look critically at my participation in groups. Also, to see if the things I was learning from the one could be applied to the other situation.

> I was taking one class (the Enhancing group) and also giving one. That's why I was analyzing so much.

DISCUSSION

Open-ended research such as that carried out in this project is like setting out on a new journey without a map. There are certain advantages to this sort of free-ranging adventure. You can happen onto wonderful new terrain and discover things previously unimagined. The disadvantage is that, having never been there before, you are never too sure what it is you are looking at. Even more unsettling, as you try to describe it, you're not too sure that what you see is what anyone else will see, once they come this way.

The only recourse is to test these analyses in public, hoping for feedback which will assist in more closely approximating a kind of consensual reality in future studies. The labels I've used are not as important as is the test of whether I've captured here the essence of the experiences of the learners in a way which gains some sort of consensus from those who study and experience these things, and which, in the long run, will allow us to become better practitioners in enhancing self-directed learning.

The unit of study in this project was the learners' experiences. Group processes could have been the focus of the study, or some other aspect of learning. It was clear, in reading the journals, that the participants did not stick to describing only their development as learners as they had been asked. All kinds of other life issues crept into their written accounts. Rather than being useless to us these data are tremendously valuable, as they tell us about their reality-that although they process issues and ideas raised in the course, life itself is being processed.

The interactive, seemingly idiosyncratic manner in which this group made sense and meaning of their own processes of learning tells us much about what one may expect of learners. While Knowles has brought to our attention the temporal and experiential nature of adult learning, through this kind of methodology we can gain a better understanding of just what that means to the individuals involved. It is quite clear that this group did not compartmentalize learning into work, personal, and course learnings. These all interacted, sometimes conflicting with, and sometimes contributing to, resolution of their various issues and agendas. This apparent randomness has been noted by Candy (1990), Spear (1988), and Danis and Tremblay (1988) the latter who report that "...in order to learn, self-taught adults seize any opportunity that random events may offer them" (p.178).

By attending to the experiences of these learners as they saw it, we are spared the temptation to try to structure the data by some other construct, such as the insidious Tylerian model through which so much of the writings on self-directed learning, let alone adult education in general, is framed (Apps, 1979; Day and Baskett, 1982). That is fortunate because neither Spear (1988) nor Danis and Tremblay (1988) found evidence of detailed pre-planning in their examinations of autonomous learners.

Self-directedness, as portrayed here, is in a sense a process of becoming. There appears to be no clear distinction between those who are autonomous learners and those who are not. Autonomous learning seems to be at least in part situational and contextual. There are people who, at various times, in regards to various issues, and under certain circumstances, are able to take considerable responsibility and have considerable control over their own learning goals and processes. There are other times, for example when resources are not available, that the individual cannot be autonomous and self-directing even though he or she may have a predisposition to learn on his/her own at that point in time. Based on my observations of these learners, I am uneasy with attempts, such as those of Bonham (1989) or Kolb (1976) to suggest that there are finite numbers of learning styles. Learning is a far too dynamic and fluid phenomenon to be captured by such simplistic interpretations.

Long (1990) has argued for a more robust theory of self-directed learning than has heretofore been offered and has suggested that environment and information, learner characteristics, and learner processes need to be considered in the amalgam. This research would support the need for a broadened theory. Such a theory would have to incorporate the way in which learners make their own unique sense of their circumstances, and act out of these constructions. Such a perspective places the focus of attention on the way in which the components suggested by Long interact on and in the learner, but, in addition, it adds recognition of learner agency. Although there is much to what has been described above to give support to Spear and Mocker's (1984) Organizing Circumstance, these findings would not support the degree of determinism implied in the concept, a criticism which Spear (1988) has since observed.

A COMPOSITE PICTURE

What would a composite picture of a professional who is trying to improve her agency in learning look like? The following is an attempt to portray a more holistic, but composite representation of these learners as they struggle with daily problem-solving and attendant learning as professionals.

These learners carry to their learning endeavors all sorts of background concerns, feelings, and issues. Some have been with them for a considerable length of time and are at various stages of resolution. Layered on and intermingled with this are the various learnings and problems with which they must cope in order to carry out their duties as professionals. These include decisions about what and how to teach something tomorrow or how to manage a difficult staff member, and although learning isn't necessarily the prime focus, some kind of learning must take place in order to resolve these issues. These various issues comprise the agendas which they carry with them, and which compete for their conscious attention, moving in and out of focus as various circumstances seem to dictate. Time, energy, level of health, primacy, immediacy, perceived outside demands, are some of those circumstances. Moving these various agendas toward resolution involves a constant balancing act.

The idea of self-directedness in learning never enters their heads. Yet,in various ways they have ongoing learning projects and they use a variety of strategies-which they probably could not label-to deal with these projects. Depending on a variety of factors, including background and foreground factors, they respond sporadically to these projects and the agendas attached. They formulate their goals in a cyclic, spiralling way, becoming a little clearer as to what they have to do to further one or more of these projects or agendas and doing what they can to get the information, or gain a conception of the task at hand. As they interact with their daily world, they become clearer about these agendas and what they must do. Everything in their world has a potential to provide clues and stimulus for resolving some or many agendas. Each time they reach a greater level of clarity, they are more able to see also their next set of options and directions.

Sometimes, they are very deliberate in resolving their agendas, and this will vary by individual and circumstance. They go to seek help, read a book, or talk to someone whom they perceive to be helpful. Sometimes they make links between disparate ideas out of sheer coincidence, when, for example they are talking about something, and the application of that idea to something else they are dealing with comes to mind.

Coincidence and accident is not the mainstay of their strategies; they also make things happen. They turn situations into opportunities to resolve one or more of their agendas. During a chance encounter with a colleague in the hallway, they may ask that colleague how they might deal with a problem, or where they might turn for information. While attending a course, they may run across a useful reference which they note; or they will hear a new viewpoint quite unrelated to their agenda, and they will make some tentative connections. Sometimes, they can be seen writing furiously, ignoring their surroundings, as they move a project ahead a bit more by conceptualizing and re-conceptualizing a problem, solution or both.

Sometimes they "talk out loud" about what they are dealing with or sometimes, depending on their predilection, they may process concerns sub-vocally. In so doing, they add life and meaning to as yet not fully articulated understandings. Even when they are not talking-they may be staring blankly into space-they could still be processing, dealing in some way with a problem or issue which has moved to centre stage in their mind at that moment.

Not only do they verbalize their issues, but they selectively listen to others, especially those whom they feel are credible. In so doing, what the other says may connect or link with ideas or issues with which they are dealing. This is an internal, non-rationale connection quite unintelligible to an outsider who would probably wonder how on earth they could make sense out of such disparate things or ideas. Somehow, in this process, they are reinforced to select this way rather than that way; to do this next rather than that.

Each situation is a test of their ideas and themselves as able problem-solvers and learners. They bounce their ideas or understandings against the outside world-using it as a mirror as well as seeing if, in their perception, it holds up to scrutiny. Depending on their degree of "inner" or "other"-directedness, they will seek internal and external cues to help them assess the validity of possible actions, decisions, or directions.

In the process, they are also revising their image of themselves as learners. These images are largely sub-conscious, but if you ask them to describe themselves as learners they are often quite able to do so: "I learn best by talking to others"; "I'm impatient with too much theorizing, I just like to try it out".

As they test their ideas, they are also sharpening and deepening them. This is a cyclic process in which various agendas are continually revisited, adjusted, added to, and revised in the light of constantly incoming data and clues. Nothing is organized or categorized as it might be in a text book. All is fluid, constantly changing and reforming. This is, in effect, these individuals' ways of making meaning of their world as they see it. It involves conceptualizing and reconceptualizing problem, solution, and circumstance. From the outside they seem at times to back into solutions, rather than dealing with issues in a linear, sequential, problem-solving manner. The logic, however, is in the eyes of the beholder.

As they attend to the demands of competing agendas and issues, these learners contend with finite time, energy and resources. Some demands are ongoing, others are short term. The ongoing demands are less manageable and seem to be simply accommodated in their life and time space. As short-term demands are dealt with, leaving room for more energy, time and resources, they have windows of space, both temporally and emotionally, to deal with new issues. Based on this, an informal, constantly revising timetable seems to be operating in which they book time to deal with whatever else is pressing for attention.

CONCLUSION

We have a long way to go in gaining a good understanding of the processes involved with helping adults learn how to learn. Works such as are contained in this and previous volumes by

Processes

Long and Associates have contributed to a much-needed dialogue. We have even less understanding of how professionals may be enabled to improve their self-direction in learning, and it is hoped that this chapter will contribute to a growing comprehension of this particular area of adult education.

REFERENCES

Apps, J.W. (1979). Problems in continuing education. New York: McGraw Hill.

Baskett, H.K. & Garrison, D.R.(1989). Research writing: Patterns and strategies of some of North America's most prolific adult education researchers. AERC Proceedings.

Baskett, H.K. & Hill, L. (1990). Enhancing professionals' autonomous learning: A report of an action demonstration project. Paper presented to the Fourth International Symposium on Adult Self-Directed Learning, February 25-27. Norman, Oklahoma.

Belenky, M., Clinchy, B., Goldberger, N., Tarule, J. (1986). Women's ways of knowing. New York: Basic Books Inc.

Bonham, L.A. (1989) Self-directed orientation toward learning: A learning style. In H.B. Long and Associates Self-directed learning: Emerging theory and practice. Norman, OK: Oklahoma Research Center for Continuing Professional and Higher Education of the University of Oklahoma.

Candy, P.C. (1990) The transition from learner-control to autodidaxy: More than meets the eye. In H.B. Long and Associates, Advances in research and practice in self-directed learning. Norman, OK: Oklahoma Research Center for Continuing Professional and Higher Education of the University of Oklahoma.

Cervero, R.M. (1988). Effective continuing education for professionals. San Francisco:Jossey-Bass.

Cervero, R.M., Azzaretto, J.F. & Associates (1990). Visions for the future of continuing professional education. Athens, Georgia: Georgia Centre for Continuing Education, The University of Georgia.

Cervero, R.M., Azzaretto, J.F. & Tallman, D.E. (1990). Renewing and redirecting continuing professional education. In R.M. Cervero, J.F. Azzaretto & Associates, Visions for the future of continuing professional education. Athens, Georgia: Georgia Centre for Continuing Education, The University of Georgia.

Danis, C. & Tremblay, N.A. (1988). Autodidactic learning experiences: Questioning established adult learning principles. In H.B. Long and Associates, Self-directed learning: Application and theory. Athens, GA: Adult Education Department, The University of Georgia.

Day, C.W. & Baskett, H.K. (1982). The poverty of programming and andragogy. International Journal of Lifelong Learning, 1 (2).

Farquharson, A. (1983). Competencies for continuing education in the professions. Canadian Journal of University Continuing Education. 9 (2).

Fox, R.D., Mazmanian, P.E. & Putnam, R.W. (1989). Changing and learning in the lives of physicians. New York: Praeger.

Garrison, D.R. (1989). Facilitating self-directed learning: Not a contradiction in terms. In H.B. Long and Associates, Self-directed learning: Emerging theory and practice. Norman, OK: Oklahoma Research Center for Continuing Professional and Higher Education of the University of Oklahoma.

Gerstner, L.S. (1990). On the theme and variations of self-directed learning. In H.B. Long and Associates, Advances in research and practice in self-directed learning. Norman, OK: Oklahoma Research Center for Continuing Professional and Higher Education of the University of Oklahoma.

Glaser, B.G. & Strauss, A.L. (1967). The discovery of grounded theory: Strategies for qualitative research. Chicago: Aldine.

Guglielmino, L.M. (1977). Development of the self-directed learning readiness scale. Unpublished doctoral dissertation. University of Georgia.

Hogan, C.R., & Champagne, D.W. (1987). Personal style inventory. San Franciso: CH Publications.

Houle, C.O. (1980). Continuing learning in the professions. San Francisco: Jossey-Bass.

Hunt, D.E. (1987). Beginning with ourselves. Toronto: OISE Press.

271

Jarvis, P. (1990). Self-directed learning and the theory of adult education. In H.B. Long and Associates, Advances in research and practice in self-directed learning. Norman, Oklahoma: Oklahoma Research Center for Continuing Professional and Higher Education of the University of Oklahoma.

Kaplan, A. (1964). The conduct of inquiry. San Francisco: Chandler.

Kolb, D.A. (1976). Learning style inventory technical manual. Boston: McBer.

Long, H.B. (1990). Changing concepts of self-direction in learning. In H.B. Long and Associates, Advances in research and practice in self-directed learning. Norman, OK: Oklahoma Research Centre for Continuing Professional and Higher Education of the University of Oklahoma.

Mezirow, J.D. (1981). A critical theory of adult learning and education. Adult Education, 31 (1).

Miles, M.B. & Huberman, A.M. (1984). Qualitative data analysis. Beverley Hills: Sage.

Peters, J.M. (1989). Self-direction and problem-solving: Theory and method. In H.B. Long and Associates, Self-directed learning: Emerging theory and practice. Norman, OK: Oklahoma Research Center for Continuing Professional and Higher Education of the University of Oklahoma.

Peters, J.M. (1990). Analysis of practical thinking in self-directed learning. In H.B. Long and Associates, Advances in research and practice in self-directed learning. Norman, OK: Oklahoma Research Center for Continuing Professional and Higher Education of the University of Oklahoma.

Smith, R.M. (1983). (Ed.)Helping adults learn how to learn. San Francisco: Jossey-Bass.

Spear, G. (1988). Beyond the organizing circumstance: A search for methodology for the study of self-directed learning. In H.B. Long and Associates, Self-directed learning: Application and theory. Athens, GA : Adult Education Department, The University of Georgia.

Spear, G. & Mocker, D. (1984). The organizing circumstance: Environmental determinants in self-directed learning. Adult Education Quarterly, 35 (1).

CHAPTER FIFTEEN

THE FUTURE OF SELF-DIRECTED LEARNING AS RELATED TO CONTINUING PROFESSIONAL EDUCATION

Jeanie Rountree, Joanne A. Lambert
Misty Rice, and Lloyd J. Korhonen

Self-directed learning over the past decade has focused mainly on the medical profession. Much of the research is also definitional, arising from the fact that "specific definitions are lacking and terms such as **learner-directed, individual instruction, individualized instruction,** and **independent study** are used inconsistently" (Bell and Bell, 1983, p. 24).

Gibbons, Bailey, Comeau, Schmuck, Seymour and Wallace (1980), analyzed biographies of famous experts and observed that patterns of self-education which began in youth remained through adulthood. Lone (1988) makes further use of biography in studying self-direction in learning. Other biographical surveys have included men and women of fame who have exhibited self-direction in learning.

Part of the literature is promotional in nature and expounds the virtues of self-directed learning, calling it the "key to personal success" (Zemke, 1982, p. 28). Researchers have found that exceptional workers in jobs requiring a high level of creativity, problem-solving, and ability to change all scored significantly higher on self-directed learning readiness than other workers (Zemke, 1982, p. 28). There is the implication, then that self-directed learning may be the key not only to personal success but to economic success as well. According to researchers at the Center for Management and Professional Development at Florida Atlantic University, "There is mounting evidence to suggest that workers of the future will need to be able to take more responsibility for the management of their learning" (Zemke, 1982, p. 28). The assumption here is that self-directed learning is a learnable skill. Indeed one of the researchers cited by Zemke, Lucy Guglielmino, believes self-directed learning skills are innate but repressed through social conditioning. She argues that "Our traditional approach to education stifles self-directed learning and decreases the desire to learn. We've been trained to undervalue our own independent learning and overvalue that which we get from authority figures" (Zemke, 1982, p. 30).

Guglielmino's comments echo that of other self-directed learning researchers battling the myths of education. These myths can be summarized as follows: (1) Learning and education occur only in schools. (2) One individual is more educated than another if he or she has completed more formal training than the other. (3) Anyone who failed to learn in school is dumb or stupid or illiterate (Sisco, 1983).

Fortunately, the research on self-directed learning exposes the flaws in these myths. Studies have shown that over 90 percent of the adult population engages in at least one independent learning project per year which lasts an average of 100 hours. Furthermore, there is no significant difference in the number of learning projects undertaken by adults with more than 12 years of education compared to those with less than 12 years of schooling (Sisco, 1983). Moreover, the statement that "Most people have the potential not only to learn, but to create knowledge given the right combination of motivation, opportunity, resources, support" was written to describe adult, not child, learners (Gross, 1982, p. 4). The key point for continuing education professionals is that most adults have an intrinsic motivation, or desire, to engage in the learning process. This realization has brought increased attention to adult learners.

In self-directed research on the cognitive development of adults, Long (1980) attributed a combination of social change, human nature, and demography with the increased attention to the study of adult learners (p. 1). As reported by Lace (1986), adult learners, or nontraditional students, have been identified as higher education's best potential student market. The National Center for Education Statistics in Higher Education (NCES) projects that by 1993 there will be an enrollment decline of 6.3 percent in traditional students in higher education. The Center also projects a 15 percent decline in the number of traditional aged college men. On the other hand, there should be a 27 percent increase in nontraditional students by 1993. Colleges will gain more than 800,000 of these older students (The Condition of Education, 1985). This change in student body population represents an exciting and challenging period for higher education.

The shift toward a nontraditional student body raises the following questions which are addressed in this study: (1) What are the characteristics of adult learners, particularly self-directed learners? (2) What academic programs will best meet the needs of self-directed adult learners?

METHODOLOGY

For purposes of this study, self-directed learning is defined as a process for which the learner takes the initiative and responsibility for learning, including evaluating the outcomes of the learning experience. The work of Gibbons, et al. (1980) have implications for this study. Through analysis of biographies of twenty experts who could be considered self-directed learners, the authors identified a number of common characteristics. Eight categories were developed to classify life experiences: Background (Personal History); Personal Characteristics; Learning Methods; Relationships with Others; Living Conditions; Key Incidents in the Subject's Behavior; Attitudes, Opinions, and Philosophy. This study of biographies found that self-directed learners tend to be curious, creative, self-confident, assertive, altruistic, charismatic, intelligent, and nonconformist. Self-directed learners also were found to possess a good sense of humor.

Two major differences between this study and the one reported by Gibbons et al. are: (1) The population for the current study is selected from a group of students involved in learning in nontraditional educational programs. The people might be considered "average" or "ordinary" individuals, not "experts" or "successful" individuals about whom biographical data would be available. (2) The data were collected from the individuals who were participating in the learning situation, affording the insight and self-assessment of the learners themselves, not the perceptions and assumptions of biographers or outside evaluators. The study presented in this paper builds on previous research by describing self-directed learner characteristics based on data collected from self-directed learners themselves.

Data for this study were collected from 372 participants in two nontraditional educational college credit programs, 220 of whom were enrolled in a liberal studies distance education program, and 152 in a weekend college program. For purposes of the study at hand, no differentiation is made between the participants in the two programs, and no comparisons are made between groups. Data were examined only to identify common characteristics of participant and to determine components of academic programs that can best meet the needs of these nontraditional students. In both programs the curriculum was general liberal studies, the students had no previous experience with the format of the program in which they were enrolled, and the selection of format and decision to participate was voluntary on the part of each student.

Sixty-two percent of the participants were female, and more than half of all respondents were in the age range 30-49. Sixty percent were married. Sixty-four percent had held three or more jobs in the past ten years.

Research focused on 15 factors relating to motivation and learning objectives, 21 on personal traits, and 23 on learning methods.

For self-assessment of personal characteristics, participants were asked to compare themselves to the "average person" by rating themselves as (1) Lowest

15%, (2) Below Average, (3) Average, (4) Above Average, (5) Highest 10%.

On 15 of the 21 items, 50% or more of the respondents ranked themselves above average or in the highest 10%. Eighty percent ranked themselves above average or highest 10% on motivation for achievement, and 76% placed themselves in this range on intellectual curiosity. Other significant categories included 72% on persistence, 73% on ability to do independent work, 69% on mental health and emotional stability, and 68% on optimism. Other characteristics noted as high ranking items were academic ability, reading ability, leadership, ability to handle stress, self-confidence, tolerance, self-discipline, personal organization, and ability to deal with uncertainty.

Among learning objectives, self-directedness in learning is exhibited by more than 50% of the respondents ranking very important or extremely important areas relating to development of intellectual skills and abilities, enjoyment of learning, and satisfaction of degree accomplishment. In response to the query regarding the extent to which high school grades are an accurate reflection of motivation to learn, participants' rankings resulted in almost even distribution among the three categories Great Extent, Somewhat, and No Extent. Ranking of several other motivational factors indicated not only high value for increased knowledge, but also high motivation for improving job skills for advancement and/or better on-the-job performance.

Of the 23 learning methods listed, all were considered Helpful or Very Helpful by 70% or more of the respondents, with more than half the items placed in these categories by 90% or more of the participants. Choices ranged from lectures and speeches to developing own project. Respondents were not asked to rank methods of learning by preference, but merely to indicate helpfulness toward accomplishing learning objectives.

CONCLUSIONS

The purpose of this study was to characterize adult self-directed learners, and to determine effective programs of study that will assist students in meeting their educational objectives. Learners' self-evaluations indicate that they consider themselves above average on all categories queried regarding motivation to learn, intellectual capacity for learning, and willingness to persist under adverse conditions.

Additional learning was deemed to be of high importance to the learners, with learning for the sake of learning considered equally as important as increasing knowledge for job improvement or advancement. All methods of learning cited were considered to be helpful to their learning needs.

The purpose of this study was to characterize the adult self-directed learners by personal traits, methods of learning, and motivation for learning, not to prioritize methods of learning by order of preference. Implications are that adult self-directed learners perceive themselves capable of participating in unfamiliar academic program formats, and find a variety of learning techniques helpful to the process of accomplishing their objectives.

Based on this study, directions for future research are indicated for:

1. A comparison between participants in the weekend college and the distance studies program to determine whether differences exist in degree of self-directedness required for accomplishment of objectives in the format chosen.

2. A survey of the participants in the weekend college and the distance studies program to determine whether they persist in the chosen format.

3. A study of participants in noncredit learning programs sponsored by academic agencies to determine whether they exhibit similar characteristics to those involved in the weekend college and the distance studies programs.

4. A survey of other participants in other nontraditional degree and/or college credit programs to determine whether similar results occur.

5. A study of how learners select and plan their learning projects, and whether they will persist in an undesirable format in order to accomplish objectives.

Further research should be directed toward studies not only of characteristics common to self-directed learners, but also toward learning methods that will best develop and enhance the competencies of self-directed learners.

REFERENCES

Bell, D., and Bell, D. (1983). Harmonizing self-directed and teacher-directed approaches to learning. Nurse Educator, 8(1), 24-30.

Brockett, R. (1983). Self-directed learning and the hard-to-reach adult. Lifelong Learning: The Adult Years, 6(8), 16-18.

Chene, A. (1983). The concepts of autonomy in adult education: A philosophical discussion. Adult Education Quarterly, 34(1), 38-47.

Gibbons, M., Bailey, A., Comeau, P., Schmuck, J., Seymour, S., and Wallace, D. (1980). Toward a theory of self-directed learning: A study of experts without formal training. Journal of Humanistic Psychology, 20(2), 41-56.

Gross, R. (1982). Arousing the passion for knowledge: A fresh frontier for adult education. Lifelong Learning: The Adult Years, 5(10), 4-6, 30.

Lace, William W. (1986). A non-traditional approach: Why you should look at non-traditional students. Currents, 8-11.

Long, H. (1980). Some qualitative performance characteristics of adults at the formal operations stage. Journal of Research and Development in Education, 13(3), 21-24.

Long, H. (1988). Studying adult self-directed learning through biography. Paper presented at the American Adult and Continuing Education National Conference, Tulsa, Oklahoma.

Sisco, B. (1983). The undereducated: Myth or reality. Lifelong Learning: The Adult Years, 6(8), 14-15, 24, 26.

Zemke, R. (1982). Self-directed learning: A must skill in the information age. Training, 19(8), 28-30.

CHAPTER SIXTEEN

ADAPTING THE CONCEPT OF SELF DIRECTED LEARNING TO ISLAMIC EDUCATIONAL PRACTICE

Kola Kazeem

The issue of "adaptation" in the educational development of Nigeria is not a new phenomenon. For a considerable period, particularly before the second World war, British colonial officials came to accept the pull of the educational system prevailing in Nigeria before their incursion. This conviction was demonstrated (further) in Muslim dominated area (Northern Nigeria) where the colonial educational officials perceived in the Islamic Schools possibilities for a combination or synthesis with western type of schools. This perhaps is due to the fact that Quranic School was available to children in Nigeria before the advent of European education. It encompasses a conscious attempt to help people live in their society and to participate fully and effectively in its organization in order to ensure its continued existence.

Islamic education practice no doubt fascinated the colonial education officers since the time of Lord Lugard to the extent that nearly every proposal for government education in the "Muslim" North before 1930 contained significant plans for a positive relationship between government and Islamic institutions.

However, the interest of the colonial officials in this project was inconsistent. For instance, it was discovered that the idea of integrating Islamic Studies in the government School's curriculum was not to give Islamic education a (purely) "modern" look per se; it was (as it were) only used as "an effective way to attract Muslims to schools where such training took place." In other words, interest in Islamic education derived from a desire for change, albeit limited, and for emulation of Western institutions.

Whatever may be the reasons for the colonial government's action, it was no doubt demonstrated that Islamic education has within it a system worthy of preserving for proper and societal development. It has equally initiated the idea of modernizing and reorganizing Islamic education practice to embrace and incorporate into its systems the Western educational ideals. In other words, Islamic education since the Colonial period has witnessed a considerable improvement. Many Muslim Scholars "cashed" in on this government initiative to introduce innovations. For instance, Taj - al - Adab - Iluri - a Muslim scholar of note, introduced books containing photographs to his students as textbooks.

Other Scholars also initiated campaign for the reformation and reorganization of Islamic education in the traditional Koranic Schools. One notable scholar is Shaykh Kamalud - deen al - Adab. He made frantic efforts to improve the method for teaching Muslims in Ilorin and elsewhere in Nigeria (Nasiru, 1978, p. 150).

It should be noted, that the reorganizations introduced by these scholars do not go beyond incorporating those aspects of Western education that serve as attractions to pupils of Koranic Schools. Such things include, ensuring an appropriate number of school years, well mapped out syllabi, beautiful classrooms with well arranged tables and desks, tidy and fitting uniforms, orderly arrangement of the opening and closing hours of these schools, with the attending music of the school band and some games (Nasiru, 1978, p. 143). All of these were to be introduced in Islamic Schools, to avoid the sacrifice of Islamic ideals/practice for Western values. Their aims in this regard was to preserve the values of Islam utilizing Western system, and not to promote Western education per se, nor change the orientation, content and perspective of Islamic education. In the words of Ansari, the efforts of Muslim Scholars:

As far as the re-orientation of education on Islamic lines are concerned, have not gone beyond a particular limit. In traditional Madrasas (schools), the highest point of our achievement is that we have added to the Curriculum some European languages, and a few modern subjects and given a new look to the teaching of the old subjects but there has been no modernization of the perspective. What we have is a discordant juxtaposition of modern and traditional ideas. (Ansari, 1978/1979, p. 61).

In short, the anxiety of Muslin scholars was to preserve Koranic Schools for subsequent transfer to posterity as they had inherited them from their fore-bears.

Islamic system of education still exists (in different forms) along side the state Western - style system in Nigeria - offering an independent source of literacy and an avenue to social promotion for those who are denied access to (or choose not to enter) the modern school system. Today, it takes place in three different kinds of settings. There are those based purely on the traditional set-up; others are based on a mixture of both the traditional and Western system, this Jimoh called, semi - formal schools; and those offered in purely formal settings. Besides, it is now pursued at different levels - the Koranic level, which is equivalent to primary school; the Ibtidai, lasting for three years, is equivalent to Junior secondary school; the Idadi also lasting for three years is equivalent to the senior secondary school; and the Thamawi, which is equivalent to advanced or tertiary education, lasts for four years. It should be noted, that each of these levels, have the Qur'an and Sunna as the central curriculum but the content of the curriculum at each stage differs significantly.

These development notwithstanding, Islamic education to many is nothing but religious education per se. It neither provides any economic opportunities for people as does Western education, nor does it help in changing and accelerating community development. Apart from this knowledge in Islamic Education is not translated in terms of a general theory or philosophy which may help review ideas of the modern sciences, and which may guide intellectual pursuits and inspire research. Others contended that as remarkable as its contributions to literature is, it is mostly concerned with issues in the social, political, and economic field and that even in those fields, it is more interested in practical problems. It was further argued that the majority of individuals with Koranic training do not achieve understanding of the language and their literacy activities are restricted to reading and writing known passages of the Koran, frequently used in prayers. In other words, critics of Islamic education, tended to describe such instruction (Arabic Knowledge based upon the recitation and copying of the Koran) as of little pedagogical value (Wilks, 1968).

These and other ideas represent the criticism of Islamic educational practice and perhaps this idea underlie the swing in the educational pendulum toward Western education, while little or no attention is given to exploring the possibilities of utilizing new trends or developments in the modern educational enterprise to suit and (or) improve Islamic education.

The object of this paper, therefore, is a humble attempt at showing the extent to which Islamic educational practice can adequately tap the benefits of self-directed learning. In other words, to what extent can the concept of self-direction be adapted to Islamic educational practice? - bearing in mind that in its practice, there is nothing to support the fact that reading and writing entails fundamental "cognitive restructuring." That is, whatever was learned, developed or translated (in Islamic education) was that which would first and foremost help establish the religion of Islam or assist it's government and community (Ummah) to retain their dominance. Stated differently, there is little evidence to show that knowledge was developed for its own sake in Islamic education.

Let us now examine the meaning of self-directed learning and how it can be utilized in instructing learners of Islamic educational schools.

The Idea of Self-Direction
Self-directed learning as a concept has come of age. The term embraces all the ways in which people may be involved in learning in institutional, formal, informal and nonformal settings (Joblin, 1988).

As an educational idea, self-directed learning was conceived as a challenge to the assumption that individuals especially adults can only learn in the presence of a fully accredited and certified professional teacher who has been trained in the techniques of instructional design and classroom management. The idea of self-direction as a delivery strategy implies that the key element in the teaching - learning process is not the external direction (i.e. managing the external conditions which would facilitate the internal change [learning] given by the teacher or other outside sources), but the arrangement of these external conditions to produce an internal change (Brookfield, 1984; Long, 1989). Thus, self-directed learning is not to describe a particular kind of internal change in consciousness, but to refer to the activities involved in acquiring particular skills or knowledge. See Long's chapter in this book for additional comments on this idea.

The assumption here is that individuals have some force motivating them internally to carry out one or a number of activities on their own and perhaps achieve commendable results for themselves, or the society at large. This to Brookfield (1981) is independent learning, and as he describes it further:

> That which takes place when the decisions about intermediate and terminal learning goals to be pursued, rate of student programme, evaluative procedure to be employed, and sources of materials to be consulted are in the hands of the learner. The learner may engage in the temporary submission of authority to an accredited expert when, for example, a budgerigar breeder visits a specialist on disease diagnosis to learn how to detect and treat common bird ailments; the overall responsibility for the learning activity, however, rests with the breeder and when the expert has provided

the specialist knowledge required the learner reasserts control over the direction of future learning (Brookfield, 1981, p. 16).

The contention is that the learner controls his learning and that such learning "occurs in settings not expressly intended for educational activities." That is, the self-directed learners act on their own behalf in much the same manner that a professional teacher acts in organizing a formal classroom experience. In other words, it implies a controlled linear process which is, to some degree, anticipated and organized by the learner (Spear and Mocker, 1984). See Long (1988) and Spear (1988) for additional but different views on the linearity of self-directed learning.

It should be noted that, though central to the thoughts of the advocates of self-directed learning is the idea that learning is indeed "a natural, normal organic part of living, as functional a part of living as breathing," they none-the-less, accept the role of the teacher in the learning process. For instance, Knowles submitted that the "andragogue, while being able to accept dependency, at a given time and moment, or time with a given person, has a built in sense of obligation to do everything one can to help that person move from dependency towards increasing self-directness" (Knowles, 1977, p. 206). The role of the teacher in self-directed learning is, therefore, to build in his instructional set-up the idea of developing in the learner some independence in the learning process. It is to help a learner become increasingly self-directed in learning.

The idea, therefore, is that, advocates of self-directed learning, especially Knowles, accept the fact that individuals enter any educational project in a state of dependency, whereas they are self-directing in every other aspect of their lives (Knowles, 1977). This assertion corresponds with the idea that self-directed learners in most instances do not engage in detailed pre-planning, neither do they bother themselves to scout for varieties of alternatives available in the learning process (Spear and Mocker, 1984). To this end, Knowles suggested, that there should be provision for some entry experience into any programme. This is with a view to helping the learner get the ideas being disseminated and to help him (the learner) acquire the skills of being a self-directed learner. To Knowles, any educational programme that does not involve the learner will be resisted. As he puts it:

> ... One of the basic findings of applied behavioral science research is that people tend to feel committed to decision or activity in direct proportion to their participation in or influence on its planning and decision making. The reverse is even more relevant: people tend to feel uncommitted to any decision or activity that they feel is being imposed on them without their having a change to influence it. (Knowles, 1984, p. 123)

In the final analysis, self-directed learning hinges on the idea that individuals needs should be involved in giving direction to any decision or activity if it is to evoke their commitment and that the inner potential of the individual as a self-directed learner must be integrated in any educational programmes.

Having undertaken a brief description of self-directed learning, the major issue now is to assess the Islamic educational practice with a view to showing what it stands for, and how it is being conducted, its curriculum, and the extent to which it has developed its perspectives over the years, along the lines of self-directed learning.

Status of Islamic Education
Education in Islam like everything in the Islamic social order is divinely ordained, and like the society it serves, it had the divine purpose of conducing approved conduct, happiness in this world and eternal bliss in the next world. That is, learning in Islamic education has purely religious motives and content. Although its message insists on the high value of learning and wisdom, basically the content of its education is closely connected with theology, morality, charity, patience, forgiveness of offenders and virtue that constitutes right conduct.

287

Islamic education started with Prophet Mohammed's experience of the divine revelation:

> Proclaim (or Read)
> In the name of thy lord and cherisher
> who created .... taught man that
> which he know not ....(Qur'an, Ch.96)

This revelation marked the first revealed words and verses of the holy Koran. It reveals that education has been ordained by Allah (God) as a potent requirement of a believer since the inception of Islam. As such, learning and wisdom seeking has been a prerequisite of a true Muslim. "Quest" for learning is a duty incumbent upon every Muslim, male and female, wisdom is the goal of believers and they must seek it irrespective of its source.

Perhaps, it was the sacredness of education in Islam that resulted in the Koran becoming the central curriculum. The Koran forms the basis of both moral and general education. This is because, the important feature of Islamic education is:

> ... the continuity of Muslim Society in which there is no distinct separation of the temporal and the spiritual. Always and everywhere we come back to the Koran. Not only because literature and art repeat Koranic verses, or are inspired by them, but also because it is the very form of the holy book, its language, its rhythm, that have determined the way in which Muslims thought and feelings find expression. (L.L. Garh, 1971, p. 12)

In view of the position of the Koran to Islam as a religion and the fact that the aim of Islamic education is to make a good Muslim (which is synonymous with being a good citizen) out of the learners - making them to be more aware of their duties and responsibilities as a Muslim, learning in Islamic education has purely religious curriculum.

This however, is not to suggest that learners in Islamic education are forbidden from acquiring knowledge of any sort. For instance, the Koram emphasizes the development of human faculties by carefully observing and understanding the phenomenon of nature:

> And in the succession of the night and the day and in the sustenance which Allah sendth down from heavens whereby He giveth life to the earth after its death, and in the changing of the winds, are signs for people who have sense. (Qur'an, Ch. 45, V. 4)

The Koran here appeals to human reason, thereby showing the importance of education.

In the same vein, the Holy Prophet Mohammed encouraged mankind to pursue other forms of education:

> God has not created anything better than reason. The benefits that God giveth .... and understanding is by it; and God's displeasure is caused by it, and by it are reward and punishment. (Naqvi, 1971/72, p. 13)

Islamic education from inception did not neglect or exclude the understanding and development of other branches of knowledge. Medicine, science and other technical knowledge were learnt at least through apprenticeship (Haqvi, 1971/72). It is important to note that the objectives of secular learning were not divorced from the main objective of the society, namely the Islamic ethical principles and values. Meaning that medicine, engineering and mathematics remain decidedly religious. Every action and every endeavor had to be justified in religious terms. Thus, the professional standard of excellence and the ethical standard of professional conduct were reinforced and safeguarded by religious ethics and values.

In fact, it has been remarked that in the early years of Islam, Muslims dominated the world academic science - that the scholarship of the earliest Muslims played a leading role in the foundation of present day civilization. This fact was reinforced by Robert Briffault:

289

> The dept of our science to that of the Arab does not consist in
> startling discoveries or revolutionary theories; Science owes a
> great deal to Arab Culture; it owes it its existence. (_____)

Arabic scholars have played an important role in helping to preserve what is today called modern civilization and modern science. They made several discoveries and delved into astronomy, geography and psychology. They greatly improved algebra, trigonometry, geometry and so on. They learned, translated and even published philosophical works of Plato and Aristotle and medical works of Hippocrates. Historiography was highly developed by the likes of Ibn Khaldun, Leo - Africanus, Ibn Batuta and others.

With special reference to Nigeria, there has been some remarkable contribution of Islamic education to the society. The system provided converts with a new means of livelihood. They function mostly as diviners, preachers, and administrators assisting kings in communication with other Muslim kings. Apart from this, many of these scholars became valuable instruments used by the colonialists (Nasiru, 1978).

These development and contributions shows that Islamic education (at inception) then was oriented towards intellectual development. Jimoh (1971) contended that if Islamic Culture were to be left as it were (in areas where it was functioning before the coming of the European) it would have evolved into a modern system. For, he noted further, "it possessed the essentials necessary for the survival of a civilization - a rich cultural heritage, a national language, and a century of stable government based on Islamic jurisprudence with al its inherent vitality and appeal to the African" (Jimoh, 1971/72).

However, the sacredness of the Holy Koran (the immutable source of the fundamental tenet of Islamic education and religion, which also forms the perennial foundation of Islamic system of legislation), and the fact that whatever is being learnt is to help preserve and ensure the continuity of Islam as a religion, its method of instruction, therefore followed the time-honored one of reading and commentary. In which the teacher reads a passage from a text, then the learner repeats this after him for a number of times - until the learner is able to master the correct pronunciation. This is the method used at every stage of Islamic education - for adult, as well as children. Even when some measure of modernization was introduced to Islamic education, (methods, such as drama technique, role - play and discussion methods), it remained largely religious - aimed at maintaining the status quo of the Koran in Islam.

Based on the fact that early Muslim scholars had played a significant role in the development of science, it shows that at one time in the life of Islamic Education, learning was pursued for its own sake (Haqvi, 1971/172). One then wonders, what went wrong over the years. In other words, where had the inspiration for scientific innovations associated with Muslin scholars gone? Is it because the orientation of Islamic education has shifted from intuitive and "cognitive" development to purely the development of all things, Islamic? Is it possible to use other delivery techniques in the present Curriculum?

Prospects of Self-Direction in Islamic Education
Teaching of religion has been transformed since the early decades of the 20th Century, when Thomas Shield (quoted in Bryce, 1978) in a paper titled "The Method of Teaching Religion" revealed that:

> Teaching is both a science and an art ... From time to time men and women rise up who possess the art in a high form and though they do not disclaim the help of Science and study and practice, their art is in them as a native power which informs all they do (Bryce, 1978, p. 5-41).

Before this time, the nature of teaching religion extolled the merits of having learners memorize and insisted on the necessity of a doctrinal manual. What Shield was advocating here was based on the psychological sequence of learning. That is:

> ... not what was first in time nor what is logically the basis of the
> body of the truth to be imported, but what the child needs now
> for his unfolding mental life and what he can comprehend now in
> the light of his own past must be presented, if it is to serve as
> food to growing mind (Shield as quoted by Bryce, 1978, p. 5-
> 42).

In other words, whatever education should be given to the learner should not necessarily be what has been but that learners should be taught the idea of appreciating their own human life of nature and of revealed religion.

Shield's idea was for educational (religion education) objectives or technique to shift from a teacher - centered, fixed curriculum to a learner centered basis for instructions. That is, the learner should become "an active agent in the educative process" and not a passive recipient memorizing what the teacher selects as ideal for learning.

It should be noted that, while Christian education has recognized the increased need of integrating Shield's ideas - ensuring the development of the human spirit in the working out of spiritual ideals at all levels, Islamic education (over the years) shunned these ideas. It's educational method remained static. This perhaps is due to the very nature of Islamic education which holds the Koran in a "revered" position. For Muslim beliefs regarding the Koran is that it is a speech articulated by God himself, revealed to the prophet through an infallible way and preserved in the form that we have it now, without the admixture of any elements contributed by the prophet or any other human being. The major task of learning in Islam (based on the Koran) is how to break words into stages - preparing for reading, establishing initial reading attitudes and skills and acquiring the mastery of Koranic texts. This process has been described by Zerdoum as imposing.

> ... a purely mechanical, monotonous form of study in which
> nothing is likely to arouse his (learner's) interest. The Scholl
> (Koranic) thus tend to curb his (learner's) intellectual and moral

activities at the precise moment when it should be developing rapidly (cited by Wagner and Lofti, 1981, p. 247).

The issue is that, no one is claiming that the Koran should be removed from the syllabus or occupy a prominent position in Islamic education, but that education developed basically on religion without recourse to intellectual development limits the scope, character and kills the natural inspiration of the learners. As A.A. Engineer (1978) put it:

> I do not view Islam as a system which had provided set answers to all our problems long ago, but as a faith, whose universal values, as a historical project are valid even today, and with the reformation of religious truth so as to be meaningful in the modern world can be realized even today ... simply being a product of one's heritage is not enough; one should feel duty bound to contribute to it too (Engineer, 1978, p. 94).

The prevailing system where the teacher is the "alpha and omega" in Koranic Schools does not augur well for Engineer's call. To achieve this, a measure of assistance should be given to the learner (by the teacher) in the process of organizing external conditions to produce an internal change. In other words, the central role of the teacher as the pivoter of the learning process should be replaced with helping learner's develop the internal consciousness naturally endowed individuals.

The learner should therefore be prepared and developed towards conducting their "own" learning successfully. Thus, instead of teaching the learners that which they only repeat without understanding, efforts should be made to first ensure that learners start out with issues that would prepare them for conducting their learning on their own.

CONCLUSIONS

So far, we have considered the questions of integrating or adapting self-direction to Islamic education. An over-view of the discussions shows that since there is nothing intrinsic in expanding and developing intellectual ability of the learners of Islamic educational settings, a measure of self-directions may be introduced.

It should be noted however, that introducing self-direction in Islamic education would require a shift in the curriculum. There is no doubt, that even the current practice, where the Koran stands at the center can still make use of self-direction. After all, self-directed learning is not to change the curriculum content but to ensure learner's initiatives in charting his own learning.

While attempts at introducing self-direction to Islamic education will no doubt help open up its educational domains, and solve the problems of rigidity - in scope and practice, it's (self direction) working acceptability rest with the Muslim intelligentsia, rather than the Ulama (Muslin Literates) to ponder over.

REFERENCES

Ansari, A.H. (1978 and 1979). Transformation of perspective in education. Islam and The Modern Age, IX(4), Nov. 1978 and X(1), Feb., 1979, 59-71.

Brookfield, S. (1981). Independent adult learning. Studies in Adult Education, 13, 15-27.

Brookfield, S. (1984). Self-directed learning a critical paradigm. Adult Education Quarterly, 35(2), Winter 1984, 59-71.

Bryce, M. C. (1978). Four decades of Roman Catholic Innovators. Religion Education, (Special Edition), September-October.

Engineer, A.A. (1978). Islam and reformation. Islam and the Modern Age, IX(1), February 1976, 94.

Hubbard, J.P. (1975). Government and Islamic education in Northern Nigeria: 1900-1940. In G.N Brown and M. Hiskett (Eds.), Conflict and Harmony in Education in Tropical Africa. London, 152-167.

Jimoh, S.A. (1972). A critical appraisal of Islamic education with particular references to relevant happenings on Nigerian scene. Nigerian Journal of Islam, 2(1), July 71 - January 72, 31-49.

Joblin, D. (1988). Self-direction in adult education: An analysis, defense, refutation and assessment of the notion that adults are more self-directed than children and youth. International Journal of Life-Long Education, 7(2), April-June 1988, 115-125.

Knowles, M.S. (1977). Adult learning processes: Pedagogy and andragogy. Religious Education, LXXII(2), March-April 1977.

Knowles, M.S. (1984). The adult learner: A neglected species (3rd ed.). Houston: Gult.

Long, H.B. (1988). Self-directed learning reconsidered. In H.B. Long and Associates, Self-directed learning: Application and theory. Athens, Georgia: Adult Education Department, University of Georgia, 1-10.

Long, H.B. (1989). Self-directed learning: Emerging theory and practice. In H.B. Long and Associates Self-directed learning: Emerging theory and practice. Norman, Oklahoma: Oklahoma Research Center for Continuing Professional and Higher Education, University of Oklahoma, 1-12.

Naqvi, S.H.Z. (1972). Islam and the development of science. Nigerian Journal of Islam, 2 (1), July, 1971-January, 1972, 11-19.

Nasiru, W.O.A. (1978). Islamic learning among the Yoruba. Unpublished master's thesis, University of Ibadam, Ibadan, Nigeria.

Omolewa, M.A. (1976). The adaption question in Nigerian Education, 1916-1936. Journal of the Historical Society of Nigeria, 8(3), 93-119.

Qur'an, Ch. 45, Verse 4; Ch. 96.

Spear, G.E. (1988). Beyond the organizing circumstances. In H.B. Long and Associates. Self-directed learning: Application and theory. Athens, Georgia: Adult Education Department, University of Georgia, 199-222.

Spear, G.E. and Mocker, D.W. (1984). The organizing circumstance: Environmental determinant in self-directed learning. Adult Education Quarterly, 35(1), Fall 1984, 1-10.

Wagner, D.A. and Lotfi, A.H. (1980). Traditional Islamic education in
    Morocco: Socio-historical   and   psychological   perspectives.
    Comparative Education Review, 24(2), Part 1, June 1980, 238-251.
Wilks, Ivor (1968).   The transmission of Islamic learning in the Western
    Sudan.   In J.   Goody (Ed.),   Literary in Traditional Societies.
    Cambridge, 1968.

DATE DUE

DEMCO 38-296

Please remember that this is a library book,
and that it belongs only temporarily to each
person who uses it. Be considerate. Do
not write in this, or any, library book.